The Shepherds of InEquality

The Shepherds of InEquality

And the Futility of Our
Efforts to Stop Them

Dawn Pretorius

To order additional copies of this book, contact:
Xlibris
844-714-8691
www.Xlibris.com
Orders@Xlibris.com
841792

To all the journalists around the world who risk their lives to give us accurate and real-time reporting, which is one aspect of their job; the other is investigative reporting, which requires systematic and painful original research activity, which contributes to the downfall of high-powered money launderers

To the many specialists who investigate suspected money laundering, such as intelligence agents, law enforcement officers, criminal investigators, and the many other people who take risks and participate in the fight against money laundering

To my sons Lyle and Dale for their moral support, to Vivienne O'Hare, a buddy senior in compliance, with similar sentiments, for her offer to assist in checking my draft work

Thank you.

CONTENTS

PREFACE

ONE OF THE world's biggest and most vociferous sustainable industries is money laundering. Irrespective of how economies fare, there are always plenty of opportunities to grasp and networks to participate in.

The skill sets required for laundering money are diverse, from highly professional and experienced, technical, academic, and scientific, to rough-and-ready hands-on practitioners. There is a job for everybody. These practitioners are also the shepherds of inequality – a troubling and growing trend around the world.

A counter-industry of painful proportions, both in terms of cost and content, known as anti-money laundering (AML), has been designed to fight back. I write from this industry.

My book looks at these two industries as it relates to power, leadership, greed, and the trillions of dollars that influence national policies, people, culture, and both vulnerable and developed economies around the world and sarcastically suggests that, after years of legal and compliance effort, the anti-money laundering industry is the one that is failing miserably despite the incredible amount of money and skills it takes to thwart, not necessarily the crimes, but just the proceeds of those crimes.

This book is not intended to denigrate the efforts of people involved in terms of investigation, law enforcement, the judiciary, and compliance. Their efforts should be applauded.

But the overall evidence suggests that while efforts are intense, we have created an industry of anti-money laundering, which might just be the biggest con of all.

I have randomly chosen approximately sixty months of news from some fifty equally randomly chosen countries on ways money has been laundered; each story or observation recounted represents a moment in time because something researched today changes tomorrow. Investigations into money laundering can take years. Many never result in satisfactory convictions; many just fall off the radar, or politics will interfere. And yes, there are some spectacular results, but they are few and far between.

The anti-money-laundering industry is similarly inconsistent; there are regulatory changes introduced at different times and differently applied around the world, all of which are dependent on physical and financial resources, skills, and political will.

Both industries are therefore moving targets, and the amount of money involved in both industries is estimated at best.

Money laundering is the world's biggest industry because it encapsulates trade, commerce, finance, business, manufacturing, production, and politics and pervades the world's economic efforts in all these areas. To fight it, a costly counter-industry has grown exponentially, but its efforts, relative to the value of money being laundered, are estimated to be less than 1 percent effective in terms of successful convictions and/or money retrieved.

INTRODUCTION

MONEY LAUNDERING IS a phrase bandied about with words such as *crime, fraud, racketeering, organized crime*, and *illegal markets*. To the average person in the street, it is just another example of nefarious activity. The words *dark, dangerous*, and *underground* come to mind.

But the term *money laundering* does not refer to nefarious activity. Money laundering refers to the proceeds of the crime, that is, the money earned from drug dealing, people trafficking, arms trafficking, illicit diamond dealing, and other illegal trading. It is also about the proceeds earned from white-collar (or corporate) crime, which includes insider trading, embezzlement, cybercrime, and identity theft. It is also about wealthy people hiding their money from tax authorities and other prying eyes. It is also about politicians and their minions wanting more power and the money to become even more powerful.

Why is it called money laundering?

When money is earned illegally, whether it be through smuggling goods, trafficking people, or performing illegal corporate transactions, the phrases often used to describe it are "dirty money" or, more formally, "the proceeds of crime."

The term *money laundering* is said to have originated with the Italian mafia criminals, such as Al Capone, who deliberately bought laundromats to fudge their illegal profits from prostitution and bootlegged liquor sales with legitimate business sales from the laundromats, thereby obscuring their illegal profits.

In the earlier days, when there were no restrictions on depositing money and, irrespective of where it came from, banks gladly accepted deposits of any kind. Once the money was in the banking system and in an account, any person or company being offered to be paid from a bank account accepted that the check or transfer represented legitimate funds, or frankly, did not care. Cash was also appreciated. No questions were ever asked.

The term *money laundering*, over time, referred to the illegally earned money having been washed clean when it is deposited in a bank account. That now, of course, is a misnomer. In most countries now, the cash deposited over a certain amount in a bank is automatically reported to a legislative reporting authority. In other words, financial institutions are alerted, through legislative requirements that need to be followed, that they should not be used to legitimize illegally earned money.

Money laundering, therefore, is not about the crime, irrespective of what it is; it is about the proceeds of crime.

It is all about the money.

CHAPTER 1

Illegal Earnings

The Traffickers

G LOBAL ILLICIT TRADE and illicit economies are responsible for transforming systems, changing rules, and altering the power dynamics in our world. We read about it, and we watch movies about it, namely, narcotics, kidnapping for ransom, the trafficking of anything from arms to humans, the trade in stolen and counterfeit goods, bribery, and money laundering, to name just a small cross-section, but are we aware of the extent of it, or quite frankly, do we care because it is a daily occurrence?

Our global economy is one of convergence where legitimate commerce and legitimate transactions perpetuate and feed off the illegal economy and vice versa.

Cities' markets, be it from New York to London, Shanghai to Hong Kong, Boston to Amsterdam, or Tokyo to Sydney, are considered attractive to many people around the globe whether it be for business, residential, travel, or education purposes. Other cities such as Caracas, Acapulco, San Salvador, Palmira, Beijing, Tehran, Johannesburg, and Jakarta are mostly associated with danger and illicit markets.

But whether it is New York or Sydney or Caracas, every city presents a myriad of lucrative opportunities to be infiltrated by illicit networks to traffic anything that holds value in the eyes of the traffickers. The more sophisticated the city, the better the opportunities.

While trafficking enriches a few, it exploits thousands, accentuates poverty, reduces productivity, disincentivizes investments in research and development, jeopardizes public health, emaciates communities' human capital, erodes the security of institutions, and destabilizes fragile governments.

Cash is still king for traffickers because it is anonymous, fungible, and portable. It bears no record of its source, owner, or legitimacy; it is used and held around the world and is difficult to trace once spent. Additionally, despite its bulk, cash can be easily concealed and transported in large quantities in vehicles, commercial shipments, aircraft, boats, luggage, or packages, in special compartments hidden inside clothing, or in packages wrapped to look like gifts.

Cash-intensive sources of illicit income include human smuggling, bribery, contraband smuggling, extortion, illegal gambling, kidnapping, and prostitution. Drug trafficking, however, is probably the most significant single source of illicit cash along the supply chain, from the individual to the mid-level distributors, wholesalers, and suppliers.

The FBI indicates that traffickers will also use money brokers to facilitate trade-based money laundering (TBML). These schemes are deliberately complicated in how merchandise is moved, the value falsified, and financial transactions misrepresented with the help of complicit merchants—all designed to disguise the origin of illicit proceeds and integrate those proceeds into the market. Once criminals exchange illicit cash for trade goods, the tracing of the source of the illicit funds is nigh impossible.

Transnational criminal organizations may dump imported goods purchased with criminal proceeds into the market at a discount to expedite the money laundering process, putting legitimate merchants at a competitive disadvantage. These days, traffickers are seldom unbanked, and significant amounts of money earned from traffickers now pass through legitimate financial services businesses and cryptocurrencies.

So how do traffickers make their money?

Traffickers are inherent in our societies and have been so for years. Trafficking has not abated; it has just become more diversified and a lot more sophisticated, thanks to technology and the many ways money can be moved around the world with impunity.

There are many examples in the history of powerful entities—names with which we are familiar. The mafia of Sicily is one such example. Sicily was an island ruled by a long line of foreign invaders over many centuries. Sicilians pulled and worked together to protect themselves and conducted their own type of justice. These mafioso, as they became known, were distrustful and apprehensive of central authority. By the nineteenth century, a number of these groups extorted protection money from landowners. The groups developed into powerful criminal and competing organizations. The dress code of the mafia in the 1920s in America, from the pinstripe suits to the black- or white-band fedora hats, and black-and-white spat shoes, became a fashion statement and an enviable brand recognition. The cigar added the final touch; it helped to synchronize groups to a single code of conduct and undivided loyalty.

On the other side of the world, the roots of the Chinese triads developed a little differently. Way back to about 1000 BC, legend has it those Chinese monks were committed to fighting injustices and were the first instigators of such groups forming; peasants started the sway to form groups to protect themselves against evil leaders. They operated as secret societies against the very harsh rule of the Manchu Qing Dynasty. The extent of their power is said to have brought down or propped up emperors at their whim. They thrived in the warlord era from the 1920s to the 1950s, the Green Gang (of some 100,000 members) being the most recognized because of its connections to Chiang Kai-shek, the military and political leader of the Chinese Nationalist Party in the mid-1900s.

The extent of trafficking is hinted at in the randomly chosen examples given below:

Drug Traffickers

Al Capone, or Scarface, was born in 1899 in New York City and was the son of Italian immigrants. During the Prohibition era, he attained infamy as a cofounder with Johnny Torrio, boss of the Chicago Outfit. This syndicate controlled the illegal alcohol, prostitution, and gambling rackets in Chicago and earned them some $100 million a year during the prime of the Prohibition. Al Capone enjoyed political protection because of his close relationship with Johnny and the Unione Siciliane. Unione Siciliane was a Sicilian-American organization set up in Chicago that, it would appear, controlled the Italian voting process in the United States at that time. During the Prohibition period, organized crime bosses fought to take control of this influential organization for their own ends and that of the Chicago Outfit. When a threatened Johnny retired, Capone expanded the bootlegging business through increasingly violent means simply because he was allowed to do so. Because bribes were paid to police and politicians, law enforcement was never a threat. But he softened opinions because he shared his illegal earnings with charities and he was loved for that, to his great delight.

The St. Valentine's Day Massacre in Chicago pushed society to demand justice, but ironically, he was prosecuted for tax evasion and jailed for eleven years. Although released after eight years, he developed neurosyphilis in prison and a stroke took him out at forty-eight.

From the 1950s onward, ethnic mobs emerged with powerful and rich gangsters. Frank Lucas, who capitalized off the heroin trade in the 1960s and 1970s by using an East Asian connection during the Vietnam War, cut off the Italian mafia who controlled the trade in his Harlem at the time. Lucas claimed to have sold one million dollars' worth of heroin a day in his prime and to have on hand a large supply of heroin. He was captured in 1975 in New Jersey, along with the $550,000 hidden in his home, for federal and New Jersey state violations. He was sentenced to seventy years in prison but became an informant, so his sentence was reduced to five. Some one hundred drug traffickers were captured as a result. Frank was again arrested and back in jail for seven years for drug dealing in 1984. Ironically, he had been caught in the act of exchanging one ounce of heroin and $13,000 for one kilogram of cocaine. He maintained the authorities had taken all his money (much of which was purported to be in the Cayman Islands) and his properties in and around America and Puerto Rico. Wheelchair-ridden and in his eighties, he died in May 2019 in his hometown.

The Cocaine Queen of Miami, Griselda Blanco, was a drug lord for the Colombian Medellin cartel. She grew up in Colombia and pickpocketed her way through her teens. She controlled the cocaine trade through vicious violence and intimidation, making $80 million a month during the 1970s and 1980s. Blanco came to symbolize the "cocaine cowboy" bloodshed of the 1980s when rival drug dealers brazenly ambushed rivals in public; she also pioneered the gunning down of rivals by motorcycle drive-by and using people to fly to Miami as her drug mules.

Griselda was caught and convicted for drug dealing and charged with murder but, for technical reasons, only served ten years and returned to low-profile living in Colombia. She was, ironically, killed by two gunshots to the head in a motorcycle drive-by shooting and is claimed to have died, nevertheless, a rich woman.

El Chapo is today one of Mexico's most infamous drug lords. He is the head of the Sinaloa cartel, which smuggles billions of dollars from Colombia through Mexico and into the United States. Joaquín Guzmán Loera became rich enough to make the *Forbes* list in 2009 as the 701st of 1,000 of the wealthiest people in the world; in 2013 he was listed as one of the top sixty most powerful people in the world. Guzmán was jailed in 1993 but escaped in 2001 with the help of many prison guards and workers.

One of them opened Guzmán's electronically operated cell door, and Guzmán got into a laundry cart that another maintenance worker rolled through several doors and eventually out the prison's front door. He was then transported in the trunk of a car driven by the same worker out of the town. He stopped at a petrol station and went inside, but when he came back, Guzmán was gone on foot, into the night. After an extensive fugitive hunt, he was again captured in 2014 in Mexico by the Mexican authorities. In July the following year, he spectacularly escaped again from a maximum-security prison; he had escaped through a tunnel leading from his shower, which was not visible from the cameras. It was sophisticated in that it was equipped with artificial light, air ducts, and a motorcycle, which presumably transported material for the tunnel construction and provided a quick getaway for Guzmán. He was caught again, charged, and will spend the rest of his life in a maximum-security prison.

Guzmán's world still extends beyond Mexico and the United States. Mexico's Sinaloa cartel is the biggest supplier of cocaine and "ice" to the Australian illegal drug market using shipping containers secretly identifiable by outlaw motorcycle gangs who arrange transport of these from the wharf to the wholesalers and by pilots flying small jets and twin-propeller planes to specific destinations. Pilots can earn $500,000 to fly five hundred kilograms of drugs (as pellets of cocoa powder, for example) into remote locations or small airports in Australia. Drugs are offloaded and cash onboarded. Often American, Canadian, or Australian pilots were used, seemingly being less suspicious than, for example, a Mexican pilot. This network still works in collaboration with Middle Eastern and Asian gangs and has tentacles into about fifty countries.

Guzmán's business is now run by Ismael "El Mayo" Zambada and continues to be lucrative—especially currently in synthetic opioids, which is a separate concern. El Mayo is seventy-one years old (2019) with diabetes; he is the last remaining member of the Sinaloa cartel's old guard. No doubt somebody will rise from the ranks and take over. But the Mexican government now says there is officially no more narcotics war, so catching drug lords and cartels is no longer their top priority. But on August 8, 2019, Mexican police found nineteen bodies in Mexico City, nine of them found grotesquely hanging from an overpass alongside a drug cartel banner threatening rival cartels.

Worst still was the incident on October 18, 2019 in which Guzmán's son, Ovidio Guzmán, who is only in his late twenties and a top figure in the Sinaloa cartel along with his brothers Iván Archivaldo and Jesús Alfredo, was captured by Mexico's National Guard. Any plan of arrest was not thought through, possibly in their need to act quickly. The Guard arrived at a safe house without a warrant, and while they were waiting for it, hundreds of cartel gunmen with bulletproof vests surrounded the area with SUVs and pickups, toted assault rifles, and viciously attacked the soldiers and civilians, leaving at least eight people dead. The carnage did not end there. Members of the Sinaloa cartel wreaked havoc across

Culiacán to retaliate against Ovidio's attempted arrest. Heavily armed gunmen riding in convoys sparked some seventy separate firefights with Mexican security forces, set fires to vehicles, shot at government offices, and engineered a jailbreak that freed fifty-five prisoners. Cartel gunmen had also kidnapped eight army soldiers and an officer. By nightfall, it was clear that the cartel held the city captive. The incident was the worst Mexico had seen in their fight against the cartels, especially after earlier incidents that week that saw gunfights and deaths played out by other cartels. President Andrés Manuel López Obrador finally released Ovidio, claiming that people's lives were at risk otherwise. A government weakened from organized crime, and with a weak economy, is now also a captured state by increasing cartel power.

The world of drug trafficking continues unabated. It is interesting too, isn't it, that *Forbes* magazine recognizes wealth built through illegality and brutality.

Semion Mogilevich roams freely. He is a Russian organized crime boss and has been described by the European and United States agencies as the boss of bosses of most Russian mafia syndicates in the world. According to the FBI, he is the most dangerous mobster in the world, accused of weapons trafficking, contract murders, extortion, drug trafficking, and prostitution on an international scale. According to the late former Russian Federal Security Services defector, Alexander Litvinenko, Semion had a good relationship with Vladimir Putin in the 1990s. The powerful collude with the powerful.

Much like Semion, the present mafia is much more polished, sophisticated, and elusive. In August 2019, the *Guardian* referred to a scathing United Nations Commission report on the Guatemala mafia.

The report said the impunity of power in Guatemala dates to colonial times and why such networks persist today is that "they have distorted democratic institutionality in their favor and they have molded the political system and designed mechanisms that allow them to occupy positions of power, manipulating legislation.

"Between 2012 and 2015, an illicit, political-economic network took over the executive [branch], subordinated the legislative, manipulated and interfered in the election of judges to high courts, and, in addition to looting the state, promoted laws and policies favoring private companies to the detriment of competition and the citizenry," the report continued.

All that benefited drug trafficking networks, it added.

Opioid drugs trigger yet another link to the above cartels. Just to get a taste of the extent of the tentacles it has in society, it is useful to refer to the Chinese company Yuancheng (meaning "extended success"), which was founded in 2001. It employs some seven hundred people and has offices all over China. This business sells, it is said, chemicals to the public and businesses and offers ten thousand compounds ranging from food additives and horror-type additives such as synthetic cinnamon to pharmaceuticals, from Viagra to collagen, pesticides, veterinary products, anabolic steroids, and precursor chemicals used to synthesize drugs, including fentanyl.

Fentanyl is the term used for synthetic substitutes. Most of the illicit fentanyl is used in America, where statistics show it to be the cause of many deaths. The fentanyl comes through Mexico, but because Mexican cartels lack trained chemists to make fentanyl from scratch, they buy precursors in bulk from China and develop the finished product for sale.

Two articles in the *Guardian* refer to this sophistication: an article by Duncan Campbell of the *Guardian* reported in July 2019 that the National Crime Agency estimated that £90 billion of criminal money is being laundered through the UK every year. This represents 4 percent of the country's GDP. London is branded as "the global capital of money laundering and the beating heart of European organized crime." The article goes on to say that crime is an essential part of the British economy, providing hundreds of thousands of jobs for professional criminals that include police and prison officers, lawyers and court officials, and a security business that now employs more than half a million people. Steve Rodhouse, the National Crime Agency's head of operations indicated that the international nature of crime and technology are the two biggest challenges, and that "high-harm" operations involve people, commodities, and money transfers across international borders.

Another article in the *Guardian* published on October 30, 2019, refers to the Italian mafia networks which, according to the Italian Interior Minister Luciana Lamorgese, have become "less high-profile in recent years as they spread their activities into new sectors, but they are just as dangerous." It further reported that organized crime groups "have made extensive transformations" while adopting "increasingly complex" models of criminal activity.

"Criminal organizations are ever more sophisticated as they manage to infiltrate important economic sectors to clean up illicitly accumulated money," said Lamorgese at a hearing with the Italian parliament's anti-mafia commission. "The mafia continues to weigh heavily on our institutions and economic system." The biggest mafia gang operating in Italy is 'Ndrangheta. The same article states that a study by the Demoskopia research institute in 2013 claimed that 'Ndrangheta made more money than Deutsche Bank and McDonald's put together, with a turnover of €53 billion (£44 billion).

A retired chief of Europol reckoned that 5,000 organized crime groups were operating across Europe. There were some 180 different nationalities operating, making them a multinational business using specialists and skills related to the movement of money, money laundering, and the forging of documents. Mixing legal business with illegal business and employing 400 to 500 experienced money-launderers means that these crime groups are effective and use the dark web to sell thousands of illegal items such as guns, drugs, fake credit cards, and counterfeit gold bars.

The stories of these cartels are long, many, secretive, and intricate, with complex interdependencies and connections.

Despite all the law enforcement, justice, and agency initiatives to have the kingpins imprisoned, the cartels remain active and operate globally and there is always another kingpin to take over from the one that is in jail. Sometimes, even jail terms provide a wonderful "office" to continue the illegal business.

The movement of illegal funds is hidden in convoluted accounting trails leading to offshore tax havens and shell companies or remains unknown, or the cash crosses borders and is exchanged. For many commodities trading around the world, cash is still king, surprisingly, so cash is still revered despite digitization. For example, Deloitte indicated (September 2019) that cash usage continues to grow in the South African economy, at a rate of 6–10 percent per annum, ahead of inflation. This suggests that there is still a long way to go concerning electronic payments. This is also applicable to most African countries, South America, and Asia. Cash will still be around for a long, long time.

Human and Sex Traffickers

"It Was As If We Weren't Human": Inside the Modern Slave Trade Trapping African Migrants

By the time his Libyan captors branded his face, Sunday Iabarot had already run away twice and had been sold three times. The gnarled scar that covers most of the left side of his face appears to show a crude number 3. His jailer carved it into his cheek with a fire-heated knife, cutting and cauterizing at the same time.

This is an introduction by Aryn Baker of *Time* on March 14, 2019, in an article that tells us the story of a thirty-two-year-old man who left his Nigerian hometown with the objective of getting on a smuggler's boat to take him across the Mediterranean to Europe. Jobs were plentiful, his friends on Facebook told him. He traveled some 2,500 miles over the desert plains of Niger and through the lawless tribal lands of southern Libya only to be captured in Libya and sold to armed men who constantly moved African migrants to favor their own labor needs and demand for ransom.

Nearly 25,000 victims of human trafficking were detected globally and reported to the United Nations Office on Drugs and Crime (UNODC) in 2016, and most of these people were trafficked to be sexually exploited. However, this figure reflects only the number of cases detected and reported to UNODC. The International Labor Organization estimates that five million people were victims of forced sexual exploitation (mainly women) in 2016, and one million of them were children. Similarly, people are trafficked for labor exploitation, with criminals taking advantage of desperate people wanting to emigrate.

The bodies of eight women and thirty-one men were found in a refrigerated trailer attached to a lorry in an industrial park in Grays, Essex, UK, in the early hours of October 23 in 2019, later to be identified as Vietnamese. How did they get there? The long journey was summarized by the *Telegraph* of the UK reporters on November 2, 2019.

The journey started in Bulgaria, and the lorry they were found in was registered in Varna on the Black Sea Coast. This route is apparently known as a route for cigarette smuggling and having links to a number of Irish Republican gangs. It passed through Portadown in Northern Island and then is believed to have boarded a ferry in Dublin, which crossed over to Wales. It is understood that only the cab of the truck boarded the ferry.

The cab then arrived at Holyhead and traveled by road to Essex. The container ship containing the trafficked people came from port of Zeebrugge—a Belgian port apparently known for migrant stowaways. This full container then arrived at the docks of Purfleet in Essex. At this time, the investigators do not understand why the cab and the container were separated nor designed to arrive four days apart.

"Maurice Robinson of Craigavon, Northern Ireland, (who drove the cab) was arrested shortly after the discovery. At twenty-five years of age, he has been charged with thirty-nine counts of manslaughter, conspiracy to traffic people, conspiracy to assist unlawful immigration, and money laundering." He is one of a few people arrested, including a woman.

Sex trafficking is seldom separate from human trafficking. When people are poor, have little control over their lives, and need money—and more so to send money home—they are vulnerable and easily lured to cross the moral line. Sex trafficking is a multibillion-dollar business.

For sensitive readers, it must be said there are many initiatives in countries around the world to stop human trafficking and there are many great testimonies; a very prominent project is the CNN Freedom Day Project #MyFreedomDay.

It is the high-profile people, their power, and their money that sexually exploit and traffic thousands of underage girls. American financier Jeffrey Epstein dropped out of university, and although he never completed a degree, he was a clever man. He worked as a teacher (what did he commit there, I wonder?), switched to the banking sector and moved on to Bear Sterns, and then formed his own company. His professional background makes for fascinating reading. While there were questions by journalists from time to time, the interested world was shocked at the revelations that the sex trafficking, which he had been doing for so many years and among so many high-profile men, were not reported. Trafficking is driven by demand, but it is said that poverty fuels the supply from the Philippines to Tanzania and the United States. Epstein took advantage of that. He was arrested on charges of sex trafficking and sex trafficking conspiracy in July 2019 for the second time in his life; his private jet, referred to as the Lolita Express for obvious reasons, included wealthy, high-profile passengers such as former president Bill Clinton, Prince Andrew, and Harvard professor Alan Dershowitz, who have all denied any wrongdoing.

Epstein committed suicide on August 10, 2019, much to the relief of many high-profile men because all charges were dropped. Epstein's most influential assistant, however, was his girlfriend Ghislaine Maxwell, who faced allegations of procuring and sexually trafficking underage girls for Epstein and others. As of April 2022, she was still incarcerated and would face sentencing in June 2022 for the enticement of minors, sex trafficking of children, and lying under oath. Technically, she could face sixty-five years in prison, but it is more likely to be twenty years. Maxwell was deemed a flight risk and therefore she was not granted bail.

In an article, "Human Trafficking in the Community Banks" by Nancy E. Lake, the author indicates that the human trafficking of twenty-one million slaves, according to a May 2014 report by the International Labour Organization, generates annual profits of $150 billion, which include $99 billion from commercial sexual exploitation. This is compared to the global sports of the same year, which generated $146 billion. The figure will be much higher now as human trafficking is a growing trend. She contends that community banks engage in processing proceeds from human trafficking whether banking personnel is aware of it or not.

Sadly, this trade is not easily exposed because those that are trapped in this way are poor, fearful, ashamed, or maltreated and have few other options even if they could manage to free themselves.

Sia Partners, who describe themselves as a next-generation consulting firm, indicated in June 2021, that "behind drug trafficking, human trafficking has become the fastest growing and most profitable international illicit crime in the world" and indicated that the International Labour Organization estimated that just over forty million people were in modern slavery as of 2016.

Human trafficking is not easy to identify, least of all by bankers or other financial institutions. Rather, hotel staff, nurses, air attendants, beauticians, factory workers, and domestic workers, particularly those that have been trained to spot the signs of trafficked victims, are where they are more likely to be identified and assisted.

Animal Traffickers

It is not only humans that are exploited; animals are exploited too.

The illegal animal trade has many moving parts, and every animal victim has a different purpose and value. But ultimately, animal trafficking only happens because there is a market for it. Every year, up to $23 billion worth of elephant tusks, rhino horns, tiger bones, bear bile, and other wildlife by-products illicitly change hands, according to United Nations estimates (2020).

Oxpeckers.org is Africa's first investigative environmental journalistic unit. Their work combines, as indicated on their website, traditional investigative reporting with data analysis and geo-mapping to expose eco-offenses and track organized criminal syndicates in southern Africa. They are one of a few units around the world that come across the dire treatment of animals used for smuggling. A small snippet from just one of the many reports opens a world of smuggling we usually do not hear much about:

> In the crime-ridden borderlands where Zimbabwe and South Africa meet, donkeys have been sought after by smuggling syndicates since late 2015 because they are silent and can transport heavy cargo across the rough terrain.

Recently, however, the beasts of burden have themselves become targets of smugglers and traders who sell them to abattoirs in South Africa, which export their hides and meat to China.

Edmore Mathibela leads a cross-border smuggling syndicate that operates in the Madimbo Corridor, on the South African side of the border, and he indicates that provided the right amount of money is paid, they are willing to smuggle cigarettes, clothing, minerals, stolen cars' parts, and stolen livestock. "Most donkey thefts on the Zimbabwean side are perpetrated by locals who are hired by South African syndicates based in Limpopo province. We help with smuggling them out to South Africa."

Mathibela said a culture of bribery and corruption has transformed the border area into a melting pot of strange bedfellows and cross-purposes as criminals and security agents collaborate. Apparently, soldiers and police are both found to be part of crime syndicates in the form of thieves, robbers, contraband smugglers, drug dealers, and muggers to further criminality. Even some officials or officers of the law are crime members, shareholders, beneficiaries, or indeed, informers. For example, they may provide updated information on border patrols for a fee for a share of the loot. "The smugglers combine bribery and evasion to run cigarettes, alcohol, gold, diamonds, people, goats, cattle, and donkeys past the border security patrols. Car theft syndicates use stolen or hired donkeys to pull top-range luxury cars stolen from South Africa across the Limpopo River into Zimbabwe."

There are so many horrific examples of how animals suffer when being transported: slender-billed parakeets transported, often with their feet and beaks taped, in one or two-liter plastic bottles with a few holes in them; stolen bird and reptile eggs are concealed in special vests so that couriers can bypass X-ray machines at airports; baby turtles are taped to trap them inside their shells and many shoved into one tube sock, and infant pythons are shipped in CD cases. People for the Ethical Treatment of Animals (PETA), in one of their articles, quoted the following:

> In one case, a man who was arrested at the Los Angeles airport had Asian leopard cats in a backpack, birds of paradise in additional luggage, and pygmy monkeys in his underwear." Their chances of survival? "We have a mortality of about 80 or 90 percent," says a German customs agent.

Their fateful journeys involve several stops along the way, from the trappers to intermediaries and from exporters, and then, for the final few that survive, to their destination. Seldom is that the end of their suffering as they are then incarcerated by unprepared or ignorant caretakers, never to be given a home in their natural habitat again, which may include pet stores and zoos. Even if animals are let free in a different environment, it changes the ecosystem and can kill native species, or they can be unknown vectors of human disease. COVID-19 of 2020/21 may be an example of how the world and its economy can be brought to its knees because of this.

Animals are taken from almost any country: pangolin parts from Nigeria, wildlife from Uruguay, infant langurs from Bangladesh, live monkeys and reptiles from Spain, and songbirds from Italy and Malta, so it is not just from Africa. Generally, few laws and penalties exist or are implemented, perhaps because animals may be considered less important in the scale of dramatic events. PETA indicates that the prices of animals' heads range from tens of thousands of dollars for a hyacinth macaw to a few dollars for a giant cockroach. It is a multibillion-dollar industry, and the buying and selling of protected wildlife are still today one of the largest sources of criminal earnings, behind only arms dealing and drug smuggling and "might very well be the world's most profitable form of illegal trade, bar none" according to *National Geographic*.

A May 2015 report on www.C4ads.org, "Species of Crime Typologies and Risk Metrics for Wildlife Trafficking," is broadly representative of the threats associated with wildlife transnational organized crime (TOC) and identifies seven key typologies that conclude that wildlife trafficking networks:

1. Nest illicit activities within licit financial and transport systems
2. Create complex means of physical obfuscation
3. Obfuscate beneficial ownership, sources of contraband, and funds by establishing shell or front organizations, or by other strategies
4. Manipulate multicountry accounts and payments schemes, including those that clear through Western jurisdictions
5. Demonstrate convergence with high-risk illicit activity

6. Demonstrate convergence with bribery and exposure to politically exposed persons (PEPs), and
7. Demonstrate beneficial, financial, or client relations with environmental product suppliers.

The fishing industry may or may not have dreadful tales hidden in its dark waters, but C4ADS has also authored a report (Strings Attached) on their investigations into the fishing industry. Illegal, unreported, and unregulated (IUU) fishing takes place. This interferes with the seafood supply chain and endangers the economic security of individuals, communities, and governments across the world. The onshore networks are as much to blame as the vessels are. I am aware that in South African waters around Cape Town, as an example, several fishing boats sell their quotas when they come onshore and appear legitimate, but meanwhile, other large quotas have been sold at sea to Chinese boats.

To give heart to animal lovers, in June 2019, Operation Thunderball was created. It was the largest ever anti-wild-life trafficking bust conducted by police, environmental authorities, wildlife and forestry agencies, border patrols, and customs agents in 109 countries in a joint operation by the World Customs Organization (WCO) and Interpol throughout June. The outcome saved thousands of trafficked plants and animals from around the world. Hundreds of arrests were made and many more are being or were investigated.

It was reported that "such initiatives will be replicated to raise awareness within the global law enforcement community on the gravity of global wildlife crime and to better coordinate cross-agency efforts, including the engagement of civil society groups to detect and deter wildlife criminal networks."

Commodities Traffickers

Mwanza's mine is at the center of one of the world's most important sources of gem-quality diamonds, so it is surprising that the Kasai Province capital of the Democratic Republic of Congo (DRC), Tshikapa, is a neglected, dusty, and derelict picture of poverty.

The mine is the death knell for miners who work in dangerous and unsafe mines. Every year, hundreds die in collapsed tunnels. This picture is mimicked in many other countries in Africa, especially where there is conflict.

Some twenty years ago, the illegal sale of blood diamonds produced billions of dollars to fund civil wars and other conflicts in countries in Africa such as Sierra Leone, Côte d'Ivoire, Liberia, Libya, the Democratic Republic of Congo (DRC), and Angola. Blood diamonds are usually mined in a war zone and sold to finance military operations. Civil conflicts proved a good reason to overtake existing governments and the control of the lucrative blood-diamond trade.

A typical such scenario was the 1991 start of the Revolutionary United Front (RUF) violence unleashed on people living and working in villages in Sierra Leone until they took control of the mines in that area. It went on for eleven years. The RUF threatened, killed, and even cut off the arms of people living and working in diamond villages until they were able to take control of the mines in the area. The RUF went from village to village, causing fear and flight. National Geographic News reported at the time that these conflicts combined had displaced millions and resulted in the deaths of more than four million people.

The Kimberley Process Certification Scheme, which prohibits the trade of conflict diamonds, was put in place to formalize the movement of diamonds. However, its limited definition and corrupt policies mean that if diamonds are sold because of conflict, there is no recourse for their sale. As long as the profits do not fund armed forces, they are considered ethically sourced, regardless of the human-rights abuses miners suffer to collect these gemstones.

MiaDonna.com reported the following on May 24, 2018: "According to Bain and Company, about 133 million carats of rough diamonds are mined each year—with 65 percent of them originating from Africa. Then consider the fact that if only one in four (25 percent) of diamond mines in Africa are well regulated, we can assume three of every four diamonds mined in Africa have a history of environmental and humanitarian abuses. This equals sixty-five million diamonds that are hitting the international diamond market each year or at least one in thirteen diamonds on the international market coming from a conflict origin."

Human Rights Watch released a report in February 2018 scrutinizing "steps taken by key actors within the jewelry industry to ensure that rights are respected in their gold and diamond supply chains." The report highlights the varying policies and practices of thirteen major jewelry brands in their efforts, and failures, to responsibly source their diamonds. The reason conflict diamonds are still a problem is that unknowing or uncaring consumers never check their origin. If they did, some further research may be necessary; some big businesses continue not to ask, and neither do some wealthy purchasers.

A Forbes article from early 2017 indicated that conflict diamonds from the Central African Republic (CAR) have found their way to Facebook's online marketplace. Despite the Kimberley Process, which implemented a ban in 2013, diamonds continue to fund wars that have killed thousands of people. According to a United Nations panel of experts, conflict diamonds are still being smuggled out of the CAR, with an estimated value of $24 million; that represents some 140,000 carats of conflict diamonds flooding the market despite the ban. The trade route is a circuitous one in that most of the smuggled diamonds are first taken to Cameroon, the DRC, and then Sudan before being released into international markets. Rebel groups can raise $3.87 million to $5.8 million a year, to continue funding their terror.

In Venezuela, all Venezuelan diamonds are labeled as being smuggled illegally, yet the country remains compliant with the Kimberley Process; Namibia extracts underwater diamonds and harms sea life. Angolan award-winning author and journalist Rafael Marques de Morais exposed hundreds of cases of murder, torture, mutilation, rape, and corruption linked to the diamond industry within Angola. In 2011, his book *Blood Diamonds: Corruption and Torture in Angola* documented the link between generals in the Angolan military and government ministers, and shareholders in mining and security companies that have committed brutality in diamond-mining districts.

It has been more than a decade since the term *blood diamonds* entered the public domain; the reality is that there are many companies, despite efforts at regulation, which sell blood diamonds.

South African gold is being looted on an industrial scale, with research estimating that the country loses about $1 billion through illegal gold mining every year. According to research by the Global Initiative Against Transnational Organized Crime (GI), there are large anomalies in gold trade data; it also shows how organized crime rings conduct mining operations on an industrial scale and gold is smuggled through Eswatini (Swaziland) and Mozambique to jewelry-manufacturing hubs in Dubai, Mumbai, and Karachi. These operations are performed by thousands of illegal miners and international networks of buyers. The modus operandi is reportedly to melt the illegally mined gold down with legitimate gold at refineries run by criminal syndicates. Then the gold is smuggled out of the country via second-hand gold and scrap-metal dealers. According to *Mining Review*, South Africa's illegal mining trade is estimated to be worth R7 billion a year, citing PwC South Africa's Mine Report 2017. The reasons behind this are thought to be gold's high value, the ease of finding willing buyers, and the high number of abandoned gold mines.

C4ADS.org is a nonprofit organization dedicated to providing data-driven analysis and evidence-based reporting on global conflict and transnational security issues. As an example of their work, their investigations and C4ADS satellite imagery and their automatic identification system (AIS) data, in November 2019, evidenced that at least two VLGCs (very large gas carriers, ships that carry between 50,000 and 80,000 cubic meters of gas) visited an export terminal in Iran to load up on liquefied petroleum gas (LPG), in violation of US economic sanctions on petroleum and petroleum-related products from Iran. After loading in Iran, these ships crossed the Indian Ocean, passed the Strait of Malacca, and arrived at import facilities at several locations in China.

Another example of C4ADS's work was the discovery of a series of large-scale sand-dredging operations in Haeju Bay, North Korea, in August 2020. They tracked hundreds of vessels that were dredging sand in Haeju Bay before transporting it to China. This sand extraction from North Korea to China violates United Nations Security Council (UNSC) Resolution 2397 (2017). "The activity in Haeju demonstrates the scale and a level of sophistication unlike other known cases of North Korean sanctions evasion at sea, providing renewed evidence of North Korea's evolving abilities to coordinate and execute complex operations with facilitators abroad.

"Sand is a critical material with various uses in modern infrastructures, such as concrete and glass in construction, and silicon chips in electronics. Although it is the world's most extracted natural resource today, its demand outstrips supply. As the price of sand has risen rapidly in recent years, so has the practice of both licit and illicit sand excavation and trade around the world."

How easy is that? Big ships, big business, and blow me down, it's brazen too. (What harm does it do to the ocean floor?)

Asia has about 7 percent of the world's old-growth forests and many unique tree species but is tragically experiencing the fastest deforestation rate in the world. It involves illicit logging; money and greed take precedence over environmental damage to the earth and its communities and pave the way for corrupt officials and violence to overrule. It is estimated that more than half of the global demand for illicitly logged timber comes from Asia and Europe and that about 20 percent of the global total of illegally felled timber is imported into the European Union and about 25 percent into China.

A 117-page report published by the Atlantic Council Global Energy Centre titled *Downstream Oil Theft Global Modalities, Trends, and Remedies*, written by Dr. Ian M. Ralby in 2017, indicates oil smuggling and theft. Part of the summary includes a paragraph that says it all: "Theft, fraud, smuggling, laundering, corruption. Hydrocarbon crime, in all its forms, has become a significant threat not only to local and regional prosperity but also to global stability and security. Combating this pervasive criminal activity is made only more difficult by the reality that many of those in a position to curb hydrocarbon crime are the ones benefiting from it."

The Stockholm International Peace Research Institute (SIPRI), the independent resource on global security, estimates that the total value of the global arms trade in 2017 was at least $95 billion. The top one hundred arms companies made an estimated $398.2 billion worth of sales in 2017 (reported on August 23, 2019). The Arms Trade Treaty, which was set up in 2014, has been a failure. Trade has grown in the last few years, and despite their commitment to regulating irresponsible arms trade, many key states' parties continue to sell arms to governments that commit serious human rights abuses. Data collected by Stockholm International Peace Research Institute shows that the global arms trade industry is continuing to supply weapons to some of the most deadly armed conflicts. China, France, Russia (suspended), the United Kingdom, and the United States, the five permanent members of the UN Security Council—a body charged with the maintenance of international peace and security—are collectively responsible for over 70 percent of the arms trade.

There is so much more illegal trafficking of almost any commodity, but the above indicates the broad extent of the world of trafficking, without giving too many statistics, which become meaningless in vast numbers.

Any product can be trafficked, whether designed for legal use or not. The ease with which these products can be moved, disguised, or pushed to and from anywhere in the world is difficult to grasp. How do they do it? How do we let it happen?

The powerful movers and shakers get their mules to do the dirty work while they live extravagantly. Mules just make a living. Those who make more than that, take the risk of losing their lives, being roughed up, or discarded from the only livelihood they know.

Most traffickers do not get caught; if they do, they may continue to traffic while serving a jail sentence. Much of the money made by traffickers is seldom found. For some traffickers, there is even recognition for their achievements: El Chapo was recognized as the sixtieth most powerful person in the world in 2013.

Traffickers escape from jail, serve shorter sentences than originally charged, or interfere for their own means in the political arena and get away with it.

Trafficking is pervasive, using any channel, platform, or commodity without a care for the environment and the disruption to communities.

The Profiteers

It is simplistic to align money laundering to criminals and terrorists because that context is misguided. It leaves out an entire population of money launderers who are rich, powerful, elite, connected, mostly educated, and self-resolute, with the world at their bidding.

Money represents the lifeblood of an organization, despite all the hype about corporate governance. For many companies around the world, we will never really know the extent of the money laundered and how it was laundered. It is unfair to mention only seven organizations as examples of what we do know about them, but these are names we all recognize:

Facebook was reported as giving several multinational companies such as Netflix, Amazon, Spotify, Microsoft, and Altaba (formerly Yahoo) the ability to access users' contact information, private messages, and friends' lists. Did users sign up for this? Mark Zuckerberg, the founder, is, at thirty-five, the sixth richest person in the world, worth $67.4 billion (at the time of writing), and faces a lot of controversies still regarding the use of this social media platform for nefarious activity purposes. The ethics behind the billions earned is questionable.

Linked to Facebook was Cambridge Analytica, a firm that combined data mining, data brokerage, and data analysis with strategic communication for political electoral processes. Cambridge Analytica acquired and used personal data about Facebook users from an external researcher who had told Facebook he was collecting it for academic purposes. Investigative undercover journalists exposed the CEO boasting about various nefarious deeds and honey traps to discredit politicians on whom it conducted opposition research on the one hand. On the other hand, Cambridge Analytica took on many election campaigns from countries around the world for lots of money. By collecting data from Facebook users to build psychographic profiles on them, Cambridge Analytica was able to create profiles of potential voters, which prompted a specific advertising message that would persuade such a voter to think accordingly. The Netflix documentary *The Great Hack* says it all and more.

The baby-friendly Johnson and Johnson has been found to have misrepresented the risk of opioid addiction to doctors, manipulating research and helping to drive an epidemic claiming thousands of lives and profiting further by buying poppy-growing companies to supply raw narcotics for itself and other drugmakers. Jerry Oppenheimer authored a book a few years ago called *The Crazy Rich*, which is a fascinating account of the Johnson and Johnson dynasty over five decades. It is difficult to know if wealth corrupted the Johnson family or merely enabled their immoral behavior. Has the company behaved similarly in the past about which we do not know? In May 2022, a documentary described a joint BBC investigation which found that Johnson and Johnson is one of three major firms that buy palm oil from companies that deprive Indigenous communities (such as the Orang Rimba) in Indonesia of potentially millions of dollars of income, despite having made promises of wealth and development. It was supposed to be a win-win, but the farmers were carelessly marginalized.

Purdue Pharma, the maker of OxyContin, filed for chapter 11 bankruptcy protection on September 15, 2019, just days after reaching a settlement with more than 2,000 local governments over the alleged role it played in adding to the American opioid addiction crisis by marketing OxyContin even though the company knew that it was addictive. The Sackler family agreed to relinquish ownership of the lucrative company and agreed to pay $3 billion in cash over several years and future revenue from the sale of OxyContin, to assist communities hardest hit by the opioid epidemic. This is an unusual settlement. Normally litigation (usually protracted over years) is the normal legal response. In this way, society benefits by having $3 billion dollars to use to fight the opioid crisis. When there is so much money, it is easy to pay fines to benefit a society that you led to need this assistance in the first place.

It was reported in July 2019 that Microsoft Corp agreed to pay about $25.3 million, including a criminal fine, to settle US charges that it made improper payments that were used to bribe government officials in Hungary and other countries. The payment of an $8.75 million criminal fine to be paid by Microsoft Hungary, according to the US Department of Justice, is part of a three-year non-prosecution agreement in which it admits, accepts, and acknowledges responsibility for employees' misconduct. Microsoft also agreed to pay $16.6 million to settle related civil charges by the US Securities and Exchange Commission over its activities in Hungary, Saudi Arabia, Thailand, and Turkey, without admitting wrongdoing. Microsoft violated the federal Foreign Corrupt Practices Act in both cases.

Amazon's federal tax bill was $0 for the second year in a row (through a combination in part of legitimate tax credits and deductions) despite nearly doubling its taxable income in 2018 to $11.2 billion, from $5.6 billion a year earlier. While other taxes were paid, and taxes paid on behalf of employees, the tax incentives Amazon gets through its company structures, intercompany transfers, expenses, and inventories ensure minimal taxation and feed the head himself, Jeff Bezos, presently the richest person in the world at some $202 billion (August 2020). It is not illegal, but the tax avoidance trails in the unethical stance of intentional greedy enrichment.

Steinhoff International is a South African international retail holding company that is dual-listed on the German and South African stock exchanges. It deals mainly in furniture and household goods, and as of August 2016, Steinhoff held retailing activities in thirty countries, counting 6,500 retail outlets belonging to forty different brands and employing about 90,000 employees. Serious accounting irregularities were performed by former executives and senior management over a few years. They performed transactions that were either fictitious or irregular. This resulted in inflating the profit and asset values of the Steinhoff Group. Why do they inflate profit and asset values? To pay themselves more, of course.

And the auditors? The auditor fees (which include actual audit fees) totaled €16 million for the 2017 financial year, €28 million in the 2018 financial year, and €11 million in the first six months of 2019. It is known to date to be the biggest example of fraud in South African history. The fraud was complex: it was not detected by Steinhoff's audit and risk committee, not by its internal or external auditors, not by its bankers, not by the rating agencies, not by the investment managers, and not by anyone else who lent money to Steinhoff. The question must be asked here: why not? That is because everybody, that is, the supply chain, was benefiting from it.

And what about the water companies in the UK? The industry is already reeling, with water companies having been heavily criticized for taking on debt and paying billions to their offshore owners while delivering poor service to households.

These are all examples of money earned illegally and, if not illegally, unethically; anything that yields profits is fit for purpose. The more complex the connections and transactions, the easier it is to launder money.

The Terror Funders

While money laundering and the financing of terrorism are two phenomena that differ in many ways, they exploit the same vulnerabilities directly through people or financial systems. The same attention to opacity hides the source of the funds; the main difference is that one system is used to make and retain money, and the other is to finance acts of terrorism.

An act of terrorism that stunned the world for its sheer audacity took place in 2001, on September 11, when nineteen al-Qaeda terrorists hijacked four airplanes intending to attack America—the first foreign force to do so on American soil. At 8:46 a.m., American flight 11 crashed into the North Tower of the World Trade Center. At 9:03 a.m., United flight 175 crashed into the South Tower. At 9:40 a.m., American flight 77 crashed into the Pentagon, and at 10:03 a.m., hijacked flight United flight 93 crashed into a field in Shanksville, Pennsylvania—the plane's target was believed to be the US Capitol, and it may have been prevented from doing so by the bravery of passengers on board. Some 3,000 people lost their lives. This was a long time ago, but it led to the recognition of the funding of terrorism.

The other brutal terrorist group that rose to prominence in early 2014 was the Sunni Islamist group known as ISIS or ISIL. As al-Shām is a region often compared with the Levant or Greater Syria, the terrorists are known as the Islamic State of Iraq and al-Sham, or Islamic State of Iraq and Syria (both abbreviated as ISIS), or the Islamic State of Iraq and the Levant (abbreviated as ISIL). Their defining feature was the public release of videotaped beheadings of people who resisted their ideology. They gained enormous physical ground in Iraq and Syria. Generating capital by way of bank robbery, pirating oil fields, and robbing other economic assets, ISIS had access to a lot of money as their revenue streams were diversified and far-reaching, including the donations from people, legitimate businesses, and charitable organizations that supported their ideology. The group was pushed out of Iraq and Syria (after killing thousands of innocent citizens) by the United States, British, and French militaries.

The fall of Raqqa, the caliphate's stronghold, and the symbolic Syrian city looked to be the end of ISIS. However, media reports in 2019 say ISIS is still operating in these countries and other countries in North Africa such as Libya, Tunisia, Morocco, and Algeria. Their tentacles are growing, and threats to the Middle East and Europe have already been felt.

Another group that is also well-known is al-Shabaab, which, for example, killed twenty-six people in July 2019 in a suicide and bomb attack on a popular hotel in southern Somalia; another suicide attack on Nairobi's Dusit Hotel and shopping complex in January 2019 killed twenty-one people.

Regardless of how terrorists raise their capital, the end goal is to ultimately disguise the funds by exploiting global financial systems.

Perhaps, contrary to money laundering, the actual acts of terrorism are relatively low-cost compared to the damage they inflict; however, the operational costs of sustaining such organizations can be significant.

Money used for terrorism is often much harder to detect, and it comes from diverse sources, ranging from a religious activist group to genuinely earned money or earned from drug trafficking. Irrespective of the source of the money, funding terrorism is considered a money-laundering event. The movement of money between corridors, for example, goes from Kenya to Nigeria or South Africa to Mozambique.

As an example, the current state of al-Shabaab and the Islamic State networks in South Africa supporting terrorism in

Mozambique has been captured in a research report by Global Initiative in February 2022, *Insurgency, illicit markets, and corruption: The Cabo Delgado conflicts and its regional implications.*

The report indicates that the main sources of funding for the Mozambique insurgency are local in that funding is mostly obtained from the support of local business people, cash and goods seized during attacks, and looting. However, the involvement in this illicit economy remains a small proportion of their funding base, which is mostly through kidnap for ransom.

The goals of the research are to ensure the stability of local governance structures, to understand what drives corruption, and to invest in the region to address economic inequality in a way that is transparent and locally based. Another focus is on professional resources to protect and serve the people of Cabo Delgado and to use specialist prosecutorial and police teams in Cabo Delgado, Niassa, and Nampula to tackle the illicit economies.

On the other side of the corridor is the Southern African Development Community (SADC), which is a regional economic community comprising sixteen member states: Angola, Botswana, Comoros, Democratic Republic of Congo, Eswatini, Lesotho, Madagascar, Malawi, Mauritius, Mozambique, Namibia, Seychelles, South Africa, Tanzania, Zambia, and Zimbabwe. Among the objectives, the research recommends that SADC member states collaborate on regional threats and improve intelligence-sharing. Another is to support Mozambique to improve security force relationships with the local people.

This is going to take a long time to achieve while the Mozambique terrorist threat increases.

Heads Of State And Their Minions

Money laundering by government officials, many heads of state, and their contacts are prolific in not many but most countries around the world. It seriously intercepts the political integrity of states and businesses, not to mention the stability and robustness of the economy and the social effectiveness of society. These rogues are individuals who have been entrusted with prominent public functions, including heads of state or government, senior politicians, senior government, judicial or military officials, senior executives of publicly owned corporations, and important political party officials. These individuals, especially when they come from countries with a significant corruption problem, abuse their official functions for their financial gain through embezzlement, receipt of bribes, and other criminal activities. Illegal proceeds are deftly moved out of the country to willing offshore havens and equally eager, greedy lawyers and accountants who set up shell companies and trusts to hide the source of the money.

Government seniors and their minions are adept at converting their illicit proceeds into clean funds by buying real estate and other assets in foreign countries. Government officials who steal from their people, extort businesses, or seek and accept bribery payments to funnel their illicit gains into purchasing assets such as luxury real estate, hotels, private jets, artwork, and motion picture companies are commonplace. This practice distorts the economy because legitimate individuals and businesses are excluded from buying or investing in those properties or assets. Moreover, theft of government funds erodes trust in government and private institutions, undermines confidence in the fairness of free and open markets, and breeds contempt for the rule of law, which threatens our national security.

The unmitigated joy of having political power or unlimited power or access to those with political power is the ease with which the country's money jar can be pillaged or, for favors, be embellished with bribes and kickbacks. These government elitists accumulate personal fortunes in their own countries and shift that wealth into the broader financial system.

Many government officials and heads of state hardly ever get prosecuted, usually refuse to resign if called to do so, simply continue to deny charges, and fight politically to stay in power. And, unbelievably, continue to have adoring fans.

Many examples given in this book in the following chapter on money laundering involve public officials that are high-ranking, including presidents and other heads of state.

The *New Yorker*, June 18, 2018, "The Reputation-Laundering Firm That Ruined Its Own Reputation," tells us of a "PR company that worked with dictators and oligarchs deliberately inflamed racial tensions in South Africa—and destroyed itself in the process."

Oakbay Investments was owned by three powerful businessmen (who are brothers) operating in South Africa, namely Atul, Ajay, and Tony Gupta. "The Guptas, brothers who had holdings in everything from uranium mining to newspapers, maintained close ties with Jacob Zuma, the president of South Africa, and were notorious for having leveraged this connection for profit and influence. Three members of Zuma's family had worked in Gupta-owned businesses." ("Operating in South Africa" is a ridiculously euphemistic description. They raped the land by the billions.)

Bell Pottinger was one of London's leading public relations firms.

On January 14, 2016, four of their publicists met with Oakbay. The purpose of the visit was to launch a public relations campaign to highlight economic inequality in South Africa and to persuade black South Africans that they "were poorer than they should be, mainly because large white-owned corporations had outsized power. The campaign, a Gupta suggested, would not only be beneficial to the country but would also bolster his family's financial position, by casting the brothers not as overstepping oligarchs but as outsiders countering white supremacy." The article goes on to say, "Bell Pottinger's work in South Africa included the covert dissemination of articles, cartoons, blog posts, and tweets implying that the Guptas' opponents were upholding a racist system." As the account became more public, the relationship with Zuma drew more curiosity and therefore exposure. The campaign was deemed as an inflammatory economic-emancipation campaign. Soon, one of the world's savviest reputation-management companies became embroiled in a reputational scandal. Bell Pottinger could not contain the uproar, and in September 2017, it collapsed.

London is a honeypot for the international super-rich and is accepted as the world's financial center. As the author, Ed Caesar, writes, "A network of services is available to oligarchs, sheiks, and mandarins with the proper investment profiles. Lawyers, accountants, fund managers, and real estate agents have become a kind of butler class to the extraordinarily wealthy, helping them to reinvest or to hide their wealth. Publicists like Bell managed the public images of rich and powerful people from around the globe. In 2010, the *Guardian* called London the world capital of reputation laundering."

Power yields anything fit for purpose.

CHAPTER 2

A Picture of Money Laundering Around the World: The Paint Is Not Yet Dry

THIS IS AN arbitrary choice of money laundering episodes taken from an equally arbitrary choice of some fifty countries that made news around the world over about sixty months. These examples are all moving targets in terms of reported crimes, investigations, charges, justice, jail terms, reprieves, and collaborations, and each true example reported here represents the news at the time of writing the example. I am grateful that much of the media and many of the journalists bring money laundering to our attention; many times it is only through their efforts that money laundering is revealed.

You may not want to read the example given in each country. This chapter is designed to give you an inkling of the pervasiveness of money laundering around the world. Believe me, it is everywhere.

After my research, this is my take on it:

Money laundering examples around the world reveal
A soaring and spiraling success in making millions of dollars
And a great penchant for pervasiveness
In this dishonest world of ours.

Money laundering examples around the world reveal
Ostentatious opportunities
An abundance of architects
All colluding, connecting, and schmoozing
In this greedy world of ours.

Money laundering examples around the world reveal
Moribund economies
Emboldened rulers
Weakened justice
Costing lives and livelihood
In this uncaring world of ours.

The United Kingdom—its nickname is Londongrad

London's nickname is Londongrad. It is named after Leningrad because it is considered home to Russia's wealthy expat community, especially oligarchs. Some twenty years ago, lots of money was pouring into London from wealthy Russians, most of the money being dirty money. How much exactly is probably not known.

In 2017, the *Guardian* revealed that it had received documents from a three-year investigation by the Latvian and Moldovan authorities on the "global laundromat." The documents revealed that between 2010 and 2014, British registered companies and British-based banks helped move at least $20 billion of the proceeds of criminal activities from Russia to London.

Before that, even the Home Affairs Select Committee, a government department that examines the expenditure, administration, and policy of the Home Office and its associated public bodies, concluded that the London property market was the corridor for the laundering of £100 billion of illicit money a year.

What was London's attraction? Because it was a financial hub of the world, with millions of transactions passing through, it was easier to get lost in the crowd. Also, knowing who the owners are of businesses did not raise any queries.

The *Guardian*, in early 2019, referred to a report on economic crime that indicated the scale of laundered money entering the UK was "was very uncertain, with estimates ranging from tens of billions of pounds upwards." An area of vulnerability is the property market and company formation. The report came after the *Guardian* and partners around the world revealed how Russian money had been channeled into the UK and used to pay for everything from luxury properties, yachts, and cars, to school fees. It went on further to reveal that hundreds of UK firms had been used to disguise the sources and beneficiaries of millions of pounds worth of transactions. A former fund manager called Bill Browder gave evidence to parliament's home affairs committee, in which he revealed how £22 million that had been stolen from the Russian state by a group of corrupt police officers and officials had come to the UK via twelve different banks and been spent on an array of luxury goods: $176,000 on chartering a private jet; $192,000 on redecorating a yacht; $20,000 on private school fees; $41,000 on a wedding dress; $295,000 to pay off an exclusive women-only credit card that offers "the most privileged and luxurious service."

The minister for national security at the time said, "Those with dirty cash to clean don't just sit on it. They reinvest it in serious organized crime, from drug importation to child sexual exploitation, human trafficking, and even terrorism."

As one journalist described it, "The ordure churned out by Russian crooks and kleptocrats is thus, thanks to the skilled attentions of the tax havens' best brains, indistinguishable from ordinary investment."

If bank analysts decided to investigate the question of money laundering, they "could have walked down the hall and asked their colleagues since it turned out that Deutsche Bank itself was a significant culprit in spiriting money out of Russia without informing the authorities. Less than two years after the report—called Dark Matter—was published, Deutsche Bank traders in Moscow were caught secretly moving $10 billion (£7.5 billion) of their clients' money out of Russia by illegally exploiting the stock market."

With examples of institutions as sophisticated as Deutsche Bank working to hide Russian money, it is no surprise that the amount of money laundered is vague. It is said that by letting Putin's allies launder their stolen fortunes and hide them in the UK, the UK is drawing a line under their crimes and rewarding the Russians for doing it.

The invasion of Ukraine on February 24, 2022, by the Russians and the abhorrent atrocities they are committing have rallied NATO members to unite in their determination to retaliate by weakening Russia by applying serious sanctions, asset freezes, and travel bans on oligarchs that have links to Putin. We do not have to question why are oligarchs only now facing asset freezes? The answer is easy. It is all about the money usually, but finally, there is a superseding cause. There are oligarchs associated with many governments around the world, but the association with the Putin regime is somehow the most acknowledged.

The United States Of America—Friends With The Russian Presidency And Russian Oligarchs

Donald Trump is a past president of the United States. Presently there are about a dozen investigations against him, and some of them include suspected money laundering, tax evasion, and links to the Russian presidency and Russian oligarchs.

Time magazine on March 24, 2019, gave a list of twelve investigations but indicates that some may not yet have been made public and there are other loosely connected players also being investigated because of the Mueller investigation. Some revelations from Michael Cohen (Trump's lawyer who is serving a three-year sentence for the Stormy Daniels affair), real estate loan transactions through Deutsche Bank, the since-dissolved Donald J. Trump Foundation and its directors that have been sued by the New York attorney general's office for a "shocking pattern of illegality" and for violating tax laws, and his personal tax history, tax schemes, and tax issues over some years are just some examples. (Whew!) The *New York Times* investigation found that he received at least $413 million in today's dollars from his father's real estate empire, much of it through tax dodges in the 1990s. Donald Trump assisted his father in many of those tax dodges and continued to participate in dubious tax schemes during the 1990s, including instances of outright fraud, which greatly increased the fortune he received from his parents.

Past president Donald Trump's former campaign manager, Paul Manafort, seventy-one, sought an early release from prison because of the threat the coronavirus posed to his health, to serve the remainder of his seven and a half-year sentence for a series of convictions on charges of tax evasion, failing to report foreign bank accounts, witness tampering, and engaging in unregistered lobbying for foreign interests.

Among the luxury goods on display during Manafort's trial on thirty-two counts of financial fraud and money laundering was a python coat for which he paid $18,500, nearly twice what he paid for an ostrich waistcoat, but a mere fraction of what he spent on clothes, rugs, and garden landscaping—all funded by lobbying for foreign governments.

Mexico—"I Will Fight Crime And Commit A Crime"

Anger at widespread corruption scandals, including the alleged bribes from Odebrecht, a lucrative house deal involving the family of past president Enrique Peña Nieto, and hundreds of millions of dollars siphoned from government coffers through fake contracts, helped leftist Andrés Manuel López Obrador win a landslide presidential victory, and he took office on December 1, 2018.

López Obrador pledged in his manifesto to clamp down on financial crime and tighten money-laundering, banking, and tax regulations. From Reuters' Stefanie Eschenbacher, September 2018: Lopez's full name is Andrés Manuel López Obrador, and he refers to himself as AMLO. By law around the world, a compliance officer focusing on anti-money-laundering measures is usually referred to as an anti-money-laundering officer (an AMLO).

Fox40.com/news posted on March 29, 2021, that AMLO proposed yet another law to allow authorities to take over private gas stations and hand their businesses over to the state-owned oil company Pemex in the name of protecting the economy and national security. This is predicted to weaken private companies, strengthen inefficient state-owned companies, and turn back private sector involvement in the energy sector.

On Bloomberg.com an opinion was published by Shannon O'Neil, a senior fellow for Latin America Studies at the Council on Foreign Relations, in New York on February 4, 2020: "Yet on corruption, voters' hopes and the president's rhetoric seem to have left rationality and reality behind. Not only has his administration overlooked high-profile cases of public graft, but it's also dismantling the institutions that could make Mexico more transparent and accountable." (Surveys show that one in three Mexicans pays a bribe every year for basic services; nearly half of businesses say they lost out to others offering kickbacks.)

Angola—In Charge Of Crime

The son of Angola's former president Jose Eduardo dos Santos has been charged with fraud over an alleged illegal transfer of $500 million while he oversaw the country's sovereign wealth fund.

Iran—Sanctions A Doorway To Crime

"[Iran's] objective is to ensure that no legitimate company or government knows that they are being used to achieve Iran's illicit aims . . . To those in the private sector, I urge you to also take additional steps to ensure Iran and its proxies are not exploiting your companies to support their nefarious activities. You may think your clients and counterparties are legitimate, but they may be part of the Iranian regime's deceptive schemes to fund terrorism and human rights abuses," said the undersecretary of the Treasury for Terrorism and Financial Intelligence, Sigal Mandelker, June 5, 2018 (www.ffd.org).

Notwithstanding the number of sanctions instituted against Iran, the risks of doing business in Iran are substantial, because of pervasive corruption, legal risk, systemic human rights violations, and persistent support for foreign terrorist organizations. In May, the US Treasury's Office of Foreign Assets Control (OFAC) designated sanctions against the governor of the Central Bank of Iran for covertly funneling millions of dollars to Hezbollah on behalf of the Islamic Revolutionary Guard Corps' Quds Force. The involvement of the central bank governor in money laundering and illicit finance illustrates the extreme degree to which Iran's entire financial system has been compromised. Iran was blacklisted by the Financial Action Task Force in February 2020 for a period of time. As of June 2022, it was no longer blacklisted.

Iraq—Commit Fraud And Get Appointed Again

Iraq issued arrest warrants for a former trade minister and two senior officials after they were found guilty of embezzling $14.3 million in public funds. This was reported by the *New Arab* on November 20, 2018.

While the minister was not named, a source at the Integrity Commission told the global news agency AFP that the most high-profile convict was former Trade Minister Malas Abdulkarim al-Kasnazani. Kasnazani and the two other officials were tried in absentia and sentenced to seven years in prison. However, it would appear they fled Iraq and therefore would not be facing justice.

Kasnazani has a history of committing fraud, having forged Saddam Hussein's signature, and for an unrelated issue, got sacked under the previous government as a trade minister. It is interesting to note that despite his background, he later got appointed as a trade minister again.

AFP reported that "the embezzlement of public goods—from land to government funds—is a deeply rooted problem in a country with such a large public sector.

"Corruption, shell companies, and 'phantom' public employees who receive salaries but do not work have cost the country the equivalent of $228 billion since 2003, according to Iraq's parliament. That figure is more than Iraq's gross domestic product and nearly three times the annual budget."

As indicated by Open Democracy in December 2019, the corruption of both US and Iraqi officials during the US occupation is well documented. UN Security Council resolution 1483 established a $20 billion development fund for Iraq using previously seized Iraqi assets, money left in the UN's "oil for food" program, and new Iraqi oil revenues. Auditors, KPMG and an inspector general, discovered that much of the money had been stolen or misused both by the US and Iraq officials.

All of this has cost the war-torn country hundreds of billions of dollars. As with almost every new government, heads of state and politicians promised to fight the corruption that is "rotting Iraq inside out, little has been done or achieved. When convictions are made, it is usually in absentia, and incarcerations, while punishingly long, are also increasingly rare."

Iraq is the eighteenth most corrupt country in the world, according to Transparency International (2019).

Albania—Government Linked To Organized Crime

In December 2018, thousands of Albanian opposition supporters called for the resignation of Prime Minister Edi Rama and Interior Minister Fatmir Xhafaj during a protest in the capital Tirana, accusing them of links to organized crime and drug smuggling. The brother of Xhafaj turned himself in to the Italian authorities to serve a 2002 sentence for drug trafficking. The former Interior Minister, Saimir Tahiri, was also reported as being involved in drug smuggling and corruption.

Ireland—The Irish Have It

The Irish government has been slow to tackle international corruption involving Irish companies and financial institutions, according to its 2018 edition of Transparency International's Exporting Corruption report, rating countries based on their enforcement against foreign bribery under the Organization for Economic Cooperation and Development (OECD) Anti-Bribery

Convention. Ireland is a member, and therefore, it is a crime for Irish companies to bribe officials overseas.

It further indicates that "while the report welcomes the recent enactment of new anticorruption legislation, Ireland has yet to prosecute any company alleged to have bribed foreign officials and is considered to be among eighteen countries that have little or no enforcement of the Convention." It is also noted that several recent money laundering investigations or cases brought in other countries have mentioned the use of Irish shell companies. Irish-based banks are also accused of failing to prevent the laundering of the proceeds of corruption from overseas.

Lichtenstein—Impenetrable Offshore Trusts

The Principality of Liechtenstein is Europe's smallest country, wedged in between Austria and Switzerland. It may be the least-visited country in Europe, but it holds enormous wealth on behalf of many of the world's super-rich, ruling dynasties, and Russian oligarchs. It is a tax haven, and it is said to have more registered companies than citizens and it has the highest gross domestic product per person in the world.

It specializes in administering impenetrable offshore trusts and foundations to protect assets and secure them for families and future generations. Even well-known companies such as furniture giant Ikea deposited an estimated $11 billion (£8 billion) in a foundation registered in Liechtenstein.

The *Independent* reported on March 8, 2018, that a luxury Tudor-like mansion called Kenstead Hall in Hampstead, London, was registered by a relatively unknown Liechtenstein entity known as the Asturion Foundation. However, the real owner is King Fahd of Saudi Arabia. This is evidence that Liechtenstein clouds these registrations with mystique and mystery. The security provided cannot easily be penetrated; no leaks of confidential information can therefore be accessed.

But within this secret veil of money management, there probably lurks further corruption. Under the law, beneficiaries of the trust can be left with not getting access to their assets. Under the laws of the principality, legal rights are held by the trustees, so even a trustee cannot be trusted. This is also known as a discretionary trust, which is widely applied almost anywhere in the world.

Liechtenstein says it is acting against fraud, tax evasion, and money laundering, and it has been removed from the blacklist of countries that have been uncooperative on tax investigations. But the article warns that the history of the ruler when it comes to financial integrity is not a healthy one. A Senate subcommittee focusing on banks registered in tax havens referred to the LGT Bank as "a willing partner and an aider and abettor to clients trying to evade taxes, dodge creditors, or defy court orders." The LGT Bank is owned by the prince of Saudi Arabia's family who also serves on the board.

Madagascar—Corruption In Rosewood

Madagascar has for some time been drafting proposals for getting rid of its vast stockpile of illegally harvested rosewood. The committee that regulates world trade in endangered species refuses to accept the proposals because it involves paying off the local timber barons.

The Environmental Investigation Agency says that Madagascar has "likely the largest and most valuable timber stockpile on Earth." The idea behind the last proposal is to eliminate all these stockpiles to improve the control and monitoring of new illegal logging.

The stockpile is estimated at two million precious logs. It is an estimate because most of the logs are hidden by the local timber barons. These logs, rosewood and ebony, fetch thousands of dollars on Chinese markets.

Government corruption in Madagascar has been a problem for more than a decade. Transparency International rates the country at the time of writing as the twenty-second most corrupt country in the world, which indicates rampant corruption.

This downward slide in ranking has been aggravated by the conflicts between agencies and levels of government, allowing wood traders to seek export clearance for bribes.

Mozambique—Easy Trafficking

On August 30, 2019, AllAfrica reported that Mozambique had the world's highest money laundering and terrorist financing risk among 125 countries assessed by the Basel Institute of Governance: "Poor border controls and weak government institutions expose the country to cross-border crimes related to drugs and human trafficking. Mozambique is also vulnerable to other predicate offenses including corruption, car theft and smuggling, robbery, cash smuggling, illicit trade in precious metals and stones, customs fraud, and goods smuggling. Mozambique has high risks associated with corruption, which is a pervasive problem in the country."

The use of the term *systemic corruption* appears in a footnote in the report in which the IMF defines it as circumstances where "corruption is no longer a deviation from the norm but is manifested in a pattern of behavior so pervasive and ingrained that it becomes the norm." The footnote continues: "Systemic corruption has also been defined as corruption that is both pervasive and organized, affecting different levels of government, and practiced by bureaucrats and politicians alike in nearly all government departments."

Panama—Trump Ocean International Criminal Hotel

Proceeds from Colombian cartels' narcotics trafficking were laundered through the Trump Ocean Club. Donald Trump was one of the beneficiaries. The chief investigator on a Global Witness Report, Narco-a-Lago November 2017, was Ken Silverstein; material from an NBC and Reuters interview with Alexandre Henrique Ventura Nogueira was contributed. The following is adapted and summarized from that report.

A series of bankruptcies in the early 2000s meant Donald Trump was shunned by most lenders. Struggling for credit, he sold his name to high-end real estate projects. The first was the Trump Ocean Club International Hotel and Tower in Panama, which attracted criminal connections and set the scene for the further disturbing hallmarks of other Trump developments.

Since he became president of the United States, numerous investigations and articles have probed his business dealings and his alleged links to criminals and other shadowy characters. His brand to the luxurious Trump Ocean Club International Hotel and Tower in Panama aligned Trump's commercial interests with crooks looking to launder ill-gotten gains such as the proceeds from Colombian cartels' narcotics trafficking, which were laundered through the Trump Ocean Club. Donald Trump was one of the beneficiaries.

A key player in the laundering of drug money at the Trump Ocean Club was the notorious fraudster David Eduardo Helmut Murcia Guzmán, whom a US court subsequently sentenced to nine years for laundering millions of dollars' worth of illicit funds, including narcotics proceeds, through companies and real estate.

Another was Alexandre Henrique Ventura Nogueira, who brokered a third of the 666 preconstruction unit sales at the Trump Ocean Club. He claims to have sold 350–400 units overall. His sales brokerage was critical to ensuring the project's lift-off and Trump's ability to earn tens of millions of dollars.

This growth took place from 2006 to 2011, a period when Panama was known as one of the best places in the world to launder money. Whole neighborhoods in Panama City were taken over by organized crime groups, and luxury developments were built to serve as money laundering vehicles. Investing in luxury properties is a tried and trusted way for criminals to move tainted cash into the legitimate financial system, where they can spend it freely. This facilitated vast profits from criminal activities like trafficking people and drugs, organized crime, and terrorism to find their way into the US and elsewhere. In most countries, regulation is notoriously lax in the real estate sector. Cash payments are subject to hardly any scrutiny, giving opportunistic and unprincipled developers free rein to accept dirty money. A certain volume of preconstruction sales was necessary to secure financing for the project, which stood to net $75.4 million by the end of 2010. Trump received a percentage of the financing he helped secure, and a cut on the sale of every unit at the development. He and his family have made millions of dollars more from management fees, which probably continues.

In an interview with NBC and Reuters, Ventura Nogueira said that 50 percent of his buyers were Russian and that they had "questionable backgrounds." He added that he found out later that some were part of the Russian mafia.

Since the Russian government interfered in the 2016 American election, a lot has been made of Trump's heavy reliance on funds from Russia for his licensing deals, some of which have come from criminal networks.

Colombia—On One Hand And On The Other

Jose Irizarry earned a good reputation for fighting crime as a special agent of the American Drug Enforcement Administration (DEA), and more specifically for overseeing undercover investigations that led to dozens of drug arrests. Jose was transferred to the Colombian city of Cartagena to continue his good work. He certainly worked hard, but just as hard at (allegedly) furthering his own goals of living an extravagant lifestyle. The *Washington Post* of February 24, 2020 reported that Jose spent money on homes, cars, and jewelry, and hosted wild yacht parties with bikini-clad prostitutes. It raised red flags within the agency. "How was someone who had declared bankruptcy years earlier able to afford homes in Cartagena, Puerto Rico, and South Florida, three Land Rovers, a BMW, trips to Europe, and a $30,000 Tiffany diamond ring?"

Ironically, Jose allegedly had been laundering money for the very cartel he was fighting against and was arrested for crimes relating to money laundering, wire fraud, bank fraud, and identity theft. The Justice Department confirmed that his wife, Nathalia, was accused of "diverting millions of dollars of drug money from the control of the DEA." She was able to do this because she used her husband's power, influence, and access to information, all to his financial benefit. Irizarry resigned in early 2018 after the DEA grew suspicious. He is believed to have laundered more than $7 million.

Jose formed part of this corrupt scheme all the while supposedly being required to investigate the money-laundering activity of drug trafficking organizations. Prosecutors, in their lengthy formal accusation, indicated that his position allowed him easy access to information to enrich himself while, at the same time, diverting drug money from DEA control to the control of him and his accomplices.

Even though Jose had shown signs of dishonesty during a polygraph test and had declared bankruptcy (being in debt to the tune of $500,000), the DEA allowed him to continue with his job of handling millions of dollars in financial transactions.

Using the DEA, he had set up an undercover operation to send money and contraband to Colombia on behalf of suspected drug traffickers using front companies and shell bank accounts. He then filed false reports and "directed DEA agents to wire money reserved for undercover stings to accounts in places like Spain and the Netherlands that were tied to his wife and his two unnamed co-conspirators." This meant the account was opened in the name of another person, who then became a victim whose signature was forged and whose social security number was used.

Pakistan—Money From Heaven

Arabnews.com reported on October 28, 2018, that a humble rickshaw driver, when he accessed his equally humble bank account, found it had been credited with three billion rupees (at the time equivalent to $22.5 million). His first instinct was to hide when he received a call from the Federal Investigation Agency, but his family encouraged him to cooperate.

This case is indicative of many other related stories of bank accounts in poor residents' names being flooded with cash and quickly emptied in a laundering scheme "that has likely seen hundreds of millions of dollars moved out of the country."

New Zealand—Not So Clean

Mike Stone, director of the AML Group, was reported in *Scoop* on March 4, 2020, as saying, "Each year about $1.35 billion from the proceeds of fraud and illegal drugs is laundered through everyday New Zealand businesses." The incident that prompted that remark was that Jiaxin Finance, a money remitter, had been fined for deliberately structuring payments so that they would not be reportable under New Zealand anti-money-laundering laws. That is aiding and abetting money laundering, or terrorist financing.

North Korea—So Much For Sanctions

North Korea—for all the sanctions against it—seems to be proficient in cryptocurrency laundering.

In 2020, two Chinese nationals were charged with conspiring with North Korean state-sponsored hackers to steal millions of dollars of digital money from cryptocurrency exchanges using intricate automated schemes to confuse their sources.

M. Orcutt (March 5, 2020) in "This is how North Korea uses cutting-edge crypto money laundering to steal millions," *MIT Technology Review*, said that the laundering of illicit crypto currency does not have it easy. There are two main considerations. The first is that big deposits of Bitcoin can be made at different exchanges without raising any red flags. The second is that Bitcoin transactions can be traced (by virtue of blockchain's public ledger), but "users are pseudonymous, represented on the blockchain by strings of numbers and letters called addresses. But if investigators can tie an address to a real-world identity, they can track its every single transaction.

"To clear these hurdles, the North Korean hackers sent the stolen Bitcoin through a long chain of transfers to new addresses, each of which peeled a small piece from the whole and sent it to yet another address, often associated with an account at an exchange."

The article goes on to indicate that these so-called peel chains can become very convoluted the longer they get. The money laundered then could be said to generate new peel chains. This makes it difficult to understand whether money is actually changing hands or if it is being moved to another address controlled by the money launderer.

The use of exchanges to launder stolen cryptocurrency is a growing problem. According to Chainalysis, in 2019, criminal entities moved $2.8 billion in Bitcoin to exchanges. Chainalysis believes it is a small number of rogue brokers who use their legitimate-appearing accounts at exchanges to help launder cash out to fiat money, which is an obstacle for many launderers.

Italy—The Mafia Has Never Gone Away

Many articles on Italy's mafia-dominated crime and money laundering can be found on researchgate.net. In an abstract of the findings in "Mafia, money-laundering, and the battle against criminal capital: the Italian case," the author, Yara El Siwi (University of Cambridge, Cambridge, the UK by Emerald Publishing Limited 2018), indicates the following:

> Evidence suggests that financial surveillance, the first pillar of the AML [anti-money-laundering] regime, is much costlier than it is beneficial to society. Reporting of suspicions has rocketed in the past years, bringing very little change to yearly ML [money laundering] convictions, and being only marginally helpful in mafia-related investigations, confiscations and arrests. The confiscation of assets from mafia members, i.e., the second pillar of the AML regime, has proven to be effective in gaining

control over large sums and goods. However, more research is needed around the question of confiscated asset-management and desirable re-investment opportunities.

South Africa—All The Government's Money Gone

Past president Zuma faces eighteen charges in connection with the now-infamous arms deal, which includes corruption, money laundering, and racketeering stemming from 783 dubious payments he allegedly received. (These charges were withdrawn in 2009 when Zuma was elected president, and they have subsequently been reinstated.)

Five years after the democratic African National Party came to power in 1994, after years of apartheid, the government signed contracts to upgrade its military, totaling $5 billion. The deal involved companies from Germany, Italy, Sweden, Britain, France, and South Africa. Even at the time, it was a questionable deal; millions lived (and still do) in poverty, and South Africa was not facing any specific threat to its sovereignty. So why was the deal done?

Within months, allegations of the purchasing of the equipment abounded, and investigations took place. But it has been a long haul; from 2005 until the time of writing this, Zuma has yet to face his day in court. Two people were convicted in the meantime: Tony Yengeni, who was found guilty of fraud as he received a large discount on the purchase of a luxury car from one of the companies bidding for a contract, and Schabir Shaik, for soliciting a bribe on behalf of Zuma. Yengeni only served five months of his four-year sentence, and Shaik served only four of his fifteen-year sentence.

For the last ten years of Zuma's tenure, state capture has been the bane of South Africa and seriously added to its economic woes as billions of rands have been stripped from the government's coffers. BBC News describes state capture "as a form of corruption in which businesses and politicians conspire to influence a country's decision-making process to advance their interests. As most democracies have laws to make sure this does not happen, state capture also involves weakening those laws, and neutralizing any agencies that enforce them."

In his article "State Capture: Zuma, the Guptas, and the sale of South Africa" (July 15, 2019), Neil Arum wrote that the inquiry revealed the close relationship between Zuma and the Guptas. These were three Indian-born brothers who moved to South Africa after the fall of apartheid; they were so intricately linked that they were referred to as the Zupta.

Already the Gupta brothers owned companies—many as a result of juicy contracts granted by the South African government departments and state-owned conglomerates. Several of Zuma's family members were employed, including his son Duduzane.

"According to testimony heard at the inquiry, the Guptas went to great lengths to influence their most important client, the South African state. Public officials responsible for various state bodies say they were directly instructed by the Guptas to make decisions that would advance the brothers' business interests. It is alleged that compliance was rewarded with money and promotion, while disobedience was punished with dismissal."

The public bodies captured a number of ministries representing finance, natural resources, and public enterprise, namely government agencies such as the South African Revenue Service, the South African Airways, the South African Broadcasting

Corporation, Transnet (rail-freight), and Eskom, one of the world's largest energy giants. South Africa today lives with an embattled economy and a poor government. South Africa is no longer the "jewel of Africa" that it once was.

It would seem Zuma could do as he pleased as he had the right to appoint the boards of directors of state-owned enterprises and, importantly, the heads of law enforcement agencies.

Their collective damage stretched to reputed firms that they did business with, such as KPMG, Abby Innes, the ultimate victim of state capture tends to be the political system that is corrupted by business interests. "Politics becomes the point of entry and exit into what is fundamentally a financial market for retaining control over the state and its assets," she said.

The allegations eventually brought the Zuma presidency to a premature end in 2018 and prompted the Guptas to leave South Africa. The Guptas now live in Dubai, dutifully enriched, and it looks like they will never serve time; Zuma denies wrongdoing and calls state capture political propaganda. I doubt he will ever serve time either. He has also given evidence to a commission (the Zondo Commission) set up to investigate corruption allegations during his time in office, referred to as state capture. He is still around, having been jailed for three months for refusing to attend his hearing, and now is said to be in a hospital. A quick update from prison authorities on 15 August 2021 indicated that Zuma had undergone unspecified surgery and remains in hospital with more operations planned.

Adding flavor to the story, India's state-owned Bank of Baroda—one of the country's largest—played a crucial role in the financial collusions of South Africa's politically influential Gupta family, allowing them to move hundreds of millions of dollars originating in alleged dirty deals into offshore accounts, an investigation by the Organized Crime and Corruption Project and *The Hindu* found.

Our current president, Cyril Ramaphosa, is stately, intelligent, well-spoken, and a far cry from the likes of Zuma. His record is clean. In my book *Beyond Play* (published 2014), I stated that Cyril Ramaphosa, deputy president of the African National Congress from December 2012 (best known for founding the National Union of Mineworkers and his role during the negotiations to bring about a peaceful democracy in South Africa), at the time of his appointment to vice president, had several business interests and was either chairman, executive chairman, vice chairman, non-executive chairman, independent non-executive director, independent director and non-executive director of some twenty-three listed companies, probably facilitated by black empowerment legislation.

Ramaphosa is a South African billionaire; estimated net worth is over R6.4 billion ($450 million) as of 2018. He also is one of only seven stud game breeders in South Africa; for example, an auction near the northern South African town of Bela Bela by a group of six farms known collectively as Stud Game Breeders raised about R99 million ($6.7 million) through the sale of animals including Cape buffaloes, kudu, and antelope. Ramaphosa's Phala Phala Wildlife farm is part of the group.

In January 2013, a glance at the holdings of Shanduka, in which the Ramaphosa Family Trust owned 30 percent, revealed a diverse range of interests across many sectors. In the financial sector, these included holdings of 1.2 percent in Standard Bank, where he was also a director, 7.8 percent in Alexander Forbes, and 1.5 percent in the Liberty Group.

Further investments, over and above Shanduka, which owned part of Bidvest, Ramaphosa also had interests in the telecom sector in South Africa and Nigeria and held a 32.7 percent interest in a cellphone tower building operation (Helios Towers, in Nigeria), 12.5 percent in Seacom, 70 percent holding in McDonald's SA, and 70 percent in one of three bottling plants for Coca-Cola. Because he was appointed deputy president (2014), he had to give up these investments because of the conflicts of interest they represented.

He was appointed president in February 2018.

It is just puzzling though, that during his term of office as vice president, we never heard a peep from him during the highly charged issue of state capture. I guess one has to show solidarity with the ruling political party when you are only second in charge.

State capture damaged the reputations of well-known companies that had done business with the Guptas as mentioned above. But it did not damage the reputation of President Ramaphosa.

India—Has Its Eyes On Modi

Ten years ago, Nirav Modi was an unknown diamond wholesaler in Mumbai. From then on, he built his business to become an owner of a chain of retail outlets in prime locations throughout the world. *Forbes* listed him in 2017 as having a personal fortune of £1.3 billion. But presently Modi is living in Wandsworth prison on Heathfield Road, London, because he was arrested on behalf of the Indian authorities, who have asked for his extradition.

He learned the trade from his father, and in his family, talking about diamonds was what Modi described as "our way of conversation." Ninety percent of diamonds mined across the world are cut and polished in India. In 2008, Modi turned to jewelry design, cleverly, because the diamond market had crashed, and suddenly rare pink, blue, and white flawless diamonds above ten carats were readily available at reduced prices. The Nirav Modi brand was launched. He became famous, and selling designer diamond jewelry to celebrities became his trademark.

Modi and his American-born wife Ami and their three children lived a life of luxury. To boot, Modi's brother married the niece of India's wealthiest man, Mukesh Ambani, chairperson of Reliance Industries. In the months following his departure from India, and as the investigation into his alleged fraud unfolded, the Indian Enforcement Directorate seized assets that were later auctioned: a Rolls-Royce Ghost, a Porsche Panamera, luxury watches, Hermès Birkin and Kelly handbags, and an extensive collection of artworks by celebrated Indian painters.

The *Telegraph* on May 9, 2020, reported that in 2015, Modi launched his first American store on Madison Avenue, and shortly thereafter established the close-by jewelers such as Graff, De Beers, and Tiffany & Co. The launch was said to be a flashy affair, attended by the actor Naomi Watts and Donald Trump Jr. The following year, Modi had the full support of Kate Winslet, who appeared on the red carpet at the Oscars wearing Modi's jewelry, displaying some 100 carats of diamonds. She was happy to acknowledge that Modi's "feminine, modern designs are among my very favorite."

Modi left India for New York suddenly on January 17, 2018, following his wife and children, who had left earlier, telling friends there was an illness in the family.

A couple of weeks later, the Punjab National Bank (PNB) filed a police complaint against Modi, his uncle Mehul Choksi, and others, accusing them of fraud costing the bank some £1.5 billion. The charges included criminal conspiracy and money laundering.

"It was alleged that Modi, with the connivance of senior bank officials, had acquired fraudulent letters of undertaking on behalf of a number of shell companies from the PNB branch in Mumbai, in order to obtain overseas credit from other Indian lenders—ultimately leading to an 'evergreening' of loans, which ballooned to an enormous sum."

Nirav Modi was arrested in 2019 and is being held in custody at South London's Wandsworth prison. He continues to fight a legal battle to avoid deportation.

Israel—Bound By Binary Options

A binary options industry is about trading binary options. This is an exotic financial investment option that is based on a prediction that can either be right or wrong, but nowhere in between. The two main types of binary options: one type is a cash-or-nothing binary option whereby it pays some fixed amount of cash if the option expires in-the-money; the other pays the value of the underlying security. This means that an investor bets that a given asset will be above or below a certain point after a fixed amount of time. That time can vary greatly, but it can be as quick a turnaround as sixty seconds. They are also called all-or-nothing options, digital options (more common in forex/interest rate markets), and fixed-return options (FROs) on the American Stock Exchange and are considered high-risk and unpredictable.

Binary options may be used legitimately in theoretical asset pricing, but they are prone to fraud in their applications. Many regulators around the world have banned them because of that; it is seen as a form of gambling. Binary-option outlets have been exposed as fraudulent in the past. The United States FBI is investigating binary option scams throughout the world, and the Israeli police have tied the industry to criminal syndicates.

The FBI estimates that scammers steal $10 billion annually worldwide. How the scams work includes using famous people's names illegally (and usually people with respectable reputations) to buy fake investments. This kind of persuasion is frequent and increasing. Articles published in the *Times of Israel* (*TOI*) newspaper explain the fraud in detail, using the experience of former insiders such as a jobseeker recruited by a fake binary-options broker, who was told to "leave [his] conscience at the door." Following an investigation by the *TOI*, a law banning the products was approved by Israel's legislative body, Knesset, in October 2017.

Despite this and despite Facebook, Twitter, and Google banning advertisements associated with binary options trading as well as for cryptocurrencies and initial coin offerings in July 2018, an article a year later (July 5, 2019) by Mint Press News, a far-left news website, discussed more disturbing news. The article is titled "Haven for International Scammers and Fraud" and makes for fascinating reading.

A hint of the content is given below:

In terms of the binary options given above, a top Israeli police superintendent said that Israeli kingpins were behind the binary options industry, which has only served to strengthen organized crime in Israel.

Israeli investigative journalists have revealed that there are many examples of how Israeli officials have deliberately obstructed international efforts against known criminals who have committed huge financial scams taking place around the world. The reason: it brings in billions into the Israeli economy "propping up a regime widely condemned for human rights abuses and ethnic cleansing against Indigenous Palestinians."

It has been said by a former Internal Revenue expert on financial crime that industries operating fraudulently are ignored because they are often important leaders in the economy; that "translates into political clout."

Even that law, however, was watered down and seemed to leave the door wide open for continued swindles. Some believed that it would allow scammers to simply relocate and/or move into similar scams. The concern was merited. A 2018 article reported that there had been no effective clamp down by law enforcement on Israel's boiler-room industries, which remain robust. Many changed their product and continued with their business as before.

In June 2018 Israeli-operated boiler rooms in Asia and Eastern Europe were raided by local police. According to *TOI*, it was "one of the hundreds of Israeli-run boiler rooms operating worldwide in a global plague that, to the mounting dismay and incomprehension of international law enforcement bodies, is being left unchecked by Israeli law enforcement." *TOI* reported, "Israeli law enforcement has yet to indict a single operative from an industry that has stolen billions."

China—For The Chinese

David Eby started a new job as British Columbia's attorney general. What he was not prepared for was the warning given to him by the casino regulators in the western Canadian province: "We are going to blow your mind." David was shown footage of people wheeling suitcases stuffed with $20 bills into casinos and using hockey bags to haul the cash. Surveillance videos showed these same people trading in the cash for casino chips.

This was Eby's introduction to the so-called Vancouver model—a scheme in which some of the province's casinos were unwittingly used to launder more than C$100 million during the past decade. It is a product of one of the largest financial flows of the twenty-first century: the money being frantically moved by millions of wealthy Chinese into safe assets abroad, in defiance of their country's capital controls. Since mid-2014, capital flight from China may have totaled as much as $800 billion, according to estimates from the Institute of International Finance.

Many more billions of illicit outflows from China take place. "Money laundering and illicit flows from China—the real estate problem," authored by Mohammed Ahmad Naheem, focus on the money that is laundered through real estate. It contaminates both the Chinese banking system as well as global banks. These illicit flows come from corruption and financial crime and not necessarily from drug or organized criminal gangs.

China, like all other countries, is now operating in an international banking context, in much the same way that international organized crime is also operating at a global level. Real estate remains a targeted sector for criminals seeking to launder funds, much like Britain is used.

The British Virgin Islands (or BVI, as it is known) is a tax haven with lots of secrets. To the Chinese elite, however, the setting up of a shell company in the BVI became shorthand in China for any offshore company, regardless of where in the world it was located. Another colloquialism used is *white glove*—an intermediary who launders your money (does the dirty deeds) while you keep your hands clean. The white gloves are more likely to be well-connected Westerners.

The reference made to Mossack Fonseca (the offshore law firm behind the Panama Papers leak) found a third of its work to be in China and Hong Kong.

Zambia—At The Center Of Government

On September 19, 2018, the *Guardian* reported on the investigation of, ostensibly, wide-scale corruption at the very center of the Zambian government. It involved international aid payments that were diverted from departments such as health, education, and community development. At the helm, President Edgar Lungu and his ministers, instead of officially increasing the social fund scheme for a few hundred thousand households, moved funds through shell companies. Other people in government looked the other way, and the president was never indicted.

The Zambian Watchdog in June 2019 reported that the Media Liaison Committee expected Edgar Lungu to task state agencies, namely the Drug Enforcement Commission, the Anti-Corruption Commission, and the Zambia police to report on the action taken on the eighty cases of money laundering reported by the Financial Intelligence Centre. The Media Liaison Committee also commented on "a growing trend of disrespecting constitutional bodies like the Financial Intelligence Centre, the head of state, and those that work with him." Two sides of the coin and both are corrupt.

Egypt—Anything Goes As Long As It Is Illegal

Ahram Online reported on February 20, 2020, that Egyptian authorities arrested seventeen people in one of the country's largest money laundering cases. The gang, who included six employees of Egypt's postal authority, created fake postal accounts using deceased persons' details, expatriates' details, and nonexistent companies to transfer or deposit illegal funds.

The funds, worth about $108 million, were earned in local and foreign currency trading as well as from illegal migration and drug trafficking. They were arrested.

Bribes are also the order of the day, day after day. The head of Giza's Al-Haram district and a previous head of the Customs Authority were arrested for receiving bribes from three construction companies in exchange for the termination of customs clearance procedures for certain imported goods. At the same time, several officials from many banks around Egypt were arrested over accusations of taking more than LE 11 million in bribes to facilitate credit procedures and loans for owners of major companies.

France—Laundering In Style

The Bankers Academy reports that money laundering in France is a persistent problem. Despite maintaining a sound and comprehensive anti-money-laundering system, France remains an attractive venue for money laundering because of its sizable economy, political stability, and sophisticated financial system. Common methods of money laundering in France include the use of bank deposits, foreign currency and gold bullion transactions, corporate transactions, and purchases of real estate, hotels, and works of art. A sophisticated, stable country? Through money-laundering spectacles, it does not matter in what state your country is, the abuse will be present.

Greece—One Defense Minister After The Other

The *National Herald* of May 11, 2020, refers to the case of former Greek Defense Minister Yiannos Papantoniou and his wife Stavroula Kourakou, who found themselves in the high-security Korydallos Prison after being convicted for hiding their income; they also faced charges of laundering money tied to alleged bribes from a state defense contract.

Papantoniou had followed another former PASOK Socialist Defense Minister who was also jailed after being convicted of stealing scores of millions from defense contracts but was let out of prison because he said he did not feel well.

Guatemala—Drugs Are Doing It

A Guatemalan banker accused of accepting hundreds of thousands of dollars in bribes from drug traffickers to move cocaine profits between Central America and the United States was arrested on money-laundering conspiracy charges. The

Miami Herald of November 13, 2019, went on to report that Alvaro Estuardo Cobar Bustamante, the director of a national Guatemalan bank, was the target of an FBI sting operation in which he accepted $20,000 from a cooperating witness convicted of drug trafficking. The banker agreed in a recorded conversation to move the purported cocaine proceeds to the United States.

Another cooperating witness, Manuel Antonio Baldizon Mendez, a former candidate for president of Guatemala, assisted federal authorities in the undercover operation after pleading guilty the previous year to accepting about $1.6 million from narco-traffickers to facilitate their distribution network.

Federal authorities said drug traffickers moving Colombian cocaine through Central America and Mexico to the United States pay off politicians and bankers in Guatemala because it is a critical transportation hub for drug shipments.

Iceland—Laundering Growing On Ice

Corruption in Iceland was on the rise for at least the past six years, according to a 2021 report from Transparency International.

According to their Corruption Perceptions Index, Iceland ranked 13th place out of a possible 180 (2021) for corruption, making it one of the least corrupt countries on a global scale. Regionally, however, Iceland is not only the most corrupt Nordic country—its level of corruption has been growing.

Transparency International's Corruption Score measures the perceived level of public sector corruption on a scale from 0 (highly corrupt) to 100 (very clean). In 2012, Iceland's score was 82, but it has steadily worsened since then, namely 77 in 2017 and 74 in 2021.

Peru—One Presidency After Another

Keiko Fujimori, the opposition leader and daughter of Peru's ex-president Alberto Fujimori, was arrested for alleged money laundering involving Brazilian construction giant Odebrecht, as reported by France24.com on October 11, 2018. The investigation centered on the company's undeclared campaign contributions.

(Alberto Fujimori was convicted in April 2009 of human rights violations and sentenced to twenty-five years in prison for his role in killings and kidnappings by the Grupo Colina death squad during his government's battle against leftist guerrillas in the 1990s.)

Three former presidents ostensibly took bribes disguised as campaign funds from Odebrecht, which is at the center of political scandals across Latin America. Pedro Pablo Kuczynski, Alan Garcia, and Alejandro Toledo all took undeclared campaign contributions in exchange for pledges to have the Brazilian construction giant win local tenders. Another former president, Ollanta Humala, is also being investigated for taking $3 million in bribes from the same company.

Kuczynski narrowly beat Keiko Fujimori to win the presidency in 2016, but he had to step down in early 2018 because of the suspicions of millions of dollars in Odebrecht payments to his companies before he took office as President.

Jorge Barata, a Brazilian who was a former Odebrecht boss in Peru, told Brazilian investigators that he doled out millions of dollars to Peruvian presidential candidates between 2001 and 2016.

The Fujimori family continues to dominate Peru's political agenda. Keiko's father, Alberto, protested that he is too weak with a chronic heart condition (he was eighty years old) to serve out the rest of his twenty-five-year sentence for crimes against humanity.

Brazil—Seventy-Seven Company Executives Involved

The scandal involving Odebrecht in Peru mentioned above is a story of bribery and corruption. Grupo Odebrecht is Latin America's largest construction giant, with many big infrastructure projects under its belt. It also signed the world's largest leniency deal with the United States and Swiss authorities, in which it confessed to corruption and paid $2.6 billion (£2.1 billion) in fines, said to be the heaviest of its kind in the world. Seventy-seven company executives were involved, and their plea bargains and public statements to investigators had strong political and economic repercussions throughout Latin America.

Odebrecht started as a small family construction group in the 1940s; by 2010, the company had 181,000 employees across twenty-one countries. It is also one of the biggest donors to politicians in Brazil.

Odebrecht was one of the companies caught in Brazil's corruption probe into the state oil giant Petrobras. Dozens of companies acknowledged paying bribes to politicians and officials in exchange for contracts with Petrobras and then agreed to confess to crimes and identify corrupt officials in exchange for shorter prison sentences. The revelations included bribery in other South American countries as described above regarding Peru.

Odebrecht signed a leniency deal with authorities in the US and Switzerland, agreeing to pay $2.6 billion in fines for its past mistakes—the largest sum of its kind in the world at the time.

The company also tried to settle cases with other governments so that it would be allowed to tender for future major infrastructure projects.

It is hard for investigators to determine whether those arrested are confessing to real crimes, or whether they are telling a story that prosecutors want to hear in exchange for shorter prison sentences.

Plea bargains can be rewarding for those who sign them. Some of the Petrobras executives who signed such deals in 2014 are now out of prison and serving their sentences at home, instead of spending years in jail. On the other hand, plea bargains have been instrumental in bringing to justice powerful people who would otherwise never have been caught. (BBC News, April 17, 2019)

The Lava Jato investigation, for example, started as a probe into a suspected money-laundering scheme at a gas station in Brasília. It has since ballooned to involve accusations of laundering more than thirty billion reals ($9.25 billion). Unlike other countries in Latin America, experts say bribes in Brazil move more laundered money than drug trafficking.

Argentina—Has A Terrorist Financier

CalvinAyre.com, part of the Ayre Media Group, reported on August 18, 2018, that police had raided casinos and hotels in Puerto Iguazú, near the triple frontier intersection of the borders of Argentina, Brazil, and Paraguay. The raids were part of an ongoing investigation into the activities of Assad Ahmad Barakat, a Lebanese national with alleged ties to the Islamic militant group Hezbollah. In July 2018, Argentina's Financial Information Unit froze the assets of Clan Barakat, a group associated with Assad, who has been designated a terrorist financier by the US Office of Foreign Assets Control.

Barakat and thirteen others linked to the Clan reportedly paid hundreds of visits to Casino Iguazú over the past few years even though they reside in either Brazil or Paraguay, with no obvious business interests in Argentina. Clan members would cross the border of Argentina with large sums of cash (without declaring the money) to exchange for chips at the casino and then cash out after minimal play and carry the newly laundered cash back across the border also without declaring the money. Authorities estimate that the Clan may have laundered over US$10 million via this method. The casino's role remains unclear.

Zimbabwe—Government Partaking In, Instead Of Fighting Money-Laundering

In AllAfrica of May 12, 2020, the Centre for Natural Resources Governance (CNRG) director Farai Maguwu was reported saying that the decision by the European Union to list Zimbabwe as a financial risk to the European Union was not surprising because of economic activities that were mostly outside formal systems.

Hundreds of unregistered Chinese criminals all over Zimbabwe are aided and abetted by ruling elites. They are also involved in the poaching and trafficking of wildlife organs. The government partakes in these activities, and there appears to be no intention of stopping them.

"There are so many economic activities and yet the government is perennially broke, mainly because the country has become a hotbed of organized crime."

James Mupfumi, Centre for Research and Development (CRD) director, also referred to the opaque mining of diamonds in diamond-rich Marange, Manicaland, as one case that exposed Zimbabwe's lack of transparency. He understood why the country has been labeled as a financial risk to the European Union.

Botswana- A Tax-haven Image

Botswana is categorized as high-risk for money laundering. In 2019, legislative amendments were introduced to force all corporations to disclose their beneficial owners, eliminate the "dormant" status, curb the abuse of transfer pricing, and dismantle a fifteen-year-old special tax incentives framework for offshore financial services companies.

Transfer pricing, or transactions within and between enterprises with common ownership and control, is abused when corporates tag prices for these transactions above or below the real value to distort profits and taxable income. The International Financial Services Centre is perceived as citing Botswana's "tax haven" image, particularly as some of the beneficiaries have been fingered in global tax-avoidance exposés such as the Panama Papers.

Given what is reported above, Botswana replicates what is happening in many other countries.

Bahamas – Nobody Goes To Jail

The *Tribune*, October 29, 2018, "US Report Names Bahamas as Money Laundering Jurisdiction," reported on the Bahamas' new efforts to deal with money laundering: The Bahamas will have resolved 99.9 percent of the remaining weaknesses in its anti-financial-crime defenses by year-end, with money laundering prosecutions having increased forty-fold.

Comment from a reader of the article at the time:

> Nonsense. There has not been one single story in this newspaper about anyone going to jail for money laundering. We have to supply banks with blood samples from our great-grandmother to open an account, meanwhile, money launderers

continue untouched . . . even if there are any money launderers.

I was asked last month by my bank to bring in my new passport for them to photocopy because the one on file is my old passport. Really? So I'm not me anymore? The same man you see in here every week for twelve years? KYC means "know your customer." Do you know me? Do you know me to be a terrorist? If so, call the police. I will stand right here in the bank and wait for them.

In 2019 though, a separate report focusing on drugs and chemical control contained a memorandum from President Donald Trump to US Secretary of State Mike Pompeo that listed this country among those considered major illicit-drug-transit or drug-producing countries for the 2019 fiscal year. The Bahamas provides an easy entry point into Florida for drugs intended for the United States market.

The cash proceeds made by criminals from drug transits are of concern. But drug trafficking is not the only problem; it extends to firearms and human smuggling and trafficking.

The Bahamas is an international business and financial center with an open economy. The high volume of large, cross-border asset transactions enhances the risk of money laundering through private banks, trust services, insurance companies, and corporate service providers. Other money laundering methodologies may include the purchase of real estate and precious metals and stones.

The Horn of Africa: Djibouti, Eritrea, Ethiopia, and Somalia—Rigorous Reporting Needed

Civipol Conseil (June 2019) Reported on Money Laundering in the Horn of Africa, and One Section Made an Interesting Point about the Understanding of Money Laundering:

> Though the impact of terrorist financing is more visible, and perhaps particularly so in the Horn of Africa where Al Shabaab is an active terrorist organization, money laundering is rarely understood to be a matter of major concern to many people. Money laundering and terrorist financing are too often considered technical, banking problems rather than activities that harm public and private sectors and that directly affect people's lives and everyday business.

This narrow view of money laundering as a technical challenge is not just an issue in Africa: a recent report by LexisNexis on the presence of money laundering and terrorist financing in the UK states that most of the general public is still unaware of the links money laundering and financial crime have with human and sex trafficking, drug trafficking, the sale of weapons, and the financing of terrorism.

The main findings of that report include an overall decline in the proportion of coverage given to terrorist financing, which may make it more difficult to provide long-term preventive solutions to terrorism. While money laundering is increasingly associated with state corruption, it is mostly disconnected from other forms of organized crime, such as the illegal trade in narcotics and wildlife. It is also indicated that articles that do focus on the financial aspects of these crimes lack rigorous discussion and questioning characteristic of robust investigative reporting.

Iran, Turkey, and the United Arab Emirates—Interconnected and Complex

On March 31, 2020, the Wisconsin Project, which tracks Iran's unconventional weapon capabilities on nuclear arms control, reported on the allegedly laundered $20 billion of Iran's oil and gas revenue in violation of sanctions imposed by the United States on Iran.

It is a fascinating read; I have therefore summarized the report, and I hope I can capture the complexity of it all.

A Turkish state-owned bank, Halkbank, violated the United States sanctions imposed against Iran. From 2012 to 2016, during the negotiations on its nuclear program, Iran used Halkbank for money-laundering purposes. In 2016, Reza Zarrab, an Iranian-Turkish businessman, was arrested and prosecuted because he devised a scheme to launder billions of dollars of Iranian oil proceeds through Halkbank under the guise of gold and food trade.

Evidence presented during the 2018 trial and conviction of Zarrab's co-conspirator Mehmet Hakan Atilla, a Turkish national and former deputy general manager of Halkbank, implicated Turkish president Recep Erdoğan. The case is still in limbo, but lessons have been learned on how to prevent further abuse of the international financial system to evade sanctions.

On October 15, 2019, US prosecutors charged Halkbank with fraud, money laundering, and conspiracy for violating the International Emergency Economic Powers Act (IEEPA).

The case has been dogged by allegations of political interference. Turkey lobbied the Trump administration to withdraw the charges against Halkbank and the scheme's mastermind, Reza Zarrab. Testimony from Zarrab during the trial of codefendant Mehmet Atilla directly implicated Turkish president Recep Tayyip Erdoğan and other senior Turkish government officials. The operation's purpose was to allow the Iranian government a means of accessing its oil and gas revenue held overseas. As part of the scheme, Zarrab funneled money from Halkbank accounts held by Iranian entities to accounts of his front companies in Turkey and the United Arab Emirates (UAE). Then after laundering the money through illicit gold exports and later falsified food trade, Zarrab used those funds to make international payments on behalf of Iranian entities that supported Iran's proliferation programs. According to the Department of Justice, the scheme "fueled a dark pool of Iranian government-controlled funds that could be clandestinely sent anywhere in the world."

Zarrab owned a complex network of exchange houses and front companies in Turkey and the UAE. In 2011, before engaging Halkbank, Zarrab did wire transfers on behalf of the MAPNA Group (a construction and power company with ties to Iran's nuclear and missile proliferation programs), and the money services subsidiary of Bank Mellat (which also supported Iran's proliferation programs). There was a short respite, however, because many attempted financial transfers to companies in China and Hong Kong via US financial institutions were blocked, because of sanctions issued by the US Department of the Treasury's Office of Foreign Assets Control (OFAC) targeting Iran's financial sector.

Zarrab, still on the treadmill to make more money, sent a letter to Iranian president Mahmoud Ahmadinejad in December 2011 expressing his "readiness for any collaboration in moving currency as well as adjusting the rate of exchange under the direct supervision of the honorable economic agents of the [Iranian] government." That helped him evade future sanctions using Halkbank.

The Gold Scheme and the Food Scheme were the hallmarks of the money laundering operation. A representative of a private bank in Iran told Zarrab that the Central Bank of Iran and the National Iranian Oil Company held billions of dollars representing the revenue from oil and gas sales to Turkey, in accounts at Halkbank. Because of the sanctions, money from these oil escrow accounts could not be transferred back to Iran or used for international financial transfers on behalf of the government of Iran or Iranian banks, but the funds from the accounts could legitimately be used to pay for Turkish exports to private Iranian companies—an exception known as the bilateral trade rule. Zarrab approached Halkbank general manager Suleyman Aslan with a scheme to channel funds to the Iranian government by exploiting the bilateral trade rule.

Aslan was initially reluctant, but Zarrab secured the support of Turkish Minister of Economic Affairs Mehmet Zafer Çağlayan, with over $70 million in bribes. Aslan also put out his hand for $8.5 million. Other Halkbank officials came in on the fray, including Atilla, who headed the department responsible for processing international banking transactions. This trio then coordinated the conspiracy with officials from high-profile institutions.

This revenue was then laundered through a gold export network by the companies transferring their oil revenue from their Halkbank accounts (denominated in Turkish lira, to avoid the international financial system) to the Halkbank accounts of private Iranian banks, such as Bank Sarmayeh. Those Iranian intermediaries then transferred the money to Halkbank accounts controlled by Zarrab's network of front companies. The Iranian connection was therefore cunningly concealed from other financial institutions.

The front companies then used the funds to buy gold on the Turkish market. Zarrab falsified records to indicate that the gold was subsequently exported to private companies in Iran, as permitted by the bilateral trade rule. In this way, even if the internal Halkbank transfers could be traced back to the Iranian oil accounts, the transactions would still appear to comply with US sanctions (this falsified documentation later underwent several changes as US sanctions evolved).

But what happened was that these companies "exported the gold to Dubai, where they then sold it on the market for cash. This step was critical to Zarrab's scheme and served two purposes. First, it allowed him to acquire currencies used for international payments, such as the US dollar and the euro. Second, it disguised the money's Iranian origin. Unlike bank transfers, cash transactions cannot easily be traced."

The cash proceeds from the gold sales were deposited into accounts held by his companies at banks in Dubai. Iranian banks, such as Bank Sarmayeh and Bank Mellat, then gave Zarrab's companies instructions to transfer the money to various entities in Iran's sanctions evasion network, composed of front companies and foreign suppliers in several countries including Canada, China, and Turkmenistan. US banks then unwittingly processed several of these dollar transactions through correspondent accounts. As a result, from December 2012 to October 2013 alone, more than $900 million of Iranian oil and gas money were transited through US financial institutions to make payments on behalf of Iran.

It was a remarkable success, and several of the conspirators met to discuss moving Iran's oil revenue in India to Halkbank so that it could be laundered through the scheme. China was another country where the scheme was attempted for some time.

The scheme made the Turkish economy appear stronger than reality because gold exports to Iran increased substantially as well as gold exports to the United Arab Emirates. It was clear that Zarrab was encouraged by the Turkish government to continue what he was doing.

The sanctions were tightened in 2013 by the United States prohibiting the supply of precious metals to any Iranian entities, whether private or governmental. The gold scheme became unsustainable over the long term.

It was Aslan's idea to disguise the transfers instead, using falsified records of food purchases. Food exports to Iran are exempt from US sanctions on humanitarian grounds, and Halkbank had facilitated food trade in the past, so its involvement would not appear overly suspicious. The conspirators were back in business with a new plan.

The food scheme was more straightforward and had similar characteristics. The same companies again transferred funds within Halkbank to intermediary accounts held by Iranian banks, which then moved the money to accounts held by Zarrab's companies. Zarrab concocted fake food purchases in Dubai, allowing him to transfer the money to his front companies in the UAE. To cover their tracks, Zarrab's Halkbank conspirators created false shipping records indicating that food was subsequently exported to Iran. Instead, Zarrab's front companies funneled the funds through the international financial system to entities in Iran's sanctions evasions network, again at the direction of Iranian banks.

Nothing was ever actually bought or sold as part of the food scheme, which relied more on the documentation to conceal the money's true path; for example, he recorded the nonexistent food as being shipped on small wooden vessels that did not require them, or listed cargo as weighing 150,000 tons on a ship with a 5,000-ton capacity. But this and other similar missteps brought down the entire operation with the help of a whistleblower.

In December 2013, Turkish law enforcement arrested Zarrab, Aslan, Çağlayan, and others on charges of bribery, corruption, money laundering, and gold smuggling. Investigators found millions of dollars in bribes stashed in shoeboxes at Aslan's residence and discovered documents detailing the scheme. Çağlayan, Aslan, and other Halkbank and Turkish government officials were dismissed from their positions. The case made international headlines, largely because it implicated Erdoğan. The Turkish justice system did not see the case through to a conclusion, however. Ironically, Zarrab bribed his way out of prison in February 2014, and the case against him was dismissed that October. Zarrab did not stop there; he continued to pressure Halkbank's new general manager, Ali Fuat Taşkesenlioğlu, to restart the food operation. With the help of Erdoğan and his son-in-law, then-Minister of Energy Berat Albayrak intervened on Zarrab's behalf, and the food scheme continued until at least March 2016, when Zarrab was arrested in the United States.

These money-laundering schemes helped Iran in two ways: first, it benefitted Iranian entities with ties to those activities. The Iranian oil money laundered through Halkbank was their payment; second, it relieved the financial pressure on Iran during the years of multilateral negotiations to restrict Iran's nuclear program; it also lessened pressure from the United States.

Zarrab and Atilla were the only two people that were arrested and sentenced. Atilla was hardly in jail for more than a year and was deported back to Turkey. All others remain at large.

The Turkish government appointed Zarrab to lead Borsa Istanbul, Turkey's main stock exchange, while the case continues to be pursued by the United States.

If the US justice system hands down a stiff penalty to Halkbank, a major sanctions violator that carried on its activities with the backing of the Turkish state, it may deter other foreign individuals and financial institutions from laundering money for Iran. If Halkbank instead gets off lightly, it may have the opposite effect. Bankers, businessmen, and officials in Iran, Turkey, and across the world will be eyeing the outcome.

Follow the case of Halkbank; an article in the *New York Times* on October 29, 2020, ("Turkish Bank Case Showed Erdoğan's Influence with Trump") indicated that former White House officials said they came to fear that President Trump was open to swaying the criminal justice system to advance a transactional and ill-defined agenda of his own.

Lebanon—Hawala

"A Lebanese businessman sanctioned for ties to Shiite militia group Hezbollah whose trial began in Paris is accused of being part of a criminal money-laundering ring that used the hawala* practice to fund the group's arms in Syria. Billions of dollars are believed to be traded via the system every year, and even though intelligence services across the world pay close attention to the practice, they cannot trace every transaction." This was reported on November 14, 2018, by the Counter Extremism Project, a nonprofit, nongovernment organization that combats extremist groups by pressuring financial support networks, countering the narrative of extremists, and advocating for stronger laws, policies, and regulations.

*Definition taken from Wikipedia: Hawala or hewala (Arabic) is a popular and informal value-transfer system based not on the movement of cash, or telegraph or computer network wire transfers between banks, but instead on the performance and honor of a huge network of money brokers (known as hawaladars). While hawaladars are spread throughout the world, they are primarily located in the Middle East, North Africa, the Horn of Africa, and the Indian subcontinent, operating outside of, or parallel to, traditional banking, financial channels, and remittance systems.

Hawala follows Islamic traditions but its use is not limited to Muslims. There is nothing illegal or wrong if a person prefers to use this method to transfer or send money to his family; however, some hawala dealers diverted this system for illegal purposes, particularly money laundering.

Because of its anonymity, hawala has also been a means for illegal activity to take place, such as money laundering and the financing of terrorism. For this reason, many countries prohibit hawala or have put regulations around it—such as Dubai.

Any money system, as must be obvious to the reader by now, can be and is abused by money launderers; however, it is a concern to some thirty-one countries that still apply Exchange Control legislation, which restricts the flow and movement of money in and out of the country. Hawala circumvents this.

Syria—Assad, The Main Beneficiary

It was reported by the same institution as above, also on November 14, 2018, that the economic discontent that helped trigger the civil war in Syria was sparked by corrupt business practices of Rami Makhlouf (Bashar al-Assad's cousin). Bashar al-Assad became president in 2000 after his father, Hafez al-Assad, died. His intent to open the economy to private capital was welcomed, but as time went by, the public became very aware that it was not for their benefit, but for Assad and his clan. The *New York Times* reported a university professor saying, "He has his fingers in so many pies. Anything you want to do you partner with him or share."

The US Treasury Department became aware that when it imposed sanctions on Makhlouf in 2008, they realized they were falling foul of the justice system, which inevitably resulted in being in the firing line of Syrian intelligence.

Philippines—Where Is The Money?

Ferdinand Marcos ruled the Philippines for twenty-one years and accumulated wealth from his own country, estimated at some $10 billion. He was ousted from power by a revolution in 1986. While the following government set up a commission to track down the Marcos family's wealth to recover the funds, it could not be found. The family had channeled their fortune into various offshore bank accounts, foundations, and valuable assets, making them difficult to find. To date, some $4 billion has been accounted for (Fintech News Singapore, February 7, 2018).

At the time, when he and his wife fled from Manila, his wife infamously left over 2,500 pairs of shoes behind! Marcos died in exile in Honolulu in 1989 at age seventy-two, awaiting trial. The remaining Marcos family were granted amnesty by the ruling president, Corazon Aquino. The family has since re-established its political dynasty, but the search for the former dictator's fortune continues.

Japan—Yumi Gumi

The Sixth Yamaguchi-gumi is the largest group in the Japanese Yakuza. The Yamaguchi-gumi is known to be one of the largest criminal organizations in the world. It is involved in drug trafficking, human trafficking, extortion, prostitution, fraud, and money laundering in both Japan and abroad. These activities generate billions of dollars in illicit funds annually for this group.

The pressure against the Yakuza has increased as Japan's Financial Services Agency ordered Mizuho Financial, one of the wealthiest financial institutions in the world, to improve its compliance regarding suspected loans to known criminal organizations. It is believed that because of this increased pressure from regulators, the membership of the Yakuza is steadily declining as it becomes increasingly difficult to launder money. However, they no doubt will find another way, e.g., cryptocurrencies.

Thailand—Pray And Commit A Crime

On August 9, 2018, Voice of America news reported that Wirapol Sukphol, thirty-nine, a former Buddhist monk, was sentenced to more than one hundred years in prison for statutory rape, embezzlement, and online fraud. He amassed an estimated fortune of US$32 million through a variety of illegal means, including the misuse of funds donated to him for religious purposes by his followers on the pretext it was for Buddhist statuary and temple improvements. Instead, he spent it on cars and luxury goods.

His shenanigans drew international attention in 2013 when he appeared in a YouTube video in monk's robes aboard a private jet, counting large stacks of US dollars and wearing designer accessories. He was arrested in 2016 in the United States and extradited in 2017.

The 114-year sentence comprised an 87-year term for public fraud, 3 years for computer crimes, and 24 years for money laundering. But the court capped his maximum prison term at 20 years, as required under section 91 of the Penal Code for multiple offenses and ordered him to compensate the twenty-nine complainants for their financial losses. He was also subsequently found guilty in October 2018 of repeatedly raping an underage girl for two years and keeping her separated from her parents.

Not the first monk to have laundered money or raped a girl.

European Union—Sports A Fertile Ground For Corruption

Byline Times updated on May 17, 2020, a report written by Mark Conrad: "Football Money Laundering: A Beginner's Guide" dated April 2, 2019.

A European Union study has warned that the sports industry is now fertile ground for "corruption activity such as money laundering and tax evasion." The annual cost of sports corruption globally is now approximately £78 billion, with Europe's cash-rich football sector attracting particular attention from organized criminal gangs.

Although national police forces and Europol have successfully disrupted these gangs' operations, the criminal justice bodies admit they "have barely scratched the surface of these snowballing threats to the integrity of the world's most popular, and increasingly wealthy, sport."

One classic method of laundering cash through football has been for criminals to take over financially unstable clubs—and then pump illegal monies through the club structure by way of donations or investments used to clean the cash. These activities may include inflating staff or player salaries, over- or undervaluing player transfer fees, and through directors' or owners' loan accounts to the club. There are also "combined football's financial vulnerabilities with increasingly sophisticated attempts to target the gambling industry through match-fixing."

The previous year, the ESSA, which is a Europe-wide sports integrity body that represents major betting firms, detected fifty-two suspicious football betting patterns, obviously intending to defraud firms through match-fixing.

Previous investigations by detectives in some cases have identified links to organized crime in Austria, Estonia, Germany, Latvia, Moldova, and the UK. Europol's Financial Intelligence

Group warned, based on previous investigations, that "the misuse of offshore companies to conceal the beneficial ownership of assets is still one of the major challenges for successful financial investigations.

"The football sector presents vulnerabilities related to its structure, finance model, and culture, which could be exploited by criminals."

And interestingly, Lewis Hamilton, the world champion Formula 1 racing car driver (not found guilty) nevertheless has been linked to the Paradise Papers in terms of tax evasion or deliberately using circuitous means to avoid tax and VAT. Well, who would want to convict him?

Andorra—High-Powered If You Give Kickbacks For Electricity

Andorra is a small country of 453 square kilometers in the Pyrenees Mountains, bordered between Spain and France. It is among the world's richest countries, and according to the international living index, Andorra is in twelfth position in the world for quality of life. Tourism is its main trade, and its status as a tax haven is well known.

AP News of September 13, 2018, reported: A judge in Andorra charged twenty-eight people, including former officials in Venezuela, with money laundering offenses over a kickbacks-for-contracts scheme that plundered $2 billion from the Venezuelan state oil company between 2007 and 2012. This investigation took five years; the opaque deposits in the Banca Privada d'Andorra proved challenging.

The accused included former deputy ministers, an official at the government electricity company, and a high-powered cousin of Venezuela's longtime oil czar Rafael Ramirez, who was managing the scheme. Ramirez was energy minister and ran Petróleos de

Venezuela SA for nine years until 2013, was a close aide of the late Venezuelan leader Hugo Chavez, and was also appointed Venezuela's envoy to the United Nations until 2017. He fell out with the country's current leadership and went into hiding.

The people charged had been receiving illegal payments from companies that were rewarded with contracts related to the oil industry, and many of them were from China. The Banca Privada d'Andorra management then hid the profits in shell companies in various countries before being made available in the bank's accounts.

The judge's formal accusation indicated that members were so close to the "circles of power of the state" that possible investigations were shared with Venezuela by Interpol.

Antigua And Barbuda—If You Are Going To Do It, Market It

The government of Antigua and Barbuda (an island sovereign state in the West Indies in the Americas) has exposed two convicted criminals who are now selling themselves as financial crime consultants through the Internet blog sites that they run in return for hefty payments.

Kenneth Rijock and Monte Morris Friesner have both been convicted of money laundering and fraud and have served time in jail. They sell themselves to damage the reputations of individuals, governments, and companies.

Their swindles attacked Citizenship by Investment programs in Caribbean countries, posting fake news during election campaigns, scandalizing governments through false claims and fabricated stories, and cleverly reconfiguring passports (Rijock admitted that thousands of bogus passports were manufactured and sold).

The government of Antigua and Barbuda has taken to transitioning their passports from machine- readable passports to ones that are fully biometric and incapable of being tampered with. That is the easy part. The difficulty is investigating the legal recourse available to the government against the two criminals for the damage they are being successful at doing on behalf of their paymasters (*St Kitts Nevis Observer*, April 18, 2018).

Azerbaijan—Get Politically Connected For Your Dreams To Come True

The ease with which politically connected and wealthy people can do anything they want by using secret offshore companies is staggering as many examples in this chapter have already revealed. The *Guardian* of December 21, 2018, reported that the daughters of Azerbaijan's president bought a £60 million London property which was merely an addition to a multimillion-pound property portfolio in Britain held by President Ilham Aliyev's family. Their father has been president since 2003, and since that time, his daughters have amassed vast personal business empires, no doubt with money also laundered from Azerbaijan.

Here are some connections: His daughter Leyla was in the process of going through a divorce with Emin Agalarov, an Azerbaijani businessman and pop star. Emin's father Aras is a Moscow-based property developer. He hosted Donald Trump on his 2013 visit to Russia for the Miss Universe beauty pageant, which Donald Trump funded and, to boot, decided on who and who were not acceptable applicants. There were also connections between Trump's business partners in the pageant and Russia's government officials that may or may not have assisted him in winning the 2016 presidential election. Leyla, an artist and socialite, is friends with Prince Andrew, Lord Mandelson, and Elizabeth Murdoch.

Meanwhile, three European politicians, a journalist, and businessmen who supported the regime through their business activities became recipients of Azerbaijani laundered money. They were also able to manipulate international organizations, such as UNESCO and the Parliamentary Assembly of the Council of Europe, to "score public relations victories for the regime."

British lawyers and financial institutions aided and abetted the transactions. The banking records leak of over 16,000 transactions disclosed that much of the money came from four Azerbaijan-funded shell companies registered in the United Kingdom. "The country's lax regulations allowed these companies to file registration paperwork that listed proxy or nonexistent shareholders and disguise their true origins."

United States diplomatic cables indicate that Azerbaijan's political system was indeed "feudal," with a few well-connected families "controlling practically all sectors of the economy."

Afghanistan—Chairman Of A Bank, In The Best Seat To Embezzle It

The *National* (United Arab Emirates), "The Kabul banker who almost brought Afghanistan to its knees dies in prison," dated August 26, 2018, reported that Sherkhan Farnood, the owner of at least sixteen luxury Dubai properties and a regular international poker player, was in his youth an informal hawala money-transfer operator operating from his university dorm.

He became the former chairman of Afghanistan's largest private bank but died in prison having served fifteen years for money laundering and embezzlement. He had an extraordinary rise to power during the chaotic times of a post-Soviet Moscow.

He founded Kabul Bank, before orchestrating a fraud that nearly ruined his homeland.

His connections at the time enabled him to persuade the government to give Kabul Bank responsibility for Western-funded payroll accounts for the country's soldiers, police, and civil servants. The bank was in business.

But it was funny business.

Executives were using the deposits to make big loans to a small elite group of shareholders, politicians, and their companies. There was little expectation that the loans would be repaid.

A forensic audit of Kabul Bank a few years later revealed the scale of the fraud. It was found that staff were ordered to forge documents. Proxy loans were granted under fictional names or names of cleaners and drivers. It was discovered that some 92 percent of the bank's loan portfolio was made up of just nineteen individuals or companies. The value: $861 million.

Bolivia—The Water In A Car Wash Is Dirty

In April 2018, further revelations from Brazil's Lava Jato (in English, Operation Car Wash*) investigation linked the scandal for the first time to Bolivia. According to a Brazilian police report, three Bolivian officials—identified only by their initials—were paid at least $550,000 in bribes by Camargo Correa, another Brazilian company that received a contract to build the Roboré–El Carmen highway in Santa Cruz.

*Note: Operation Car Wash (Portuguese: *Operação Lava Jato*) was a criminal investigation by the federal police of Brazil, Curitiba Branch. It began in March 2014 and resulted in more than a thousand warrants of several types. According to the Operation Car Wash task force, investigations implicated administrative members of the state-owned oil company Petrobras, politicians from Brazil's largest parties (including presidents of the republic), presidents of the Chamber of Deputies, the Federal Senate, state governors, and businessmen from large Brazilian companies. The federal police consider it the largest corruption investigation in the country's history. (Refer to the country Brazil.)

Democratic Republic Of The Congo (Drc)—Gertler And Glencore

The *Guardian*, December 5, 2019, reported that the UK's Serious Fraud Office launched an investigation into suspicions of bribery at the mining and commodity trading listed group Glencore, worth £30 billion, and its work with Israeli billionaire Dan Gertler and the leader of DRC.

Glencore is the world's biggest commodity trader in fifty countries in everything from oil to cotton, wheat, and sugar. It also has significant mining operations in gold, silver, platinum, nickel, iron, and aluminum.

This investigation came on the heels of another investigation by the US Department of Justice for alleged money laundering and corruption in Nigeria, Venezuela, and the DRC, Africa's biggest copper producer.

Gertler's notoriety in the DRC had been known for some twenty years, during which time he made billions from being the unofficial gatekeeper to natural resources deals in the DRC. His friendship with its former president, Joseph Kabila, from 2001 to 2019, was a source of controversy cited by a 2001 UN investigation that said he had given Kabila $20 million to buy weapons to equip his army against rebel groups in exchange for a monopoly on the country's diamonds. Gertler is also named in the 2013 Africa Progress Panel report, with deals that made the country poorer by some $1.3 billion.

In addition, a leaked document that formed part of the Panama Papers (see the end of this chapter) showed how "Glencore had secretly loaned tens of millions of dollars to Gertler after it enlisted him to secure a controversial mining agreement in the DRC." Gertler pleaded innocence.

Glencore has a history of notoriety. It was founded in 1974 by the commodities trader and financier Marc Rich, who in 1983 was indicted on charges described by the then US attorney for New York, Rudolph Giuliani, as "the biggest tax evasion case in United States history."

"Rich was also charged with buying millions of barrels of oil from Iran during the 1979–81 hostage crisis, flouting a ban on trading with the enemy. He fled to Switzerland and remained on the FBI's most-wanted list until he was controversially pardoned by Bill Clinton in the final hours of his presidency in 2001."

After a buyout, and under its billionaire chief executive Ivan Glasenberg, Glencore grew to become the world's biggest commodity trader, supplying the raw materials used in products from cars to smartphones.

Venezuela—A Special Kind Of Evil

In May 2019, Stephen Sackur of BBC *Hardtalk* interviewed Vanessa Neumann, the appointed UK ambassador to Venezuela's opposition Juan Guaido. His question to her was "Has the missteps of Guaido's campaign made a regime change in Venezuela less likely?"

A political crisis has been in process for a long while. But it is not so much about politics as it is about money: the downfall of Venezuela.

Hugo Chavez's economic policies pre-2010, such as deficit spending and price controls, led to severe socioeconomic crises and the worsening of corruption and murder rates. Under President Maduro in 2013, the economy deteriorated, exacerbated by the low oil prices in early 2015 and a drop in Venezuela's oil production from a lack of maintenance and investment. The government did not cut spending; as a result, it denied that the country was in crisis and violently oppressed the opposition.

Venezuela has been wracked by gross economic mismanagement resulting in hyperinflation of an estimated 10,000,000 percent for 2019, chronic utility and medicine shortages, closure of companies, hunger, unemployment, deterioration of productivity, and human rights violations. Some of the massive emigrations have also been forced. High crime, of course, is a result of such poverty and hardship and has helped to cause it.

The protest call by Guaido—the head of the National Assembly legislature has been recognized as interim president by fifty-seven countries—urged the military to peacefully and civically rise against Maduro through a proclamation to the armed forces to listen to the people of Venezuela. Maduro must go. While some military personnel heeded Guaido's call, the effort petered out and protests failed.

Venezuela's military is 160,000 strong and paramilitaries, *colectivos* (armed leftist groups that support Maduro), and criminal gangs collectively have more than 100,000 members.

Brian Fonseca, a defense and security expert at Florida International University, says President Maduro effectively tied the survival of his government to the military leadership by allowing them to participate in corruption. It is estimated that $300 billion to $500 billion are earned from illicit trade.

When the economy went into free fall, Maduro consolidated his power through political repression, censorship, and electoral manipulation. Protests were banned and any political adversaries were imprisoned.

As 2016 concluded, the Organized Crime and Corruption Reporting Project (OCCRP), an international nongovernmental organization that investigates crime and corruption, gave President Maduro the Person of the Year Award: "His negligence, incompetence, and corruption are the cause. When a country's leader can watch his people starve and still oversee a government stealing $70 billion a year all while his family deals drugs, it's a special kind of evil." His corrupt, mismanaged, and oppressive reign left citizens starving and begging for medicines. Maduro and his family steal millions of dollars from government coffers to fund patronage that maintains his power in Venezuela. The reality is that most of the military is not prepared to give up the good space that they are in.

Politically, Venezuela is still in limbo. Maduro's government has accused the United States of organizing a coup d'état to remove him and take control of the country's oil reserves.

At the time of writing, there is a $15 million bounty on Maduro after he was accused of drug trafficking by US prosecutors. The US State Department also proposed a plan for a transitional government, but Maduro will not cave.

Despite an economy in which over 92 percent of the population are poor, the unequal society persists, and Maduro's power remains surprisingly absolute.

Panama Papers From Around The World—Where The Company Could Not Even Find Its Clients

The Panama Papers refers to thousands of leaked confidential documents belonging to a Panama law firm called Mossack Fonseca. Panama is a tax haven, meaning that it imposes no income, corporate, capital gains, or estate taxes on any offshore entities that engage in business outside the jurisdiction.

Thousands of leaked documents (in fact, a staggering 2.6 terabytes of information) were released to the public by the International Consortium of Journalists, *Süddeutsche Zeitung* (*SZ*), and more than 100 global media partners in April 2016. These were infamously referred to as the Panama Papers.

Further documents revealed "Mossack Fonseca couldn't identify tens of thousands of owners of companies it had registered in opaque, low-tax jurisdictions. Two months after the firm became aware of the records breach, it still hadn't identified the owners of more than 70 percent of the 28,500 active companies it had registered in the British Virgin Islands, the firm's busiest offshore hub, and 75 percent of its 10,500 active shell companies in Panama" (OCCRP.org: "The fall of Mossack Fonseca," 2018).

Many employees were charged with a string of offenses ranging from tax evasion, wire fraud, and money laundering because of their alleged roles in a longstanding criminal scheme. This was only the beginning.

The Panama Papers have unearthed many wealthy people, namely celebrities, prime ministers, presidents, kings, politicians, oligarchs, criminals, and their family members around the world who have spirited away their investments (some ill-gotten) in trusts and shell companies. Some have been charged; some are still being investigated.

Transparency International in April 2019 commented that the unfolding developments indicate that not all crimes committees have been revealed yet. "As investigations into the Panama Papers continue across the world and more authorities examine the evidence contained in the Panama Papers, we can expect to see more investigations, more arrests, and more accountability in the years to come."

With the emphasis on "years."

CHAPTER 3

Ingenious Bankers

Financial Institutions Are Misused Willingly Or Unwillingly

COMMERCIAL BANKS HANDLE trillions of dollars of daily transactions. Banks hold accounts with other banks to facilitate transactions in the country of the bank where the account is held. Such corresponding relationships enable banks to function as intermediaries or agents, facilitating typical bank transactions on behalf of another bank. The sheer volume of transactional activity that banks manage daily means that banks are susceptible to significant money-laundering risks. Laundered money, at some stage, passes through a bank.

Money service businesses (MSBs) are also part of the fray providing financial services such as money transmitters, check cashers, currency exchangers, or selling money orders, prepaid access devices, and travelers' checks, and engaging the services of commercial banks to settle transactions. MSBs have been granting unbanked access to alternative financial services for over a century, but in the last five years, fintech companies are aggressively popping up, particularly in emerging markets, to satisfy the need for financial inclusion. Unfortunately, it provides yet another vehicle for criminals to access. Some of the MSBs and fintech are subject to the same anti-money-laundering regulations too, but new entrants into the market, especially in undeveloped economies, operate under the radar and operate unlicensed, making it likely that anti-money-laundering violations go undetected. Illegal funds transfers can attract good fees because of the risk taken. The irony of being unlicensed is that the regulators are unable to take any action and it is left up to clients to lay charges. Many clients prefer to remain silent: who wants to be taken for an idiot?

The big money, though, still passes through the big banks. In the previous chapter, big banks' involvement as facilitators of money laundering is clear.

The world's most sophisticated financial regimes cannot stem or control the flow of suspicious funds passing through its systems. But it is not always about negligence; it is about trafficking money.

There is also no doubt about the unintended consequence of AML legislation: A pen picture of some of the later involvements by banks in money laundering should give cause for concern. The very protectors of the financial economy fall within the bankers' domain, and since the advent of anti-money-laundering legislation relative to banks, including penalties, fines, and a handful of incarcerations, little has changed.

But we also thought erroneously that men of the cloth would have been protectors of the young, didn't we? (These cardinals were promoted, protected and their behavior held as open secrets among the elite of the Catholic Church: Australian Cardinal Pell, ex-cardinal McCarrick, the late Cardinal Law of the United States, Cardinal O'Brien from Scotland, Cardinal Daniels from Belgium, Cardinal Groep from Austria, Cardinal Sodano of the Vatican, and two cardinals Errazuriz and Ezzati from Chile.)

The world's most sophisticated financial regimes cannot control the flow of suspicious funds passing through their systems. But it is seldom about negligence or ignorance; it is about making money. A bank is an intermediary, so there is either collusion where illegal money passing through its doors is aided and abetted or deliberately, bankers turn a blind eye to the source of the money, the (wealthy) account holders, and the reasons for the accounts and their transactions.

Halkbank—Crime Does Pay

Although this same example was given under Iran, Turkey, and the UAE in chapter 2, here we are looking at it more keenly from the bank's perspective.

From 2012 to 2016, during negotiations on its nuclear program, Iran relied on Halkbank, a major Turkish-owned state bank, to launder money to relieve the economic pressure of international sanctions. In this way, Iran successfully evaded the United States and international sanctions that were meant to constrain its proliferation of weapons of mass destruction; Halkbank was indeed the great facilitator.

In 2016 Reza Zarrab, an Iranian-Turkish businessman was arrested and prosecuted for masterminding this scheme to launder billions of dollars of Iranian oil proceeds through Halkbank under the guise of gold and, later, food trade. During the 2018 trial when he was convicted, Reza's co-conspirator, Mehmet Hakan Atilla, a Turkish national and former deputy general manager of Halkbank, also implicated Turkish president Recep Erdoğan. The case, politically charged, remains in legal limbo. However, as the United States mounts pressure against Iran, Iran simply strengthens its nuclear program. (Political nuances became tenser after Trump's peace deals announced with UAE and other Middle East countries in September 2020 and 2021, and Biden's current intent to roll back on some of the most stringent Trump-era sanctions imposed on Iran to return to compliance with the landmark 2015 nuclear accord.)

On October 15, 2019, US prosecutors pounced with a punchy six-count indictment against Halkbank, charging the bank with fraud, money laundering, and conspiracy to violate the International Emergency Economic Powers Act. The US Department of Justice's decision to prosecute Halkbank is an unusual step because US prosecutors usually seek to settle out of court with banks accused of sanctions violations, through deferred prosecution agreements.

The US-Turkey relations were already tense: Turkish troops were sent to attack the Kurdish-led Syrian Democratic Forces—a key United States ally in the campaign against the Islamic State. This was considered an intrusion, and in Washington, the House of Representatives passed the Protect Against Conflict by Turkey Act, which called for sanctions against entities affiliated with the Turkish government, specifically including Halkbank.

The story is complicated (refer to the previous chapter under Turkey) as all successful money-laundering schemes usually are. People may be jailed, companies fined, protests held against government corruption, and banks fined, but most of the money earned has already achieved a lot of what it set out to do in the years before exposure.

How was it done? The scheme allowed the Iranian government a way of accessing its oil and gas revenue held overseas. Zarrab funneled money from Halkbank accounts held by Iranian entities to accounts of his front companies in Turkey and the United Arab Emirates (UAE). Then, after laundering the money through illicit gold exports and later falsified food trade, Zarrab used those funds to make international payments on behalf of Iranian entities that support Iran's proliferation programs. According to the Department of Justice, the scheme "fueled a dark pool of Iranian government-controlled funds that could be clandestinely sent anywhere in the world."

Visit https://www.iranwatch.org/our-publications/articles-reports/major-turkish-bank-prosecuted-unprecedented-iran-sanctions-evasion-case to read this complicated and interconnected story published March 31, 2020, involving several banks, government officials, senior bankers, some twenty companies, and other individuals. The scheme orchestrated through Zarrab and Halkbank was worth approximately US$20 billion of Iranian funds, which successfully served to feed its nuclear program. Prosecution through the US is going to be another hurdle as described in an article, "The Strange Twists in the Investigation and Prosecution of Turkish Bank Halkbank," by Norman Bloch and Samir Varma on June 30, 2020, at www.doescrimepay.com.

Danske Bank Denmark—More Than Half Of Its 15,000 Customers And Their Transactions Were Suspicious

Danske Bank is under investigation for money laundering. Thomas Borgen, at the time CEO of Denmark's biggest bank, resigned after admitting that some €200 billion of "questionable money" flowed through its Estonian branch between the years 2007 and 2015. The amount, when compared against the GDP in 2017 of Estonia, which was €29 billion, and Denmark's GDP of €394 billion, illustrates the scale of abuse. It was a massive scandal in Europe. Its Estonian branch came about when Danske acquired Sampo Bank, a small Finnish bank in 2007. Sampo Bank had a nonresident portfolio in Estonia, and it is this that caused the problems.

In the words of the independent report into the scandal written by a Danish law firm, which prompted the CEO Borgen's resignation (*White-Collar Crime Online: Deviance, Organizational Behaviour and Risk* by Petter Gottschalk and Christopher Hamerton, 2022), "anti-money-laundering procedures at the Estonian branch had been manifestly insufficient and inadequate." Danske Bank has also admitted there were "major deficiencies in controls and governance that made it possible to use Danske

Bank's branch in Estonia for criminal activities such as money laundering."

Danske shut down the nonresident portfolio in 2015. An independent investigation found that more than half of Danske's Estonian 15,000 customers and their transactions were suspicious. The source of funds passing through the portfolio was identified as more than 58 percent coming from Russia, Estonia, and Latvia. The destinations of the funds were worldwide.

The difficulty in identifying the true source of the funds came from the lack of transparency as to the real owners of the customers in the portfolio. A proportion of them was found to be UK-based companies registered as limited liability partnerships. At the time, they were not required to publish details of their ultimate beneficial owners. Therefore, ownership passed through a series of shell companies making it difficult to locate the owners (which, of course, is the whole point of shell companies).

Some £475 million was involved in 2019, but the outcome for all parties remains unclear. Other European banks, namely Deutsche Bank, Swedbank, and Raiffeisen Bank, have been suspected of transferring illicit funds from Danske Bank.

Goldman Sachs Malaysia (1MDB)—Its Tentacles Reach Far And Wide

Hong Kong CNN Business on August 9, 2019, reported that Malaysia filed criminal charges against seventeen current and former Goldman Sachs employees including Richard Gnodde, the CEO of Goldman Sachs International for their role in the 1Malaysia Development Berhad (1MDB) scandal. 1MDB is a government strategic development company that controls the government's sovereign wealth fund.

Malaysia's attorney general said that Goldman Sachs arranged three large bond offerings for 1MDB. Malaysia accused Goldman Sachs and some of its bankers of misleading investors about the bond sales and fraudulently diverting $2.7 billion of the proceeds. The US Justice Department claimed that $4.5 billion was stolen from 1MDB by senior officials and pumped into New York condos, hotels, yachts, a jet, and yes, used to fund movies such as *The Wolf of Wall Street*.

That raised questions about who at Goldman Sachs knew about the questionable integrity of the deals, and when they knew it. The bank repeatedly denied wrongdoing and blamed it on rogue employees who deceived compliance. Malaysia charged Goldman Sachs and individuals for grave violations. In March 2017, Malaysia issued a ten-year prohibition order against former Goldman Sachs banker Tim Leissner for making false statements on behalf of his bank without its knowledge. Lawsuits are being filed over billions in missing cash. Goldman Sachs says it is cooperating with authorities and contests the charges.

The tentacles in the case are spread around many parts of the world. This gives you an example of how intricate these investigations can get:

Australia (Avesta Asset Management) had accepted funds from 1MDB and subsequently has closed; the Monetary Authority of Singapore and the Commercial Affairs Department have investigated investment companies and seized several bank accounts there. Hong Kong has investigated Credit Suisse branch deposits; Bali, at the request of the United States Department of Justice, handed over the superyacht *Equanimity* as part of this criminal investigation; Luxembourg's private bank Edmond de Rothschild Group investigated transfers of hundreds of millions of dollars to an offshore company; Swiss authorities, under the direction of the Office of the Attorney General of Switzerland, froze a bank account amounting to several million US dollars linked to 1MDB, and the Swiss prosecutor said that money had been deposited into Swiss bank accounts of former Malaysian public officials and current and former officials of United Arab Emirates. The United Arab Emirates issued travel bans and froze bank accounts of former Abu Dhabi sovereign-wealth fund International Petroleum Investment Company's employees who had close connections to 1MDB, and may have used the British Virgin Islands-based Aabar Investments PJS to funnel money from 1MDB into various accounts and companies around the world; the United Kingdom's Serious Fraud Office investigated 1MDB after it was reported that funds were moved from Malaysia to Switzerland involving the Royal Bank of Scotland's branch in Zurich.

How is that for intricacy? Being a government fund, of course, it included the Malaysian prime minister at the time, Najib Razak. He was hit with dozens of corruption-related charges in the case because of channeling millions of dollars from 1MDB to his bank accounts.

Yet another character is involved: Low Taek Jho, often called Jho Low, is a Malaysian fugitive also sought by the authorities of Malaysia, Singapore, and the US in connection with the above scandal. Reports indicate that he is the beneficiary of numerous discretionary trust assets said by the US government to originate from payments out of the 1MDB fund. The prosecutors alleged Low to be the mastermind of a scheme to siphon altogether $4.5 billion from 1MDB into his accounts. He has been associated with numerous high-value transactions, including acquisitions of businesses, luxury real estate, and art, as well as philanthropy.

After their 2018 election, the Malaysian authorities, under a newly elected prime minister, barred Najib Razak from leaving the country. A huge haul of cash and valuable items from premises linked to him was seized, and he was charged with criminal breach of trust, money laundering, and abuse of power. Jho Low was charged with money laundering. Having filed complaints alleging that more than US$ 4.5 billion was diverted from 1MDB by Jho Low and other conspirators including officials from Malaysia, Saudi Arabia, and the United Arab Emirates, the US Department of Justice said it would continue to pursue investigations into 1MDB.

The whistleblower was the Swiss ex-banker and former director of PetroSaudi, Xavier Justo. Justo's story makes a fascinating read and is a lot more complex than stated here. 1MDB and PetroSaudi were in partnership, but the partnership, Justo felt, needed to be terminated as he no longer "got on well" with friends there. All he wanted was the final US$2 million former associates at PetroSaudi had promised him as part of a US$6.5 million unwritten agreement on leaving. He did, however, ask a loyal IT colleague to copy all the contents of the company's servers onto a hard drive as insurance against the withholding of his payout, "just in case." It was reported that he thought he might one day leak the ninety gigabytes of data (about 230,000 emails) to the press. Four years later and still no US$2 million forthcoming, journalist Clare Rewcastle Brown convinced him to blow the whistle rather than to sell the information or give it away to cover the outstanding US$2 million. That is another interesting story.

Punjab National Bank—Collusion With Bank Staff

Punjab National Bank (PNB) is one of India's biggest banks and the country's second-largest state-run lender. A US$177 billion fraud was detected at its Mumbai branch in 2018. (Its assets at the time stood at $120 billion.) The fraud benefited a few select account holders. Billionaire Nirav Modi has jewelry stores in a few of India's cities. It is alleged that Modi and companies linked to him acquired guarantees worth $2 billion, which were used to obtain loans from abroad. They admitted to colluding with bank staff. Other banks were also involved. PNB indicated that two junior officials had issued illegal letters of undertaking dating back to 2011. Among the further characters involved is jeweler Mehul Choksi of Choksi's Gitanjali Group; both he and Modi managed to leave India before Punjab filed a complaint.

The State Union Bank of India was exposed to about $300 million, the State Bank of India to about $212 million, and state-run UCO Bank to $412 million because of fraudulent transactions conducted at PNB. Law enforcement found millions of dollars' worth of diamonds, gold, and jewelry at Modi's home, luxury cars, twenty-one properties including a farmhouse, a solar plant, and land worth approximately $68 million. Furthermore, law enforcement was investigating more than one hundred shell companies allegedly used by Modi and Choksi in their myriad of transactions.

The scandal seriously affected the very loans needed for India's small- and medium-size businesses to help steer the government's ambitious growth programs.

European Banks

As reported by My Office News on March 6, 2019, and posted in Crime Alert, Tech News, *"Several European banks have been drawn into money-laundering allegations centered on dirty Russian money. Much of the information has been made available to media outfits by the Organized Crime and Corruption Reporting Project. Investigations into the scandal are underway in the Baltic nations, the US, the UK, and the Nordic countries. Below is a list of the main banks touched by the scandal."*

A few are indicated below:

Nordea Bank AB—from our bank to shell companies

Nordea Bank has been under investigation since 2016, and Nordea put aside a €100 million provision in April 2019 for a potential fine related to money laundering. Nordea was accused of handling millions of dollars in suspicious transactions for several years.

Allegations are that the biggest Nordic bank managed about €700 million in potentially dirty money, with funds arriving from failed Lithuanian bank Ukio Bankas and heading to shell companies in countries such as the British Virgin Islands and Panama, according to Finnish broadcaster YLE.

Nordea Bank—saluting a pesky Russian client and a tax company

Nordea is suspected of being part of a major international money-laundering scandal involving a Russian client and a tax company. For almost four years, the fraud squad tried to pursue a criminal case against a Russian client and a company in Belize in Central America, suspected of having 'washed' approximately 322 million Norwegian kroner using bank accounts in Nordea.

Deutsche Bank AG—its fingers in many pies

More than $889 million went from accounts at Deutsche Bank to those of the so-called Troika Laundromat between 2003 and 2017, according to German daily *Süddeutsche Zeitung*—part of the Organized Crime and Corruption Reporting

Project, which is a global network of investigative journalists. The report comes on top of regulatory scrutiny of Deutsche Bank's role as a correspondent bank in Danske Bank's money-laundering scandal and a probe by German prosecutors of its involvement in a tax-evasion scheme unmasked by the Panama Papers in 2016.

ABN AMRO Group NV—happy to help

The Troika Laundromat moved about €190 million through ABN AMRO Group NV, a unit of the Dutch bank that became part of the Royal Bank of Scotland.

Deutsche Bank—spiriting money out of Russia

The Global Laundromat was a channel that Russian criminals used to move money, estimated at $8 billion from 2010 to 2014 into the Western financial system. Shell companies, mostly based in the UK, "loaned" money to each other and then defaulted on these fictitious debts. The corrupt judges in Moldova authenticated the debt, with billions transferred to Moldova and the Baltics via a bank in Latvia. Deutsche Bank was used to launder the money via its corresponding banking network, thereby facilitating illegal Russian payments to the United States, the European Union, and Asia. Deutsche Bank was a significant culprit in spiriting money out of Russia without informing the authorities. Less than two years after a report—called *Dark Matter*—was published, Deutsche Bank traders in Moscow were caught secretly moving

$10 billion of their clients' money out of Russia by illegally exploiting the stock market. It was called *Dark Matter* because these flows over time produce distinctly nonrandom patterns.

Raiffeisen Bank International AG—linked to the Hermitage Fund*

This Austrian bank is one of the biggest foreign lenders in Russia. It was, in 2019, the main target of a filing by the Hermitage Fund, detailing $634 million allegedly transferred to it from Lithuania's Ukio Bankas and from the Estonian unit of Danske Bank. Hermitage said the bank ignored signs that should have triggered money-laundering prevention measures. Raiffeisen launched an internal probe, yet also pointed out that Hermitage had filed similar allegations before and those Austrian authorities dismissed them.

*Hermitage describes itself as an activist fund. Its main tactics include the exposure of corporate corruption in the companies it is holding, in the hope of improving managerial behavior and lessening the significant discount that corruption has on share prices. Most famously, Hermitage has helped to expose several high-profile cases of corruption in Russia's largest company Gazprom between 1998 and 2000. In October 2000, Hermitage reported, "Investors are valuing this company as if 99 percent of its assets have been stolen. The real figure is around 10 percent so that's good news."

VBS South Africa—By the ANC For the ANC and the EFF to Boot

The state-owned VBS mutual bank (a small lender) in operation since 1992 in South Africa was looted of more than R1.5 billion by its management and the ruling African National Congress; the party in power has been a beneficiary of this corruption and fraud. In terms of some idea of how money was flaunted on frivolous lifestyles, bank statements proved that VBS financed tribal Vhavenda King Ramabulana's five cars worth R6.5 million.

The VBS piggy bank, as reported by the City Press on June 24, 2018, had bank records that revealed the "incestuous relationship" between Vele Investments and VBS Mutual Bank. VBS was, it seems, allowably funding other Vele subsidiaries with multimillion rand overdrafts and hundreds of millions of rands, which were suspiciously transferred between these entities. Some of Vele's subsidiaries managed their daily operations with access to large VBS overdrafts and complicated intercompany loans. There were also customers that did not pay home loans, vehicle loans and overdrafts. "It was like a Ponzi scheme that was going to fail."

The third strongest opposition party in South Africa is the Economic Freedom Front (EFF), and it was also a beneficiary. Brian Shivambu is the brother of the EFF deputy leader, Floyd Shivambu, and this is how he benefited: The South African Revenue Services auditors and investigators found that Brian Shivambu had fraudulently enriched himself, compliments of VBS Bank, for about R16 million and had not declared this for income or VAT purposes, either of which is considered tax evasion (a legal money-laundering offense).

Overall, journalists investigating VBS fraud, after studying bank statements, contracts, and other relevant documents, found that VBS was defrauded of some R21.5 million; the beneficiaries of this money were Brian Shivambu, Malema (leader of the EFF), and their families and businesses.

"An analysis of the spending habits recorded in the Grand Azania bank accounts, cross-referenced with Floyd Shivambu's social media posts, suggested that the bank card linked to this account was following Shivambu across southern Africa—including to Zambia, where he spent his birthday at a luxury hotel. And the bank card of Mahuna Investments tended to follow Malema across the country, including to his hometown, Seshego, and the Durban July."

Again, a complicated trail of the movement of money, but none of it has found its way to the taxman as with all stolen money. The South African Revenue Service charged two companies that Brian Shivambu was the sole owner of, with approximately a $2 million bill for evading tax for the periods 2017, 2018, and 2019 (*Business Maverick* of August 16, 2021). The interesting thing is that usually, tax authorities want to charge tax and related penalties on illegally earned money, most of which has long gone and been spent. Charging tax has the unintended consequence of legitimizing the laundering of money.

Fourteen municipalities had funds deposited in VBS, so in the event of a liquidity stress, when the bank did not have cash to settle transactions, it was easy enough to call up a municipality or two to provide further funds.

City Press broke the news on March 11, 2018, that VBS was broke and about to go into curatorship, and at this point, no one knew about the skeletons that were about to come tumbling out of the closet. VBS was a registered mutual bank and regulated by the South African Reserve Bank. It is interesting, given how transparent all the shenanigans were just by looking at bank statements and following through on the trails of intercompany links, that the regulator had no idea. Shortly after VBS was put under curatorship, City Press raised red flags around the tiny bank's statutory reports to the South African Reserve Bank being inaccurate.

What is the point of regulatory reporting?

Sadly, and as usual, the ordinary people were compromised. Unsuspecting clients across Limpopo were left stranded and had to stand in long queues in a desperate bid to draw their money for days on end. The majority of South African municipalities are in a crisis through corruption and bad management. Nevertheless, some municipalities were persuaded to deposit money into the VBS. This was done even though it was in direct contravention of the Municipal Financial Management Act and forbidden by the National Treasury's instructions. Mayors were said to have "essentially sold their municipalities to the highest bidders."

In the overall scheme of things, the money-laundered value is not big; but in a severely ailing economy in SA, where millions of people are poverty-stricken, yet another compromised country is beset by indigenous money laundering.

HSBC And Westpac In Australia—We Say Sorry And Do It Again

HSBC, Europe's biggest bank, paid a $1.9 billion fine in 2012 to avoid prosecution for allowing the deposit of at least $881 million in proceeds from the sale of illegal drugs. In addition to facilitating money laundering by drug cartels, evidence was found of HSBC moving money for Saudi banks tied to terrorist groups. That was history. On April 8, 2020, the *Financial Times* in Sydney reported that HSBC (Lender's Australia subsidiary) told the Australian financial crime agency that it may have underreported potential money-laundering transactions it facilitated with foreign banks and other institutions.

The same regulator also initiated a legal case against Westpac Banking Corporation, commonly known as Westpac, an Australian bank and financial services provider headquartered at Westpac Place in Sydney. It is one of Australia's "big four" banks and is Australia's first and oldest banking institution. The bank failed to report international fund transactions worth more than A$11 billion between 2013 and 2019 in a timely manner, as required under the law. When it emerged that some of these payments may have facilitated child exploitation by pedophiles, chief executive Brian Hartzer was forced to resign.

Société Générale—Concealing Transactions Connected To Sanctioned Countries

Toward the end of 2019, the French bank agreed to pay $1.34 billion in penalties to settle allegations by US and New York state authorities that the bank had processed and concealed billions of dollars in transactions connected to sanctioned countries, namely Iran, Sudan, Cuba, and Libya, between 2003 and 2013. Federal prosecutors found that the bank engaged in more than 2,500 transactions valued at about $13 billion from 2004 to 2010. The transactions violated US sanctions laws. Mostly it involved a dollar credit facility designed to finance oil transactions between a Dutch commodity trading firm and a Cuban company with a state monopoly on the production and refining of Cuban crude. Investigations found that Société Générale had deliberately made inaccurate or incomplete notations on payment messages that accompanied the transactions to conceal the Cuban nexus of US dollar payments.

Credit Suisse—State Officials And Bankers Collude

A detailed indictment unsealed on January 3, 2019 in the Eastern District of New York alleges that former Credit Suisse bankers, a Lebanese businessman, and former top officials in Mozambique, including the former Minister of Finance, participated in a $2 billion corruption, fraud, and money laundering scheme (the indictment). They face charges of conspiracy to commit money laundering, wire fraud, securities fraud, and Foreign Corrupt Practices Act (FCPA) violations. There was a deliberate covering up of information and circumventing controls to convince the bank to fund illicit investment projects and to include bribe and kickback payments in part through US correspondent bank accounts as the money traveled from one foreign country to another.

As an example of just how convoluted these deals are, an article published by JD Supra.com ("Former Bankers Allegedly Concealed 'Master of Kickbacks' from Internal Compliance Department") reported that those charged used three public companies to obtain more than $2 billion in state-backed loans. These loans were to have funded projects to benefit the country of Mozambique in providing coastal surveillance, tuna fishing, and shipyard projects. Instead, the defendants undertook so-called maritime projects that conducted little legitimate activity—just enough to channel some $200 million in bribes and kickbacks to themselves, the Mozambican government officials and others.

The indictment refers to the beginning of the corruption around 2013, when representatives of Credit Suisse allege that around 2013, representatives of Credit Suisse (known as Investment Bank 1 and Investment Bank 2) arranged the government-backed loans. The companies then entered into contracts with Privinvest—a holding company registered in the United Arab Emirates—and paid nearly all the loan proceeds to them as the so-called contractor on the maritime projects.

Privinvest charged inflated prices for the equipment and services it provided, which were then mostly used to pay the bribes and kickbacks.

The companies then defaulted on the loans. The effect of the guarantees meant that the Mozambican government would be held liable for repaying the loans. However, the guarantees violated two aspects of law: the budget laws of 2013 and 2014 and the Mozambican constitution. Their guarantees were declared unconstitutional by the Constitutional Council of Mozambique.

JPMorgan Chase—Good At All Sorts Of Money-Laundering Schemes

"JPMorgan Chase Istanbul 2019" (*Daily Sabah* on March 26, 2019) reported on some of the history of JPMorgan Chase, which is one of the top ten investments banks in the world. It, therefore, holds a lot of power in the global market to manipulate and speculate over the segments of the markets yielding consequences for national assets, bonds, stocks, and currencies. It follows that JPMorgan Chase plays a significant role in financial crimes.

In October 2018, it cost JPMorgan billions for the violation of Cuban Assets Control Regulations, Iranian sanctions, and weapons of mass destruction sanctions eighty-seven times. It also violated sanctions on narcotics and Syria when it processed eighty-five transactions and maintained accounts for six sanctioned individuals.

About two months later, JPMorgan was fined for mishandling US securities that represent shares of foreign companies. The bank gave American depository receipts (ADRs) to brokers when neither the brokers nor their clients held shares in foreign companies that were required to support such transactions. An investigation by US authorities found out that JPMorgan Chase hired children of Chinese authorities from 2006 to 2013 to do jobs in China. The bank had to pay a $264 million fine to settle claims that its hiring violated the Foreign Corrupt Practices Act.

Also, JPMorgan Chase's role in the well-known Bernie Madoff Ponzi scheme is telling too. In 2014, the bank failed to alert federal courts about the largest Ponzi scheme fraud in US history, the Bernie Madoff scandal. Serving as Madoff's primary bank for more than two decades, JPMorgan had a unique window into his scheme. The prosecutors reported that the Madoff Ponzi scheme was conducted almost exclusively through various accounts held at JPMorgan. A fraudulent investor, Bernie Madoff was estimated to have swindled $65 billion into his accounts. He was given a 150-year prison sentence, and during his term, a kidney disease got the better of him in April 2021. In 2013, JPMorgan was fined for its manipulations on the quality of the mortgages it had been selling to investors in the run-up to the 2008 financial crisis as well as other manipulative bidding strategies in commodities trading.

It has paid out billions in fines, but JPMorgan still stands big and strong.

Malta And Pilatus Bank—Flouting Its Money Laundering Policies; It's Only Paper After All

When the Pilatus Bank started its business in Malta in 2014, its chairman and owner Syed Ali Sadr Hasheminejad was under investigation in the US for evading US economic sanctions and defrauding US banks by concealing the role of Iran and Iranian parties in US dollar payments sent through the US banking system. Surprisingly, the Malta Financial Services Authority

(MFSA) permitted the owner to conduct banking activities in Malta while he was still under investigation in the US.

But two years later, a whistleblower reported that the bank was conducting illegal activities and flouting its own AML and CFT (counterterrorism financing) policies. Following these revelations, the Financial Intelligence Analysis Unit of Malta did nothing, and the bank simply continued its activities. When the FIAU did investigate Pilatus Bank, members of the MFSA were also present, yet the only step taken by the MFSA against Pilatus Bank was freezing the bank's operations after the arrest of its chairperson by the US authorities. Reuters reported on November 5, 2018, that the European Central Bank withdrew the banking license of Malta's Pilatus Bank as the European Commission acted to step up a disciplinary procedure against Maltese authorities.

ABLV Bank Latvia—Facilitating Illicit Transactions For Sanctioned Entities

In February 2018, the US Department of the Treasury accused Latvia's third-largest bank of institutionalized money laundering, because it facilitated illicit transactions for sanctioned entities in North Korea, Azerbaijan, Russia, and Ukraine. The treasury's Financial Crime Enforcement Network (FinCEN) blamed ABLV for dabbling in money laundering and as an institution of primary money laundering concern and invoked Section 311 of the USA Patriot Act, which meant that the bank could no longer open or maintain a correspondent account in the US. This resulted in an exodus of nonresident deposits from ABLV within a week at an estimated value of $600 million. The bank's liquidity was therefore seriously compromised, leading to its closure.

Cyprus And Malta Banks—EU's Smallest Members Make Big Friends

In May 2018, the American treasury official in charge of tackling money laundering accused ABLV, Latvia's third-largest bank, of laundering Russian money and starving it of American dollars, forcing it to close. Later that summer, Malta felt similar heat from European officials who said there had been serious regulatory gaps in Malta's handling of scandal-hit Pilatus Bank (discussed above).

A European Commission report on the sale of passports warned that their investor citizenship schemes exposed the rest of the EU to money-laundering risks. Some complain that the countries have been unfairly singled out because they are small and efforts have been made to clean up their act. The question at the time posed: is this sentiment compatible with their continued zeal for offshore banking?

A big scandal regarding FBME, previously known as the Federal Bank of the Middle East, was based in Tanzania but about 90 percent of its banking was conducted in Cyprus. A report by the US Treasury's Financial Crimes Enforcement Network (FinCEN) in 2014 said the bank was an institution of "primary money laundering concern."

It was found that the bank was evading efforts by the Central Bank of Cyprus to supervise its activities and that FBME was facilitating money laundering, terrorist financing, transnational organized crime, fraud, sanctions evasion, weapons trading, and political corruption.

A 2014 internal report by the Central Bank of Cyprus about FBME that was obtained by the *Guardian* found that FBME had banking relationships with several politically sensitive Russian clients, including Vladimir Smirnov (who is close to Putin) and Aleksandr Shishkin, a member of Putin's political party.

Two years later, FBME was subject to "fifth special measure," which is a tough US regulatory tool set up after the 9/11 attacks to address law enforcement concerns in the banking sector. This prohibited the bank from doing business in the US or using US dollars, and barred US banks from opening or using any bank accounts on FBME's behalf. The bank was effectively shut down. FBME challenged the decision, but US courts continue to uphold their decision.

It is a complicated story, and many depositors have been sadly marginalized (2022).

Bloomberg reported (January 10, 2019) that Cyprus is no longer a Mediterranean haven for Russian businesses.

Two Russian businessmen with accounts in Cyprus for over a decade said they were contacted by their banks over the past few months, asking for documents from many years ago on the source of the money in their accounts. Unable to provide them, they were forced to close the accounts, they said, declining to be named.

The central bank directive on money laundering involves avoiding dealings with entities deemed to be shell companies, which hits at the heart of Russian investments. Cyprus banks now prefer not to deal with Russian money and Russian clients, "even those who've had accounts in Cyprus banks for many years," said Evgeny Kogan, former director of the Center for Protection of Shareholders and Investor Rights of Cypriot Banks set up in 2014. "Russian clients are becoming toxic."

Cyprus/Libya—Easy To Hide The Billions

Wednesday, July 25, 2018, "Cyprus Records Shed Light on Libya's Hidden Millions"

Leaked records from Cyprus revealed how a procurement official stole millions from his country's government using offshore companies and multiple bank accounts to channel and launder the proceeds abroad—and had been doing it for years. Ali Ibrahim Dabaiba served under Moammar Gadhafi and is believed to have stolen 20 percent of the value of the contracts his office managed.

The alleged crimes revealed apparently form only part of his hidden global empire of more than 100 companies, luxury real estate, and other assets.

Dabaiba was once mayor of the coastal city of Misrata and controlled the Organization for Development of Administrative Centers (ODAC), a major public agency tasked with developing the country's infrastructure and with a budget in 2008 of $6.8 billion.

In the prelude to the fall of the Gadhafi regime in 2011, Dabaiba cunningly switched his allegiance to the rebels. He was able to live very well in exile during the brutal Libyan war as a lot of his money was offshore. Dabaiba and a friend by the name of Landlum, through their network of shell companies around the world, invested in properties from Canada to mainland Europe.

"Banks ranging from Credit Suisse to the Central Bank of Cyprus, as well as countries such as Canada, the United Kingdom, and Germany, were all there to help."

Rizal Commercial Banking Corporation—shadowy hackers

A Manila ex-banker was handed a lengthy jail term and a $109 million fine in the first conviction over one of the biggest ever cyber-heists, which saw $81 million stolen from Bangladesh's central bank (Firstpost, January 10, 2019). Shadowy hackers transferred the cash in 2016 from Bangladesh's US accounts to a Philippine bank, Rizal Commercial Banking Corporation, where it was swiftly withdrawn. The theft exposed the Philippines as a haven for dirty money, where some of the world's strictest bank secrecy laws protect account holders from scrutiny.

ING—Admission Criminals "Use Our Account"

On January 16, 2020 (Reuters), an Italian court supported a decision made in March 2019 by the Bank of Italy supervisors that forbade Dutch lender ING, Netherlands' largest financial services provider, from onboarding new customers in Italy. The reason for the decision is ING's involvement in money laundering. ING admitted that it did not do enough to prevent criminals from being able to launder money through its accounts and agreed to pay $856 million to settle the case in its own country.

Yes Bank In India—Aptly Named

Rana Kapoor was cofounder of the private bank Yes Bank. Apparently, he never turned a borrower away, even if the business seemed risky (hence the name Yes Bank?). As a veteran banker, he used his ability to lend and recover loans, distinguishing the bank from others that "depended more on process rather than relationships."

When the business cycle turned and the central bank became tough on bad loans, Yes Bank was left with a suspiciously high level of nonperforming assets in the accounts of many well-known Indian companies. Kapoor was therefore removed by the Reserve Bank of India in 2019 and his shares offloaded to lenders under pledge. His successor could not keep the bank afloat, and the bank was closed.

According to the *Economic Times* of March 16, 2020, Rana's seventy-eight companies linked to his family members would be investigated for alleged tax evasion. It would appear these companies were used to accommodate kickbacks received instead of the loans sanctioned by him.

Standard Chartered Bank—A History Of Financial Crime

Frances Coppola of Forbes.com reported (April 10, 2019) on the long history of financial crime by Standard Chartered Bank (SCB).

SCB was at that time fined $1.1 billion for sanctions breaking and money laundering. The fines were jointly imposed by the US and UK. For SCB, an emerging-markets specialist lender with no retail presence in the UK or US, this was considered substantial.

SCB has done this several times. In 2004, SCB agreed with the Federal Reserve and New York regulator to undertake the required changes, policies, and procedures to comply with the anti-money-laundering laws. A cease-and-desist order issued in 2012 disclosed that even after SBC had signed the Written Agreement, SCB's New York branch continued to deal with sanctioned countries by deleting information from payment messages that were necessary for the branch to determine whether these transactions were carried out in a manner consistent with US Office of Foreign Assets Control (OFAC). The branch engaged in unsafe and baseless practices and rendered inadequate responses to examiner inquiries relating to the transmission of funds to and from parties subject to OFAC. This transgression cost SCB $670 million in regulatory fines.

Concurrently, the New York District Attorney's offices imposed on SCB a penalty of $292.2 million, the Federal Reserve imposed $164 million, and the UK's Financial Conduct Authority imposed $131.47 million, making this the largest penalty imposed on SCB. SCB has since indicated it has no longer broken sanctions since 2014.

But during that same year, the French bank BNP Paribas paid a record fine of $9 billion for sanctions breaking, and certain areas of its business were temporarily shut out of dollar clearing.

The size of this penalty caught the attention of the financial world, but for SCB, interference with dollar clearing was a greater threat. As an emerging-markets specialist, much of its business is in dollars, so being shut out of dollar clearing would greatly damage its business, evidenced by the Latvian Bank ABLV and Danske Bank, which at the time was still awaiting its fate from the US Treasury.

"The lesson from this is that financial penalties alone are insufficient to deter banks from criminal activity. There must be a serious risk to the business. BNP Paribas's penalty seems to have influenced SCB's business behavior more than any of the cease-and-desist orders and regulatory fines imposed on SCB itself."

The fact is that there are no charges against any senior executives who supervised during that time of sanctions-busting. "The latest cease-and-desist order prohibits those people from working at SCB, but they are still free, rich, and working in the financial industry.

"Until regulators start to hit bankers where it really hurts, banks will not change their ways."

Australia—Royal Commission Into Misconduct In The Banking, Superannuation, And Financial Services Industry, Australia, Final Report February 1, 2019 (Seventy-Six Recommendations)

The conduct identified and described in the commission's interim report includes conduct by many entities that have taken place over many years, causing substantial loss to many customers but yielding substantial profit to the entities concerned. Very often, the conduct has broken the law. And if it has not broken the law, the conduct has fallen short of the kind of behavior the community not only expects of financial services entities but is also entitled to expect of them.

Four main observations are taken from this report:

First is the connection between conduct and reward: in almost every case, the conduct in issue was driven not only by the relevant entity's pursuit of profit but also by individuals' pursuit of gain, whether in the form of remuneration for the individual or profit for the individual's business. Providing a service to customers was relegated to second place. Sales became all-important. Those who dealt with customers became sellers. Incentives have been offered, and rewards have been paid, regardless of whether the sale was made or profit derived, under the law.

Second, entities and individuals acted in the ways they did because they could. Entities set the terms on which they would deal, consumers often had little detailed knowledge or understanding of the transaction, and consumers had next to no power to negotiate the terms. At most, a consumer could choose from an array of products offered by an entity, or by that entity and others, and the consumer was often not able to make a well-informed choice between them. There was a marked imbalance of power and knowledge between those providing the product or service and those acquiring it.

Third, consumers often dealt with a financial services entity through an intermediary. The client might assume that the person standing between the client and the entity that would provide a financial service or product acted for the client and in the client's interests. But in many cases, the intermediary is paid by, and may act in the interests of, the provider of the service or product. Or if the intermediary does not act for the provider, the intermediary may act only in the interests of the intermediary. The interests of the client, intermediary, and provider of a product or service are not only different; they are opposed. An intermediary who seeks to 'stand in more than one canoe' cannot. Duty to the client and self-interest pull in opposite directions.

Fourth, too often, financial services entities that broke the law were not properly held to account. Misconduct is deterred only if entities believe that misconduct will be detected, denounced, and justly punished. Misconduct, especially misconduct that yields profit, is not deterred by restraining those who are found to have done wrong; they just paid compensation.

Global Banks In General—Defy Law Enforcement And Continue To Serve Oligarchs, Criminals, And Terrorists

The above is a report written by the International Consortium of Investigative Journalists, or ICIJ (September 20, 2020).

The Department of Treasury's Financial Crimes Enforcement Network, known as FinCEN, is an intelligence unit at the heart of the global system to fight money laundering. The FinCEN files show trillions in tainted dollars flow freely through major banks, swamping a broken enforcement system.

ICIJ organized a team of more than four hundred journalists from 110 news organizations in eighty-eight countries to investigate the world of banks and money laundering. In all, an ICIJ analysis found that the documents identify more than $2 trillion in transactions between 1999 and 2017 that were flagged by financial institutions' internal compliance officers as possible money laundering or other criminal activity—including $514 billion at JPMorgan and $1.3 trillion at Deutsche Bank.

This investigation produced the FinCEN files and below is a taste of what their report revealed (taken from their website, https://www.icij.org/investigations/fincen-files/global-banks-defy-u-s-crackdowns-by-serving-oligarchs-criminals-and-terrorists/).

"Secret US government documents reveal that JPMorgan Chase, HSBC, and other big banks have defied money laundering crackdowns by moving staggering sums of illicit cash for shadowy characters and criminal networks that have spread chaos and undermined democracy around the world.

"The records show that five global banks—JPMorgan, HSBC, Standard Chartered Bank, Deutsche Bank, and Bank of New York Mellon—kept profiting from powerful and dangerous players even after US authorities fined these financial institutions for earlier failures to stem flows of dirty money."

Megabanks are seldom prosecuted by the relevant regulators; their actions have little effect considering "the ripple the flood of plundered money that washes through the international financial system." Warnings had negligible effect.

Leaked documents reveal that JPMorgan, the largest bank in the United States, moved money for people and companies tied to the massive looting of public funds in Malaysia (including the fugitive financier behind the 1MDB scandal discussed in chapter 2), Venezuela, and Ukraine.

Then there was the Bernie Madoff Ponzi scheme scandal. Let us just digress for a moment to consider the extent of the punishment for what is said by the courts, media, and public to be the largest fraud in history, namely $65 billion. Joseph T. Wells, with four decades of experience in the antifraud field and the study of white-collar crime and punishment, indicates that the amount is "not hardly—not even close." He further indicated that "what has been lost in the hysteria of the largest fraud in history is that the lion's share of that money doubtlessly went to investors who did not show up in court to demand Madoff's maximum punishment. Why would they? They're laughing all the way to the bank because these investors were paid off early in the Ponzi scheme." JPMorgan was fined $2.6 billion in January 2014 for its role in facilitating the scheme—which represented hardly 12 percent of its profits for just that year alone.

But even after that, the FinCEN files show that JPMorgan continued to move money for people involved in alleged financial crimes, among them 1MDP and its main financier mastermind Jho Low, who "moved money for companies and people tied to the corruption scandal in Venezuela that helped create one of the world's worst humanitarian crises."

The FinCEN files also reveal that banks handling cross-border transactions have little idea who they are dealing with—even when they are shifting hundreds of millions of dollars, e.g., a shell company called ABSI Enterprises sent and received more than $1 billion in transactions.

"Compliance watchdogs based at the bank's Columbus, Ohio, operations hub decided to try to figure out ABSI's actual owner in 2015 after a Russian news site reported that a similarly named shell company—which JPMorgan's records indicated was the parent of ABSI—was linked to an underworld figure named Semion Mogilevich.

"Mogilevich has been described as the 'boss of bosses' of Russian mafia groups. When the FBI put him on its Top Ten Most Wanted list in 2009, it said his criminal network participated in weapons and drug trafficking, extortion, and contract murders. The chain-smoking, beefy Ukrainian's signature method of neutralizing an enemy, the *Guardian* once reported, is the car bomb."

The report goes on to say that even though compliance officers searched in vain through their files on that shell company, they could not find anything that indicated who was behind the company and what its true purpose was.

Despite the lack of information, though, JPMorgan had plenty of reasons to examine ABSI years earlier. ABSI Enterprises, in fact, had operated as a shell company in Cyprus. It was also known at that time as a major money-laundering center, transacting through JPMorgan to the tune of hundreds of millions of dollars.

Mogilevich is featured in *World's Most Wanted*, a Netflix documentary series released in August 2020.

Records show that JPMorgan also processed some $50 million in payments over a decade for Paul Manafort, the former campaign manager for President Donald Trump, and some of those millions in the fourteen months after he resigned from the campaign "amid a swirl of money laundering and corruption allegations spawning from his work with a pro-Russian political party in Ukraine."

Tainted transactions continued to surge through accounts at JPMorgan despite the bank's promises to improve its money laundering controls as part of settlements it reached with US authorities in 2011, 2013, and 2014.

BuzzFeed News obtained records that showed that HSBC, Standard Chartered Bank, Deutsche Bank, and Bank of New York Mellon were the most prolific in filing suspicious-activity reports with the US Department of Treasury's FinCEN. While suspicious activity is merely that, suspicious, it reflects the concerns of bank watchdogs.

The above is simply a "tip of the finger" dip into the role of banks in the laundering of money. It is a sobering thought that the protectors of our money, the essential players in our economy, and the most regulated industry around the world are, in fact, a great contributor to the downfall of an equitable and free world.

CHAPTER 4

Cryptic Cryptocurrencies

BITCOIN, A NAME most of us are familiar with but maybe have not experimented with, is a form of digital currency that is held electronically. There is still some mystery surrounding Bitcoin in that it was created in 2008 by a developer who was not keen to give his name and used Satoshi Nakamoto as a pseudonym. It would appear nobody knows who he or she is, and of course, many people have come forward claiming to be him (or more unlikely, her) but to the collective knowledge out there, nobody is the wiser. It is understood that Bitcoin was created as an alternative payment system to the conventional financial infrastructure that was designed to operate anonymously and peer-to-peer, eliminating a third party.

While the outcome is that, like conventional currency, Bitcoin can be used to buy things electronically, it is the advantages that distinguish it from conventional currency transactions. What stands out to users is that the Bitcoin network is not controlled by a bank or any other financial institution, or indeed, any kind of institution and it is not government-backed. It is decentralized; one machine talks to the other. So, if you own Bitcoin, nobody controls the money but you. It follows that there is almost (but not impossible) impenetrable privacy and the only information disclosed is the addresses of Bitcoin to which the payment has been sent or received.

Bitcoin transactions are faster than banking transactions, but as the Bitcoin usage has grown, that advantage has waned, contributing to the rise in other versions of Bitcoin coming into existence. Other altcoins (alternative to Bitcoin) have therefore been designed specifically with transaction speed in mind or improving on what the program developer perceives needs improving. Wikipedia indicates that as of early 2020, there were more than an estimated 5,000 cryptocurrencies in circulation. Ethereum is the next well-known; others include Unibright, Komodo, Basic Attention Token (BAT), and Brave Browser.

On February 9, 2020, Wendy McElroy (Bitcoin.com), author of *Crypto Is Banking for Anarchists and Average People*, indicated that an impressive number of users have made a fortune through early adoption, it is true, but the greatest beneficiary of crypto has been average people. Crypto levels the financial playing field between the rich and the working class.

"It is comparatively easy for the rich to preserve privacy, avoid the highest taxation, and be treated decently by financial institutions. They have lawyers, accountants, and other informed experts who zealously guard their interests. They have foreign bank accounts, diversified holdings, and tax write-offs. It is also easy for the rich to become accredited investors—a legal status that opens access to the most profitable investments, such as stock in start-ups."

But to deal in cryptos, it is not necessary to have any of the above.

The purpose of mentioning all of this is to look at it from a money-laundering perspective for the following reasons. The first is the freedom of doing your own thing. The second is the relative privacy with which you can do it. The third is the lack of regulations or differing stances taken by countries around the world. The fourth is that for law enforcement, it's a whole new dynamic platform for investing in crypto assets—just one more thing to learn about and investigate. The fifth is that it can be used as a form of payment (but the value of Bitcoin is very volatile, even more so than trading in fiat currencies, so if one person or business wants to pay another, the receiver may well be receiving it for less the value that it was intended at the time of the deal). The sixth point is the most telling of all because, at some stage for some time to come, criminals will want to, or have to, get fiat money for their Bitcoin.

The Library of Congress (https://www.loc.gov/law/help/cryptocurrency/world-survey.php) provides information on countries around the world about where they are in the development or implementation of regulations concerning the cryptocurrencies and indicates that "the past four years have seen cryptocurrencies become ubiquitous, prompting more national and regional authorities to grapple with their regulation."

The expansive growth of cryptocurrencies makes it possible to identify emerging patterns in terms of regulations. Some countries are declaring any profits made from cryptocurrency as being income and therefore taxed as income; other countries look at the profits for attracting capital gains tax, and yet other countries indicate they are defined as commodities, but VAT is not applicable. The most common actions identified across the jurisdictions are government-issued notices (usually from the central banks) about the pitfalls of investing in the cryptocurrency markets, designed to educate citizens about the difference between actual currencies, which are issued and guaranteed by the state, and cryptocurrencies, which are not.

The Library of Congress indicates that many of the warnings issued by various countries also note the opportunities that cryptocurrencies create for illegal activities, such as money laundering and the financing of terrorism. Some have expanded their laws by going beyond just warning the public and have indicated that organized crimes include cryptocurrency markets. Legislation, therefore, requires banks and other financial institutions that facilitate such markets to conduct all the due-diligence requirements imposed under such laws. For instance, Australia, Canada, and the Isle of Man recently enacted laws to bring cryptocurrency transactions and institutions that facilitate them under the ambit of money laundering and counterterrorist financing laws.

Japan was the first country in the world to have enacted a law defining "crypto asset" as a legal term. To provide crypto asset exchange services to residents in Japan, an entity is required to register as a crypto asset exchange service provider. The purpose of the legislation is to protect customers of exchange providers and combat money laundering and the financing of terrorism. After Coincheck Inc., which is one of the largest crypto asset exchanges in Japan, announced in January 2018 that it had lost US$530 million worth of cryptocurrencies through a hacking attack on its systems, it led to certain pieces of legislation being reassessed and revised (as of May 1, 2020).

"Some jurisdictions have gone even further and imposed restrictions on investments in cryptocurrencies, the extent of which varies from one jurisdiction to another. Some jurisdictions (Algeria, Bolivia, Morocco, Nepal, Pakistan, and Vietnam) ban all activities involving cryptocurrencies. Qatar and Bahrain have a slightly different approach in that they bar their citizens from engaging in any kind of activities involving cryptocurrencies locally but allow citizens to do so outside their borders. There are also countries that, while not banning their citizens from investing in cryptocurrencies, impose indirect restrictions by barring financial institutions within their borders from facilitating transactions involving cryptocurrencies (Bangladesh, Iran, Thailand, Lithuania, Lesotho, China, and Colombia)."

But *Gulf News* of March 10, 2021, reported on the Experts at the World Government Summit Dialogues held in Dubai. They discussed how cryptocurrency could be the greatest wealth trend in the world today and explained how prosperity and the future are anchored on a digital economy.

A comment made by Brock Pierce, founder of Blockchain Capital and IGE: "Nearly half of the world's billionaires now have made their money in crypto. As we live through what could be the greatest wealth trend in the history of the world, it's important to have more people participate in it."

Denelle Dixon, the CEO and executive director at Stellar Development Foundation highlighted the role of cryptocurrency in creating access to financial tools that are not available to many people. "We need to encourage central banks that issue these types of currencies not to ignore the private sector and all the work it has done to innovate. We can make the transition seamless for the end-users. Interoperability is one of the most important aspects in terms of payments and financing infrastructure."

Experts felt that governments should play a vital role in adopting these innovative models, which will prove successful alternatives to giant financial institutions and be more efficient and reliable.

While banks are taking significant steps to de-risk the entire crypto sector, the Financial Action Task Force, which is the anti-money-laundering world body (refer to chapter 7), pointed out that this de-risk approach is not sustainable in the long term because the crypto sphere will continue to grow. Therefore, avoiding exposure will be impractical.

This seriously complicates, I would think, the understanding and implementation of law enforcement for cryptocurrencies and crypto assets. Cryptocurrency can be said to be a crypto asset or a subclass of crypto assets, but not all crypto assets are cryptocurrencies.

A cryptocurrency is a store of value and a way to transfer that value among users of the currency. It does not do much more than that. However, crypto assets usually have many of the same features as a cryptocurrency in that there will be a physical token that serves as a store of value with the ability to transfer that value but there is usually a second layer of functionality added to that, namely the technology and/or network that enables certain functions to be performed. Ethereum is an example of a crypto asset network, where the token used as a currency is Ether.

Crypto assets are a digital representation of value that can be traded or transferred digitally and used as a form of payment. Bitcoin is the most popular digital asset used today. In the media, Bitcoin is frequently associated with the infamous Silk Road—the first online modern dark-net marketplace—where online users purchase items like weapons and illegal drugs anonymously. In 2013, the United States Federal Bureau of Investigation shut down the market's first iteration.

From the European Central Bank, August 7, 2019: "The fact that a crypto asset does not constitute a claim on any identifiable entity means that its value is supported only by the expectation that other users will be willing to pay for it in the future, rather than by a future cash flow on which users can form their expectations.

"The main characterizing element of a crypto asset is that it is not a claim on either an issuer or a custodian. However, its users attach value to it because they believe that (i) its supply will remain limited, and (ii) market participants will agree on who is entitled to sell any of the units in circulation. The scarcity of a crypto asset and the possibility to prove who can dispose of each of its units allow the existence of a crypto-asset market, where users on the supply side can offer their units for sale and users on the demand side are willing to bid."

It is felt that mainstream media content on Bitcoin and digital assets focuses on criminal activities rather than technology and innovation. Typical rhetoric goes like this: Because of its anonymous nature, Bitcoin can help criminals. Looking deeper into this statement, is Bitcoin the preferred method for criminals to conduct money-laundering activities?

2019 was a world record year for imposing fines for laundering money and two countries paying in seven digits were France and USA. Two thirds of AML penalties were imposed on banks, while approximately 17 percent was given to organizations in the gaming, gambling, and cryptocurrency sectors.

In the same year, stronger AML regulations were established concerning money and digital assets such as cryptocurrency, but despite this, the crypto sphere continues to grow.

With new technology comes new adoption. India, South Korea, and France have granted more favorable legislation in 2020 to the public concerning crypto. These actions have been driving discussions within government circles about establishing a central bank digital currency, with its own regulations and monetary authority.

As indicated, criminals who are paid in cryptocurrency, at some stage, need to receive their final payout in cash. This requires obscuring where their funds come from. Unfortunately, several sophisticated services and tools help criminals do so. After all, if there were no way for bad actors to cash out cryptocurrency that they had received through illegal means, then there would be far less incentive for them to commit crimes involving cryptocurrency in the first place.

By examining the money-laundering process, you will see that it is no difference whether one uses fiat currency or cryptocurrencies. It is the same process, just using a different vehicle.

The first thing a novice is taught about the laundering of money is the process. Placement is the starting point whereby the cash is moved away from its source. Money is placed into circulation within the existing money system by going through intermediaries, such as financial institutions, casinos, shops, and currency exchanges. Examples of these activities include currency smuggling out of a country, bank complicity, currency exchanges, and the purchase of assets. For fiat purposes, Bitcoin can be a useful tool to exchange fiat currency for Bitcoin and then Bitcoin again into another fiat currency and moving this from one country to another.

The second phase (layering) is the efforts criminals undertake to make the trail of the illegal money difficult to trace and identify. Usually, this happens by converting cash into monetary instruments or buying assets with illicit funds to resell them. Bitcoin is more practical for this phase because it is a digital currency that can be used to make purchases across the network without constraints from physical boundaries. It is possible to spend Bitcoin to buy assets or cash it out through over-the-counter brokers.

It is worth pointing out that, unlike cash, cryptocurrencies are inherently transparent since all transactions are recorded in a public ledger. As included in the report released by Chainalysis, all these illicit funds leave traces behind them. If one accumulates a significant amount of information, then it becomes possible to identify who is behind the Bitcoin address used to launder money.

The third phase involves the integration of the laundered money back into the economy, usually through the financial system, using approaches such as property dealing, front companies, foreign banks, and false invoices. When criminals use Bitcoin to receive money, their main issue is integration; that is, putting the illicit funds back into the economy to hide their illegal activity.

According to the Chainalysis 2020 Crypto Crime Report, many criminals launder their cryptocurrency with the assistance of over-the-counter brokers. These are agents or firms that facilitate trades between buyers and sellers who do not want to (or cannot) transact on a cryptocurrency exchange.

There is an added phenomenon to dealing with Bitcoin. Each Bitcoin exchange shows its Bitcoin price, and this allows for arbitrage transactions to take place. Briefly, arbitrage is the process of buying Bitcoin on one exchange and selling them at another where the price is higher. That is because the price of Bitcoin is determined by the last trade made on that exchange. Because there are different exchanges, different numbers of buyers and sellers, and different preferences, the prices do not correlate 100 percent. This is an obvious route for some people to take advantage of this and literally generate a profit out of thin air.

As with any type of trade to make money, it is never perfect. Some examples may include the time it takes for verification (especially with a large trade) and during this time, the price of the Bitcoin might change. There are exchange fees to be paid, and the transaction volume needs to be high enough on both exchanges to satisfy any large orders of buying and selling. Price differences can also reflect technical or reputational issues of an exchange.

As things stand at the time of writing, arbitrage is legal as the only thing that is being done is exploiting price gaps between exchanges. A person conducting arbitrage is just buying and selling as any other trader would do.

Over-the-counter brokers are common among traders and miners who want to divest themselves of large holdings of crypto assets at a negotiated price, as using an open exchange to sell off large volumes can impact market prices. Most traders collaborate with exchanges, but many of them are less concerned about client identification (Know Your Client) than the exchanges they operate on. Many traders take advantage of, and specialize in, providing money-laundering services to criminals. Exchanges are still the preferred way to clean illicit Bitcoin. Throughout 2019, more than $2.8 billion worth of Bitcoin was sent from criminal entities to exchanges, and 52 percent of it went to the top two exchanges, Binance and Huobi (Chainalysis study, January 15, 2020).

The question is, does it provide a less-crime-ridden alternative to the current fiat currency system? Only 1.1 percent of the total cryptocurrency volume is deemed to be illicit. Crypto-related crimes tend to be scams with transaction volumes totaling more than $8.6 billion. Excluding PlusToken, Bitconnect, and OneCoin (the three largest crypto Ponzi schemes), scams have accounted for about 0.46 percent of all cryptocurrency activity.

The reason for less abuse may be because of the blockchain technology that underpins it. It is thought that because of its anonymity and identity, Bitcoin is a better tool to launder money. But that is not so because each identity is associated with an alphanumeric string called a private key. One of its inherent features is that all transactions of a blockchain are shared among peers, whose consensus is required to validate the chronology of transactions.

Dave Weisberger, the CEO of CoinRoutes, argues, "The goal of money laundering is to create a chain of transactions that can't be traced, so since the Bitcoin blockchain is designed to have an indelible public record of all transactions, it makes laundering more difficult."

Because every cryptocurrency transaction is recorded in a publicly visible ledger and with the right tools, it is possible to investigate which cryptocurrency activities are associated with crime, gather insights on their muddying techniques, share insights with law enforcement, and stop the abuse of the system. The United Nations Drugs and Crime Office and Chainalysis both estimate that for each dollar in Bitcoin spent on the dark web, at least $800 is laundered in cash.

Bitcoin cannot accommodate the enormous volume of money that would be needed to be laundered by criminals. The Bitcoin network sees a low daily volume compared to other asset classes—$25 billion on January 27, 2020. Moving such a sum of money would immediately sound the alarm for blockchain forensic companies and would require further resources such as intermediaries and centralized exchanges.

There were 5,457 Bitcoin ATMs worldwide as of September 1, 2019. Bitcoin ATMs allow anyone with a credit or debit card to purchase Bitcoin. Additionally, they may possess bidirectional functionality, allowing users to trade Bitcoin for cash using a scannable wallet address. Bitcoin ATMs can also accept cash deposits, providing a quick response (QR) code that can be scanned at a traditional exchange and used to withdraw Bitcoin or other cryptocurrencies.

Regulations used by financial institutions to obtain a record of customers and transactions for these machines vary by country and are often poorly enforced. Criminals can exploit loopholes and weaknesses in cryptocurrency ATM management to get around Bitcoin money laundering risks.

Investigators, law enforcement, and regulators are encouraged to become experts to improve their ability to prevent and respond to various forms of crypto crime. Exchanges are also expected to carry out extensive due diligence on users, over-the-counter traders, and any other third party operating on their platforms, which still represent the preferred destination to which criminals send their illicit cryptocurrencies.

Business Insider India reported on the top cryptocurrency frauds of 2019—and how most hackers got away with it, as per an article posted on businessinsider.com in December 2019. The authors say that, as with any heist, a cryptocurrency hack is only successful when the perpetrators can make a clean getaway, which includes finding an exit so that the currency can be spent in the real world. But that is not how it always plays out.

Below are some of the biggest cryptocurrency scams and arrests of 2019:

Japanese cryptocurrency exchange BITPoint was hacked for $28 million in July 2019; $19.3 million out of the total $28 million that was stolen was from customer funds, while the rest was from BITPoint Japan.

Among the stolen financial assets were Bitcoin, XRP, Ether, Litecoin, and Bitcoin Cash. The company had to suspend all deposits and withdrawals of their crypto assets and reimburse customers (but not in cash).

Binance, one of the world's largest cryptocurrency exchanges, had Bitcoin worth $40 million stolen along with two-factor authentication codes and API tokens; this represented 2 percent of the exchange's overall holdings, so it was considered a small loss for them.

In a statement on their website, Binance wrote, "The hackers had the patience to wait and execute well-orchestrated actions through multiple seemingly independent accounts at the most opportune time. The transaction is structured in a way that passed our existing security checks. It was unfortunate that we were not able to block this withdrawal before it was executed."

According to CipherTrace, two brothers from Israel were arrested on June 21 for an alleged phishing scam that lasted for three years, and over that time, they had allegedly stolen $100 million in cryptocurrency. The authorities are still probably trying to retrieve the missing funds. Their modus operandi lured investors from crypto trading forums such as Reddit onto websites that mimicked prominent crypto exchanges.

A further six people were arrested in the UK and the Netherlands over a $27 million "typosquatting" scam and compromised some four thousand victims from about twelve countries. Typosquatting is a method that entails creating a fake online cryptocurrency exchange to gain access to victims' Bitcoin wallets.

Another example of a hack occurred in about five minutes. Kraken, a major Bitcoin trading platform, experienced a flash crash that resulted in the price of the cryptocurrency suddenly falling from $8,400 to $75. But the price quickly stabilized, so it was considered an electronic glitch in the system. But it was a clever hack whereby the hacker compromised the account of a user with a large amount of cryptocurrency and stole 1,200 Bitcoin with the value at that time being worth more than $10 million.

Bitrue, a cryptocurrency exchange based in Singapore, had $4.2 million in user assets stolen in June 2019 because hackers were able to break through the exchange's security system by exploiting "a vulnerability in the Risk Control team's second review process."

Below is a good example of how technology can fight technology:

In May 2021, Colonial Pipeline paid a Bitcoin ransom to a cybercriminal gang (known as the Darkside Group) responsible for a ransomware attack on its company. This crippled critical fuel supplies in the United States. The value was some seventy-five Bitcoin. It is a good news story because Colonial Pipeline notified the FBI quickly after the act and the US Department of Justice reached into a Bitcoin wallet to seize 63.7 Bitcoin currently valued at approximately $2.3 million.

By reviewing the Bitcoin public ledger, the FBI traced multiple transfers of Bitcoin representing the proceeds of the victim's ransom payment that they were able to identify as having been transferred to a specific address, for which the FBI had the private key needed to access assets. (How they did that is another subject to be researched!) Because Bitcoin represents "proceeds traceable to a computer intrusion and property involved in money laundering, they could be seized according to criminal and civil forfeiture statutes."

"Following the money remains one of the most basic, yet powerful tools we have," said Lisa Monaco, the deputy attorney general at the US Department of Justice. "Ransom payments are the fuel that propels the digital extortion engine, and today's announcement demonstrates that the US will use all available tools to make these attacks more costly and less profitable for criminal enterprises.

"We will continue to target the entire ransomware ecosystem to disrupt and deter these attacks."

Stephanie Hinds, acting US attorney for the Northern District of California, commented, "Cybercriminals are employing ever more elaborate schemes to convert technology into tools of digital extortion. We need to continue improving the cyber resiliency of our critical infrastructure across the nation, including in the Northern District of California. We will also continue developing advanced methods to improve our ability to track and recover digital ransom payments."

However, fraudsters have also leveraged the increased fear and uncertainty of the COVID-19 pandemic to steal money and launder it through the cryptocurrency ecosystem. FBI.gov provided the following on April 13, 2020:

> The blackmail attempts take the form of threatening emails. The messages claim having access to your personal information and hint at

other knowledge of your dirty secrets. Payment to a Bitcoin wallet is demanded in Bitcoin to release your information. While this is not a new scam, scammers used COVID-19 as a further threat. Not only will they release your personal information, but the writer will have you and your family infected with the virus.

Work-from-home scams include scammers posing as employers. You are asked to accept a donation of funds into your bank account and then to deposit them into a crypto kiosk. This so-called donation, reports the FBI, "is likely money stolen from others. Your acceptance and transfer of the stolen money are considered illegal money mule activity and potentially unlicensed money transmission."

Criminals also pitch fraudulent investments in an apparently new cryptocurrency, such as an initial coin offering. These offers obviously paint scenarios that claim exceptionally high returns over a short period for relatively small investments. The scammers then steal the investment and use the complexity of cryptocurrency to obscure the destination of the stolen funds.

There are, of course, legitimate charities, investment platforms, and e-commerce sites that accept payment in cryptocurrency; however, the FBI warns that pressure to use a cryptocurrency should be considered as a significant alert regarding money laundering.

The bottom line: Digitization is growing exponentially; it means that the money-laundering landscape is also a moving target and, for fraudsters, just another method that can be used to launder money.

Here are a few more great examples:

Toward the end of April 2021, Africrypt, a crypto investment company in South Africa, suddenly stopped operating. At that time, the crypto investment company's founders claimed Africrypt's trading system had been breached, which compromised client accounts, wallets, and nodes, thus forcing Africrypt to freeze all its accounts.

But the reason appears to be a lot more sinister. Not long after the breach, two brothers, both founders of the company (Ameer and Raees Cajee), disappeared with billions of dollars in investor funds, or rather, the brothers fled to the UK, but the funds disappeared. Raees was only twenty-one and matriculated with five distinctions, achieving 100 percent in applied mathematics, information technology, and economics. He started the company when he was only thirteen years old. His brother was an equity and derivatives trader working before as head of macro trading for RaeCreate Wealth.

The article reporting this explosive news, "R54 bn crypto 'hack' shocker hits SA investors" (but one presumes it included international investors), was written by MyOffice News on June 23, 2021, and posted in Crime Alert and Tech News. The law firm, Hanekom Attorneys, representing the victims of the Africrypt fraud, revealed that the Africrypt directors had used mixers to muddy the flow of the funds. It goes on to report that First National Bank (FNB), a leading South African financial institution, denied allegations of a banking relationship with Africrypt and insisted it did not enable the investment company's transactions that obviously must have facilitated the disappearance of the investors' funds. Of course, the jury is still out on this one.

Darren Hanekom suggests that Africrypt's accounts with FNB have already been drained and that "the entirety of investors' funds" may have been subjected to the mixing service.

The law firm further reported, "R54 billion has been transferred from its South African account(s) through Bitcoin on the blockchain, and has regrettably, now been dissipated in its entirety. Whilst we are still in the process of investigating the transfer of funds, with transactions on the blockchain being active up to and until even date, upon an initial reconciliation, the funds were subjected to various dark web tumblers and mixers, resulting in severe fragmentation."

If you can understand the dark web tumblers and mixes, good luck to you. The bottom line is that somewhere, somehow, the story of the absolutely safe blockchain is not so safe.

Then there are the crypto scams that are growing exponentially; it is all online, of course, and they could be investment scams, romance scams, digital wallet hacks, digital art thefts, and pyramid scams. Therefore, cybercrime usually involves crypto.

Time magazine of March 29, 2022, in the article "Why Crypto Scams Are Driving an Online Crime Boom—And How to Outsmart Them" refers to a report from Chainanalysis, which tracks the movement of cryptocurrency across the Internet. It found that in 2021, $14 billion worth of cryptocurrency was sent to illicit wallet addresses, which had grown threefold from 2017. There were so many crypto-romance victims that they formed an advocacy group, the Global Anti-Scam Organisation, and in 2021, fraud reports totaled $73 million in losses.

We now know that criminals become vulnerable when they try to cash out their crypto into fiat currencies such as dollars and euros. To do this requires an exchange such as Binance and Coinbase. Blockchain transfers are almost impossible to intercept in any way as they make their way across borders and cannot be reversed.

The world is on a fast trajectory in terms of financial services development, particularly with the role of fintech growing exponentially; they provide traditional banks with opportunities for fulfilling open banking. Open banking, as described by Wikipedia, is the system of allowing access and control of consumer banking and financial accounts through third-party applications. It has the potential to reshape the competitive landscape and consumer experience of the banking industry. Coupled with that are technologies being developed for payment systems—it is called convergence—such as the use of social media platforms for online retail, e-commerce, retailers offering consumers "buy now, pay later" solutions, mobile banking, and online payment gateways. This is likely to lead to less cash in circulation and more financial inclusion in the longer term, with emphasis on the longer term. Cryptos only add to the complexity.

Will money laundering be easier to investigate or more difficult? Will it be more difficult to launder money, or will it be easier? Only time will tell.

CHAPTER 5

Money, Power, Culture, and Leadership

MONEY DEFINES OUR world and our way of living and has a profound effect on how we interact in society, engage with reality, and seek opportunities to change our fortunes and futures. No matter from which strata of society you originate in life, a little taste of success leads to a desire for more.

How quickly does this journey lead to money laundering?

The Money

The world of money consumes much of our lives: we either have an ongoing desire to get the money one way or the other if we have not got it or enough of it, or we are engaged in investing and spending it somehow to build up a reputation of having influence and being more respected (which is important in terms of how we are perceived) than the next person—sometimes deservedly so.

The old adages "the love of money is the root of all evil" and "money makes the world go around" are surely true. Money is indeed the basis on which we all survive, thrive, or contrive.

My take on it is as follows:

Money is hard to find to help the have-nots sow seeds to feed a family, but it is in abundance for the haves to throw away

Money backs political will, sets the stage for dictatorship
and rule of law, yet supports freedom and constitutionality
Money funds progress and innovation, forging a better
life for the few but leaving behind the many
Money protects our environment but abuses it all the same
Money funds the honorable deeds it can perform,
and for the bad deeds it does perform
Money therefore defines who we are and how we live.

A general perspective of society and money that we can all identify with is that there are poor people, rich people, and somewhere in the middle, the middle class.

It is easy for people who have money—and the amount of money is unimportant for this point to be made—to say that the best things in life are free. Clean water to drink is seldom free, and if it is, it is not easily available. Having light or a candle is not free. Taking away pain or disease is seldom free. Sure, hugs and smiles and family warmth are free, but who hugs, smiles, and laughs when you have no electricity, walk miles to collect water, and forage in the waste for food to eat?

Sometimes, the poor have little choice but to do many things for money and, in the pursuit of it, subject themselves to dreadful conditions, participate in the most degrading circumstances, and spend precious resources and time.

The middle class is said to be the mainstay of an economy. Indeed, but at what personal cost? For the middle class, money is about hope and opportunity. So the money keeps the middle class going, conditioning them to believe that if they work harder, life will get better. Some people do eventually make enough money to move into the loosely defined elite, but at what cost? Such an achievement is more likely to come through some lucky break or who you know rather than through hard or skillful work. There are incredibly talented people in this world, but so much of that talent goes unnoticed, may be overlooked or not locally recognized, not be currently needed, or gets lost in the time it takes to continue to make money to live on.

Think about the illogical things that the middle class does to make more money: they go to work to earn money to pay for the transport to get to work, which can take up to two hours a day; they work to pay for the food that gives them the energy to be a productive worker; they work to earn money for vacations to get a well-deserved rest from work before starting the next twelve-month cycle; they pay for after-school care or a nanny to look after the children when at work; they need better clothing for work; medical costs tend to be centered on stress, sleeplessness, and mental health because of competitive structures at work; they need to overperform and continually be accessible 24/7.

The paragraph above was written pre-COVID-19 lockdowns and in slowly opening economies, maybe there will be a new norm, but how different might that be? The more you are likely to slog at it from home, the less likely you are going to be noticed as standing out among the crowd. I do not necessarily think it will change the world of the middle class much. It is interesting to note that in the many jobs now available, such as waiters in restaurants or truck drivers as examples, as lockdowns ease, workers are not going back. *Sod it! I need to be cleverer about what work I do for that amount of money!*

Middle-class life also carries with it the burden of financial care for older relatives and needy friends and anxiously providing educational opportunities for the young; in the same breath, many older middle-class folks are providing important support for their married children and their grandchildren. Either way, it means the middle-class efforts are often focused on making money for other people.

Let us not forget the debt that comes with the middle-class designation. Money is also the prerequisite to life which affords people the opportunity of shelter or education, but this also saddles them with a lifetime of debt. Students leave university these days with years of debt that still is required to be paid off.

The money earned does make it possible to sustain a lifestyle of sorts; it provides for the basics of what is considered good living and may well give the next generation a better chance—to what? To hopefully make more money.

The top three countries that have the highest household debt-to-income ratio in the world in 2021 stand at 256.7 percent for Denmark, 246.9 percent for Norway, and 235.7 percent for the Netherlands (compared by market.com.au). This means that the debt accumulated by Danish households is two and a half times as big as the volume of their disposable income. However, Denmark is a strong and historically stable economy, and it supports a high standard of living—its per capita gross national product is among the highest in the world. Danish financial institutions are liquid, well capitalized, with regulatory capital amounting to 20 percent of risk-weighted assets and have set aside adequate buffers to withstand reasonable increases in nonperforming loans to the household sector. But for economically vulnerable countries, a 70 percent household debt-to-income ratio on a personal level can be tough. People who earn less than $600 (approx. R9,339 a month, which for many people in South Africa is a monthly salary) need 63 percent of their income to repay their creditors and are also charged higher interest rates over longer periods. While there are many more countries with higher debt-to-income levels, these figures confirm that the average middle-class citizen works hard just to maintain a respectable life.

The COVID-19 pandemic reveals just how many people lived just within their income from one month or one week to another, and how many people had more than one job to earn a respectable income. The United States was a prime example, despite an initial pre-COVID robust economy.

For the rich, life is not necessarily easier; it is just a different kind of upkeep. But the problem is that it is never enough. Greed becomes an enabler for power; power becomes an enabler for more money. There are discrepancies about how people are paid for their contributions to their work or skill—more because it is dependent on what money can be further accumulated by such contribution.

How do people get rich? Rich simply means having more money to spend on more things than the average middle-class person. Employees can get rich working for a company. Advice given on the Web to get rich explains how it is done: "Those that live, breathe, and eat their profession, those that are obsessed, become great. I have never met a great person who wasn't all in and completely consumed by their trade. Have you? The fact is, if you aren't great, you are average. The rich get great." People can get rich building their businesses, cofounding business ideas, winning an award, or opening other opportunities. They can get rich by stinting and saving and making good investments that take guts, skill, and appropriate knowledge and advice. Or they were born rich. Maybe some feel obliged to give some of it away for a worthy cause.

Or they can get rich by being unlawful in terms of their business dealings. Does it affect the average person? Probably not. Does it affect the world economically? Very much.

Just one example: Think about child labor and its role in enriching the rich. It still happens. A CBS News investigation found child labor being used in the dangerous mining of cobalt in the Democratic Republic of Congo. The mineral cobalt is used in all batteries in common devices such as smartphones, laptops, and electric vehicles. A report by Amnesty International first revealed that cobalt mined by children was ending up in products from several companies, including Apple, Microsoft, Tesla, and Samsung. The work is tough for an adult male but unthinkable for a child. Even after many exposures in the media, tens of thousands of Congolese children are still involved in every stage of mining for cobalt. The latest research by the United Nations Children's Fund (UNICEF) estimates that half of the world's twenty-eight largest companies have used cobalt garnered from the estimated 40,000 children working in DRC cobalt mines. For a shift of up to twenty-four hours underground, most earn less than or only half of US$2 a day. Many children are often physically ruined as a result or buried by collapsing excavations—which they have dug up with their bare hands using machetes and spades.

It is not only children that are compromised. The wealthy profit from adult labor minimalism; Ivanka Trump's fashion clothing is manufactured in Indonesia and China. The *Guardian* and other activists reported on employees at these factories being paid one of the lowest minimum wages in Asia (and below China's legal minimum wage). They have impossibly high production targets and are sporadically compensated for overtime. This is just a taste of thousands of ways in which the rich profit from the poor. It is only when this is brought to the attention of the wider international public several times over that the big companies take action; quite frankly, who cares otherwise? The rich get richer, the middle class gets cheaper goods, and the poor earn another meal.

The poor can be lifted from despair through simple investment, and while it does happen in small pockets, it is seldom initiated by governments, or if it is, it is very minimal.

The Power

If you have money, you have power. That is because power is highly respected (in many cases, idolized) in this world.

Noam Chomsky, 93 (2022), is an American linguist, cognitive scientist, philosopher, historian, social critic, and political commentator who has written extensively on the subject of power in his 1999 book *Profit over People: Neoliberalism and Global Order*, and he has this to say: "If taken a step further, it could be shown that money and power are both forever linked to each other. They are different things entirely and can be separated from each other, held on to, and owned. Each is the other's catalyst. One is used to make the other useful. Some may argue that people use power every day throughout the world without trading money for it. In these instances, the money is still there, it's being held by all parties in these transactions. Their money is owned by them, somewhere, somehow, in the chain of several separate exchanges eventually one will lead enough money to support the group of exchanges. Like dark matter, we can't see but we know it is there because we can see the gravitational effects. Those people holding power, trading power, have the money behind that power somewhere, bank on it."

The Culture

Does this say something about the culture, then, and what does it have to do with money laundering? The word *culture* denotes the way of life of groups of people, meaning the way they think or do things. Culture, therefore, can refer loosely to country, religion, behavior, knowledge, beliefs, customs, values, attitudes, morals, or goals.

Cultural groups might be less divided if we look at common goals around the world. Common goals are likely to include freedom, human rights, equal opportunities, good health, stability and security, and the opportunity to earn a decent living.

The problem is that freedom is dependent on politics and money, human rights are dependent on politics and money (because having more money means it is easier to be free or buy freedom), equal opportunities and good health are facilitated by having more money, stability and security can be bought with money. It could be said, therefore, that money plays an important part in our lives. Nearly all cultural groups around the world are consumed with earning money. It is a desire to achieve a quality of life. Quality, of course, is in the eye of the beholder.

For many, the more money we earn, the more of the above we achieve, and the more of the above we achieve, something then happens to our psyche. We become greedy, but being greedy is difficult to define. Coupled with earning more money, a competitive spirit steps in, and more risks are taken, until ultimate power is the only further thing to strive for.

Culture can change depending on our environment; the culture in our world of work and how we earn our money, which consumes most of our waking hours, infiltrates our very being. There are different genres of work: the government culture is different from a corporate culture (less customer-centric), which is different from a small-business culture (very customer-centric); the artistic and creative world is different from the construction world, and so on.

As an example, In 2013, Deloitte published a report, *Culture in Banking Under the Microscope*, and the second summary of the feedback to the survey undertaken, referred to as "the buck stops here," indicated the following: "Bankers say that the main causes of the industry's cultural problems were misaligned incentives and poor leadership, which are predominantly within their sphere of influence. Respondents believe that neither senior managers nor the boards which monitor them were up to the job. Inadequate board oversight and management's limited understanding of their balance sheet ranked #2 and #5 as causes of cultural problems. These management and governance failings were amplified through employee incentives; compensation structures, excess pay, and misaligned performance metrics ranked #1, #3, and #6 as causes of cultural problems."

It is interesting though, that of every senior banker completing the survey, 65 percent indicated there were significant problems across the industry in this respect, but the problems were less extensive in their bank. That alone says something about corporate culture.

There is no public shame in making money, no matter how it is earned. The author R. J. Eskow on December 9, 2015, (in an article published by salon.com) refers to the celebration of investment opportunities created by the wave of criminality and fraud in JPMorgan Chase involving billions in funds during the tenure of CEO Jamie Dimon.

Greedy CEOs, Eskow writes, continue to have credibility in the media: "A lobbying organization called Fix the Debt is trading on what remains of Wall Street's credibility, and that of other greed-driven corporate leaders, in its campaign to cut desperately needed social programs like these. Astonishingly—or not, especially if you look at their ownership structures—American news outlets accord these CEOs an extraordinary and unearned measure of respectability and authority. Very few articles about Fix the Debt mention the massive fraud settlements and fines levied against these CEOs' institutions." He goes on to say that Fix the Debt is one of several interlocking organizations that are largely financed by right-wing billionaire Pete Peterson, who made his money in the hedge fund business and yet is treated by many journalists as if he were Mother Teresa.

He cites how executives are trained to think sneakily; for example, the Gillette Company ropes customers in with low-cost razors and then charges an outrageous amount for replacement blades. "If you multiply our experience ten thousandfold, you have an idea of the enculturation which is taking place every day in companies across the country. That's not to say there aren't companies that still believe in customer service; there are, and I'm grateful every time I encounter one. But the corporate culture of America has become a culture of cheating, manipulation, and greed." He also goes on to mention that insight, spirituality, and kindness are commercialized; he sat through a 2011 Clinton Annual Global meeting, and "it occurred to me that I had just seen several different photographs of happy African children dancing in the water from wells they might not have needed if not for the economic predation of corporations like the ones that had dug the wells." Irony at its best.

This author encapsulates a sad reality. A decade later, nothing has changed. Outside the corporate corridors, it is easy to paint a holy picture of the company and tick all the boxes for nondiscrimination, employment equity, wellness programs, regulatory adherence, and have an archive of meaningless (or only applied for legal purposes) corporate policies. Inside the corridors, whether these are virtual or not, a different picture emerges, especially as the companies grow bigger and more powerful.

Despite initiatives around the world to stop human trafficking, it persists because there is money to be made. But culture also plays a part in its continuation despite the efforts to stop it. Dressember. org in "Cultural Barriers Present in Human Trafficking" contends that when attempting to help sex trafficking victims, it is important to consider the cultural context; two key elements are religion or spirituality and family structures. Culture usually brings people together, but in some circumstances, the author indicates, culture can act as a barrier and this is particularly so in sex trafficking, where cultural differences stop the victim from seeking assistance.

The author referred to the last fifteen years, during which thousands of young women left Nigeria for countries like Italy, Spain, or the Netherlands in the hope of securing jobs and the opportunity to financially support themselves and their families back home. What typically occurs is that the women sign a contract with the trafficker promising to repay the traveling debts incurred to get to their destination. Typically but sadly, the young women have an experience dissimilar to what had been promised once they crossed the border. The debt, of course, is much greater than they were led to believe.

This is usually far more than what the young women will be earning, leaving the women with the only option to pay off the debt through prostitution.

The UN's International Organization for Migration (IOM) reported sex trafficking victims entering Italy via the Mediterranean Sea increased by 600 percent between 2014 and 2017. It is estimated that 80 percent of these women are Nigerian.

The barrier keeping these women from trying to escape or even from leaving when given an opportunity to do so, as reported by Dressember, is rooted in the payment contract. These contracts, drawn up between a young woman and the madam sponsoring her trip, are not only signed but also sealed with a spiritual pact, binding the woman to the contract through a juju (or voodoo) ritual performed by a priest. Once done, even breaking the contract before paying off the debt will mean that the woman is cursed, and any amount of harm will come upon her or her family.

Another example referred to is in a case study presented by Dr. Mary de Chesnay in her book *Sex Trafficking: A Clinical Guide for Nurses*. It was about a Cambodian girl named Botum, who was forced to be married at an early age because her parents could not support her and her siblings. "Not long after, her husband sold her to a brothel and arranged for the brothel owner to send Botum's parents a small portion of her earnings. Botum quickly learned that if she cooperated, she was helping her family, a strong Cambodian cultural value."

Botum was later trafficked into the United States, where she was put to work in an illicit massage parlor owned by a local gang. The gang members told her that they would begin sending money to her parents as soon as she paid off her travel debts, but Botum was arrested in a police raid and sent to a clinic for medical treatment. The health-care providers tried to help her escape the sex trafficking situation, but Botum refused. She feared that if she stopped working as a prostitute, she would never get another opportunity to help her family. "In her culture, the value of helping family trumps personal freedom."

What one culture desires, the other dismisses. Animal trafficking also absorbs cultural views and customs.

> Rhinos are slaughtered for their horns, and elephants for their tusks, destined for Asian markets. Lions may be farmed, killed in canned hunts, or poached for their bones, which are sometimes used as a substitute for tiger bones in traditional Chinese medicine. Leopards are poached for their skins, which some South Africans wear during important ceremonies. Although it is legal to own leopard skin, a permit is required to do so. Illegal pet traders regularly target cheetah for export to the Middle East, while wild dogs may be killed because they are seen as pests, or because it is a rite of passage for boys. (Scielo.org.za, June 2017)

The SAGE journals refer to "The social construction of the value of wildlife: A green cultural criminological perspective" by Daan P. van Uhm, first published as a research article on August 30, 2018. The following is a summary of the essence of the report, but justice to this information is best done if you read the full report yourself.

The history of wildlife trafficking is an international problem of the twenty-first century and still grows despite the best efforts to curb it. Cultural and social aspects are an important part of the problem, and once again, they are linked to power and greed.

Various cultures a long time ago used animal products for uses such as clothing (fur to keep warm), food, tiger bones, and rhino horns as medicine. This is understandable in times when populations were small. As civilization became more sophisticated in the days of the ancient Greeks and Romans, exotic animals were considered attractive objects to trade by the elite because animal skins, for example, were associated with class. As time went on, imported exotic animals and their products became a sign of modern colonial power and a symbolic representation of the conquest of all distant and exotic countries. The growing prosperity among the middle class such as corsets made of whalebone and feathers in hats were then displayed as status symbols. For the bourgeoisie, it was a fashion trend. Around the turn of the twentieth century, much of this morphed into exotic animals being displayed in zoos, circuses, world exhibitions, and retail stores all over Europe. As an example, a lion cub was bought by two young students at Harrods.

We know the damage trafficking does to economies, ecosystems, and impoverished communities because society generally has good access to information, but the organized crime and militias involved in wildlife trafficking add additional concerns in terms of human safety and security.

The Leadership

What does the concept of leadership bring to the problem of money laundering?

In every university, college, or school, leadership is inevitably part of the curriculum. Who is a good leader, and why was he (and to a far lesser extent, she) a good leader? What are the characteristics of a good leader?

We, for some thirty years and more, have been exploring and affirming the concept of good leadership; books on leadership still abound in academic circles and corporate corridors, and on social media. Slogans at these institutions persist: We are creating leaders for the future. The question is, would power and money form part of the good leadership equation?

After many years, the definition of what leadership is, and specifically what good leadership is, is still elusive. What does it mean to be a bad leader? If a leader is bad, how is it that they are still leading people?

Therein lies the nub. We follow leaders for personal gain or perceived personal gain; otherwise, why would we follow them? That means that the perfect leader is in the eye of the beholder. Defining leadership is fraught with inconsistencies, variations, and disparities.

The more followers, the more powerful the leader; the more powerful the leader, the more likely a greater number of followers.

Donald Trump (now a past president of the United States of America) is such an enigma that he comes to mind as the first example. Why has he got to where he is? He is arrogant and conceited, has no shame in giving false or misleading claims (12,019 of them in the 928 days of his presidency as reported by the *Washington Post* on August 11, 2019, and in May 2020, Twitter started fact-checking his tweets), is a narcissistic disrupter who has no concern for the consequences (how many times does he say, "We'll see what happens"?), and is a bigot. His erratic briefings on COVID-19 revealed laughable ignorance and distracting political nonsense, not for the people, but for his salvation. But his base is very loyal to him; they love the fact that he is bombastic, that he can say whatever the hell he likes, irrespective of whether it is true or not. His strongest pull is his enthusiasm for himself and his confidence in himself. He is also a wonderful form of entertainment.

I loved one of Trevor Noah's quips on *The Daily Show* that explained one of Trump's strong points. When talking to the people of America to secure the 2016 election, the Democrats carefully attempted to explain their policies; Trump's message was "We'll build a wall and Mexico is going to pay for it." The message was simple, and the audience could repeat it with him. The outcome (of building the wall) was never going to be an issue. And it never was.

Vladimir Putin has been around for some twenty years as president of the Russian Federation and, in that time, has moved from a veritable unknown Russian spy to an authoritarian. In the first ten years, there were heady opportunities for some Russians, while others barely survived. But Putin is still the strongman, the popular leader, and the aggressor—the man that represents the interests of oligarchs, the army, and the security bloc. Restrictions on civil rights and society were introduced that were outrageous, especially because of their irrelevance other than to show power. In 2008, instead of changing the constitution to stay on as president, he chose Dmitry Medvedev to be president. By doing so, he still had control, and power was courteously handed over. Medvedev had several wins much to Putin's irritation: he tried to modernize the economy and society by lessening Russia's reliance on oil and gas, signed a nuclear arms reduction with the United States, recovered Russia from the 2008 financial crisis, and launched an anticorruption campaign. However, when Putin returned to the presidency in 2012 as planned, he undid a lot of what was done by Medvedev, just like Trump reversed many of the achievements of the Obama presidency. Politics is not about the people; it is about the person. And more sadly, the war in Ukraine started by Putin in February 2022 only suggests ego and power with absolutely no emotion or feeling whatsoever.

These leaders have strong and loyal followers and a never-ending inflow of money (from where?) to enhance and maintain their power.

Democracy and equity are already compromised because of the pervasiveness and extent of money laundering, which continues to be nurtured by a skewed legal and justice system—skewed to benefit the rich and powerful.

Aljazeera.com on August 13, 2021, reported that Samsung's vice chairman and the world's 202nd richest person walked free on parole after serving seven of a thirty-month jail term for bribery, embezzlement, and other offenses in connection with a corruption scandal that derailed the South Korean ex-president Park Geun-hye. In 2014, she was ranked as the forty-sixth most powerful person in the world by *Forbes* and the third highest in South Korea. Two years later, she was impeached by their National Assembly and, after further charges were brought later, imprisoned for an overall twenty-five years for corruption, abuse of power, and election interference. She was also fined many millions of dollars.

There were calls for the release of Samsung's J. Y. Lee from both politicians and business leaders because they claimed a possible damaging leadership vacuum at South Korea's biggest conglomerate. The justice ministry announced his parole (among approximately eight hundred other early releases), citing concerns about the coronavirus pandemic's effect on the economy.

Lee bowed to reporters and apologized: "I have caused too much concern to the people. I'm really sorry."

But ex-president Park is expendable now that her money and power have gone; J. Y. Lee is not. "There is a long history of top South Korean tycoons being charged with bribery, embezzlement, tax evasion, or other offenses.

"But many of those convicted have subsequently had their sentences cut or suspended on appeal, with some—including late Samsung chairman Lee Kun-hee, who was convicted twice—receiving presidential pardons in recognition of their 'contribution to the national economy.'"

The rich and powerful have it.

CHAPTER 6

Globalization and Inequality

G LOBALIZATION AND MONEY are inextricably linked.

Globalization has helped to shrink our world, and technology has hastened the closing of gaps in terms of reach and mobility.

Perhaps one of the earliest examples of globalization was the use of the Silk Road, a network of trade routes that connected China and the Far East with the Middle East and Europe during the Middle Ages. Although it has been six hundred years since the Silk Road has been used for international trade, the routes had a lasting impact on commerce, culture, and history. The Silk Road has been such a defining feature of global trade that there have been many conversations about reviving it, but China is up against resistance from people affected along the planned route because of polluting the local ecosystem and disrupting their livelihoods.

One hundred ninety-five countries are member states of the United Nations, and two countries are nonmember observer states, namely the Holy See (Vatican City) and the State of Palestine.

Most of these nations today are also members of the World Trade Organization multilateral trade agreements. Special economic zones, known simply as free zones, were set up in designated areas, usually next to seaports, airports, or between two or more nations. These began in the 1960s and steadily increased from the 1980s. There are over 5,400 such zones in the world according to iContainers.com as of August 20, 2019.

The globalization of most of these markets means there is growth in international trade, an expansion of the global financial system, the lowering of barriers to international travel, and a surge in the internalization of organized crime. These factors combined provide the source, opportunity, and means for converting illegal proceeds into legitimate funds.

All the above simply means it is easier to move physical goods and cash around legally and illegally, and with the advent of technology, the financial infrastructure has developed into a perpetually operating global system in which megabyte money (i.e., money in the form of symbols on computer screens) can move anywhere in the world with speed and ease. While large transfers are said to distort the demand for money on a macroeconomic level and produce unhealthy volatility in international capital flows and exchange rates, we live with it daily.

As of 2020, trade between China, Hong Kong, and the USA, the restriction on Huawei operating 5G in the USA, and ongoing questions about China's role in spreading the coronavirus to the USA may hinder free trade between two big contenders or may change the global money-laundering landscape.

Globalization means that businesses have opportunities to increase their profits, compete in bigger markets with more innovative products, lower the price of their goods, and easily transfer capital, which allows businesses and corporations to invest in overseas property to expand their operations. That usually leads to access to a cheaper labor force available from emerging or less-developed economies. It also means that as people, we have so many more opportunities to experience, more people to connect with, and more ways to earn money or, of course, launder it.

In general, attitudes and values around the world are more tolerant and emancipative; for example, young people in the

Middle East now hold social views comparable to the ones held by young Western Europeans in the 1960s.

Globalization has done a lot to grow and enrich societies, not only economically but also socially, culturally, ideologically, and politically. It has enhanced the integration of capital, technology, and information (in this highly charged technological period), resulting in a single global market that is absurdly referred to as a global village. It also provides poor countries, through infusions of foreign capital and technology, with the chance to develop economically and, by spreading prosperity, creates the conditions in which democracy and respect for human rights may flourish.

But as always, there are two sides to this coin.

Democracy and respect for human rights tend to be an esoteric goal; it has not been successfully achieved in many or most of the countries in this world.

In general, economists and economic historians contend that current levels of trade openness are the highest they have ever been. However, this discounts protectionist policies that are introduced to support local challenges such as protecting employment in which case some tariffs are applied to imports or subsidies to exports. Other barriers to free trade include import quotas, taxes, and regulations.

According to the G20 World Trade Report for the period mid-May to mid-October 2019, the trade coverage of import-restrictive measures has soared since July 2018. In addition, the stockpile of import restrictions implemented in 2009 and still in force suggests that 8.8 percent of G20 imports ($1.3 trillion) in 2018 were affected by import restrictions. The report notes that while G20 economies collectively continue to take measures aimed at facilitating trade, the trade coverage of the new import-facilitating measures implemented is significantly lower than that reported in the last report.

Global politics are not merging successfully and may well be digressing from good decisions to benefit people all over the world to a *laager* mentality of self-isolation. Concerns over stolen or copied technologies contribute to this unease in their bid to be competitive; for example, despite Huawei's international success, the company's devices are difficult to buy in some markets, as in the United States. It is believed by some governments that Huawei equipment contains back doors that allow the Chinese government to snoop on customers in the foreign country.

Multi-corporations are also likely to contribute to unfair working conditions and likely to abuse the environment (such as mining waste) if they can get away with it, and usually, they do. There are plenty of examples of mismanagement of natural resources such as the Amazon in Brazil, where wealthy, *Dallas*-like prize-cattle farms take precedence over the environmental importance of the Amazon. Human trafficking, child labor specifically, and any other type of trafficking, are facilitated.

There are always rules, of course, but some countries, specifically China, ignore the World Trade Organization's rules with reckless abandon. We can enforce the trade laws, force the competition to play by the same rules, and stop giving our competitors the tools (technology and R & D) to win the global war. It is, however, tiresome.

The general complaint about globalization is that it has made the rich richer while making the non-rich poorer. "It is wonderful for managers, owners, and investors, but hell on workers and nature." The World Trade Organization states on its website that the richest 20 percent of the world's population consumes 86 percent of the world's resources while the poorest 80 percent consumes just 14 percent. Research findings indicate that income inequality has increased in nearly all world regions in the last few decades, which, in turn, shapes domestic politics and international relationships.

In a list of 149 countries and territories, the World Bank estimates (April 2018) the following in terms of income inequality around the world. On a scale of 0 to 100, 0 represents total equality. A scale between 0 and 1, called the Gini coefficient, is usually used to measure this. It works like this: the closer a score is to 1, the greater the income inequality. So in a country where the score is 0, everybody earns the same, which represents perfect equality. In a country with a score of 1, one person earns everything, and everybody else earns nothing, which represents absolute inequality. As an example, South Africa's Gini coefficient is 0.65—a staggering score by any international comparison— and is the world's most unequal society (followed closely by its neighbors Namibia and Botswana), where 3,500 people own more than the bottom thirty-two million people. To rub it in, while the most impoverished people in South Africa own little more than hard cash, the top 10 percent own more than 99 percent of all bonds and stock held in the economy and the wealthiest 1 percent alone owns around 90 percent of the country's bonds and corporate shares.

As another example, Nigeria is the largest economy in West Africa, is the third largest in Africa, and ranks 157 out of 189 countries on the Human Development Index (HDI) of the United Nations Development Programme (UNDP). It has a reputation as a regional economic powerhouse, but inequality leaves many needs unfulfilled.

Among Nigeria's population of 200 million, more than one in four (57 million) do not have access to safe water, and two- thirds (over 130 million) lack adequate sanitation. Ten million children are out of school, and more than half of the population (112 million) live in extreme poverty with less than $1.90 a day.

Although it possesses the resources to end extreme poverty and tangibly improve financial inequality between rich and poor, women and men, Nigeria remains a country where the government is the least committed to reducing inequality, based on Oxfam's Commitment to Reducing Inequality (CRI) Index 2019.

Most of Africa follows that trajectory. The United States' count is at 41, and much of Europe and Asia settle at between 30 and 35. The least inequality is experienced in places such as Denmark, Norway, Finland, and Ukraine in the upper twenties. Inequality. org (2019) reveals that in terms of global wealth inequality, the richest 1 percent of the global adult population owns 45 percent of the world's wealth.

Global income inequality, looking at it from any angle, "is rising or staying high nearly everywhere."

Globalization has also caused large shifts in the ownership of capital around the world. Understanding this is critical in trying to determine inequality in the assets of individuals. In other words, net private capital (the assets of individuals minus their debts) has risen enormously in recent decades, but public capital (the assets of the government minus debt) has declined in nearly all countries because of the large-scale privatization of rising public debts. This means that public capital is approaching zero or below zero in rich countries, which has strong implications for governments to find the money to invest in education, health care, environmental protection, and innovation. This dramatic decline in the net wealth of governments over the past decades poses a challenge for tackling inequality.

The bigger the gross domestic product, the wealthier the billionaire class in countries such as the United States, Germany, and Japan; for example, the wealthiest three men (most of the time) in the United States—Jeff Bezos, Bill Gates, and Warren Buffett—have more wealth than half their country combined but when viewed from the perspective of GDP per capita, a country like Swaziland with a low GDP per capita can have a billionaire's wealth weighing nearly 90 percent of the country's GDP, a performance only surpassed by the exclusive Monaco on the French Riviera. Rapid economic growth in Asia (particularly China and India) has lifted many people out of extreme poverty, but the global richest 1 percent have earned a greater share of those economic gains.

The IMF has warned repeatedly that certain numbers should be taken with a grain of salt. It cannot be automatically assumed that in nations where GDP is particularly high that the overall population is visibly better off than in most other places in the world. This is because the figures are averages in any given country, but structural inequality can tip the balance in favor of the already privileged.

Research from the World Inequality Lab 2018 report indicates that income inequality has increased in nearly all world regions in recent decades, though at a different pace, highlighting the important role of governments to mitigate inequality. Since 1980, income inequality has increased rapidly in North America, China, India, and Russia, while growing moderately in Europe. However, there are exceptions to this pattern: in the Middle East, sub-Saharan Africa, and Brazil, income inequality has remained relatively stable but at extremely high levels. The fact that inequality trends vary among countries, even when countries share similar levels of development, highlights the important role of national policies in managing inequality. For instance, consider China and India since 1980: China recorded much higher growth rates with significantly lower inequality levels than India. "The positive conclusion of the World Inequality Report is that policy matters—a lot."

On https://stats.areppim.com/ it indicates that "the share of wealth grabbed by the super-rich is staggering. From a constant

US$1.6 trillion in 1996, it climbed to 8.7 in 2019. Billionaires make just 0.00003 percent of the world population, but they currently own the equivalent of 12 percent of the GWP (gross world product)." In plain terms, the good ordinary people are letting go of a growing portion of their share of the wealth to please the ultra-rich and render them richer. "Crises may hit the planet, but billionaires hardly sneeze, while the rest of humankind struggle with economic suffocation. In the last seventeen years, their aggregate assets suffered only three slumps, a harsh one in 2008, and two comparatively minor ones in 2016 and 2019."

The May 28, 2018, copy of *Time* magazine, a feature article adapted from author Steve Brill's *Tailspin: How My Generation Broke America* indicates that [American and of America] "Income inequality has soared: inflation-adjusted middle-class wages have been frozen for the last four decades while earnings of the top 1 percent have tripled. The recovery from the crash of 2008—which saw banks and bankers bailed out while millions lost their homes—savings and jobs were reserved exclusively for the wealthiest. Their incomes in the three years following the crash went up by a third, while the bottom 99 percent saw an uptick of less than half of 1 percent. Only a democracy and an economy that has discarded its basic mission of holding the community together, or failed it, would produce those results."

It is now March 2020, and the COVID-19 pandemic has millions of people around the world in lockdown in almost every country. Economic activity, as a result, has come to a standstill for many industries and stock markets have been in a free fall, which has led to a combined $57 billion drop in the fortunes of the ten biggest billionaire losers (March 13). Of course, the stock markets should not feature as an economic issue but as a political issue because it depends on what political move finds favor with the wealthy. If investors like what is happening (for example,

Trump being upbeat about his COVID-19 experience), the stock market will bounce back. Billionaires survive disasters better and sometimes benefit from them. The poor only get poorer, and they are forced to look to the government (usually also weaker) or charitable acts by others for handouts, more handouts, and then some.

The reality is, of course, that the powerful and the rich, in general, favor the powerful and the rich or those in the position to assist the rich—lawyers, savvy accountants, tax consultants, and politicians—so that they too can get rich. It is a wonderful circle of empowerment and enrichment.

Many competing political debates given by presidential hopefuls, understandably, include ways to tackle inequality but nothing much has changed the graph of an increasing trend of inequality around the world.

Scientists work for the greater good of the world, medical health professionals work for the greater good of the world, and humanists make the world a more humane one than it has ever been before. In the last decade though, there has been a movement away from the once-revered concept of democracy. The global financial crisis of 2008 and its lengthy recovery gave populist parties the ecosystem they needed to survive and strengthen. The populist approach is becoming popular. For example, globalization invited and celebrated migration, but in the last four years, migration is a troublesome word.

Larry Diamond, a political scientist at Stanford, in his book *Ill Winds*, proves that world democracy is challenged by examples of countries becoming rather more oppressive than more free—the thirteenth consecutive year of more decline than progress, such as China holding a million Uighurs and other Turkic Muslim minorities in "political education" camps, and barring online gamers (it is a massive industry there) under the age of eighteen from playing on weekdays and limiting their play to three hours most weekends; tyrants ruling in Vietnam, Belarus, Egypt, and elsewhere through police monitoring, ethnic division, and brute coercion; and Burma's bloody expulsion of some 730,000 Rohingya Muslims into neighboring Bangladesh. Autocrats are elected like Viktor Orbán in Hungary and Recep Tayyip Erdoğan in Turkey, who hijack the courts, stifle opposition parties, and muzzle the press. For Diamond, the menace also comes from the outside: a transnational surge of authoritarian populism across Europe, along with a rising China and an assertive Russia that are "avidly undermining democracies and liberal values around the world." In the United States, once the beacon of democracy and freedom, Diamond tallies the degradation that "Trump's lawless, norm-busting presidency has already inflicted: stuffing the courts, assaulting the Justice Department, demonizing the free press, and mainstreaming extremist ideas like mass deportations and the Muslim travel ban—now shamefully validated by a Supreme Court majority." (I hasten to add that Diamond's book fights for democracy with practical examples of how change can be implemented.)

Populist leaders present themselves as representatives of "the people." They are charismatic or dominant figures who present themselves as "the voice of the people." Some are well connected to their country's political and economic elites, such as Trump, Johnson, and Orbán (from Hungary). Italy's Salvini, who is the leader of the far-right party, pledges to return to power as prime minister and forge alliances with the like-minded Donald Trump and Boris Johnson. Other nationalists and populists have come from simpler backgrounds, but with good contacts and hard work, populists Bolsonaro, Erdoğan, Widodo, and Modi swell the crowd. Populists not only see themselves as the voice of the people but as the savior of the people. They brag about their abilities to do just that; for example, Sarah Palin, a United States vice presidency right-wing contender in the 2008 election referred to herself as "hockey mom" and "mama grizzly." Cute. It looks like mama grizzly will be back on the political scene in 2024.

You may well be wondering about the link between inequality and populism. Why are democracies around the world failing to curb rising inequality? What explains the ascent of populist parties and politicians?

Sophie Hardach on April 30, 2018, (World Economic Forum) referred to a paper written by French economist Thomas Piketty, who argued that not only are inequality and populism linked, but that both can be explained by dramatic shifts in the traditional two-party system that favor different elites.

"Citing historical data from France, Britain, and the US, Piketty suggests that left-wing parties, which used to attract and represent less-educated voters, are now more associated with highly educated voters. Right-wing parties, on the other hand, have consistently attracted and represented wealthy voters. Consequently, low education, low-income voters might feel abandoned." In short, the rise of populism is related to what Piketty calls the rise of elitism.

Populism is said to be more about money and greed than it is about being the savior of the people. It brings about inequality.

Inequality and globalization have exacerbated the international financial system into a money launderer's dream, siphoning off billions of dollars a year from economies around the world and extending the reach of organized crime. This unintended consequence of globalization and the disrespect for inequality presents a serious challenge to law enforcement agencies, financial regulators, and for some countries, agitated and frustrated governments; for other countries, it is a government's dream.

In *Enlightenment Now: The Case for Reason, Science, Humanism, and Progress* (2018), the cognitive scientist Steven Pinker looks at recent studies and finds that majorities in fourteen countries—Australia, Denmark, Finland, France, Germany, Great Britain, Hong Kong, Malaysia, Norway, Singapore, Sweden, Thailand, the UAE, and the United States—believe that the world is getting worse rather than better (China is the only country that expressed optimism). However, he presents statistics and charts that show life has improved in most respects, from health care to better education and nutrition, less poverty, fewer injuries, fewer people killed and injured through war, and surprisingly, a less-polluted world.

In fact, *Enlightenment Now* suggests that there is something bratty about humankind in that we just do not want to admit how good we have it. At the risk of being bratty too, I believe that the growing inequality and globalization are bringing to the fore issues the world is now having to battle with on a more intensive basis.

Freedom of movement of people has been an increasing human right since the Second World War, whether as war refugees or economic opportunists. Slowly, that door is partially closing. Economically, most countries around the world, since the last financial crisis in 2008, have struggled to recover fully. Refugees, asylum seekers, migrant workers, and others have left their countries, looking for a better life, from Mexico to America, from Guatemala to America, from Libya to Egypt, from Zimbabwe and Malawi to South Africa, from South Africa to New Zealand, from Britain to Europe, from Burma to Pakistan, and from Syria to the shores of Europe, and globalization initially facilitated these movements. The number of people moving from one country to another to seek a better life is increasing, but there are pushbacks from populists. Arguments abound. One argument believes that there is sufficient proof that immigration (legally and illegally) has enriched society both economically and socially. The counterargument believes that there is sufficient proof that immigration (legally and illegally) leads to cultural differences that are purported to increase racial bias, make the encroached country less safe, and take away jobs from the locals.

There may be little choice in the future. Extreme climate, war (such as Putin's full-force invasion of Ukraine in February 2022 after years of tension and earlier attempts) and struggling (and corrupt?) economies will force further migration by the millions. How will we manage that? Even now, visas and residency applications and other entry requirements are getting stricter and more expensive, migrants at borders are being treated more tersely, and refugee camps are becoming a permanent headache or a form of permanent residence.

The aggressive, nonsensical, bloody, and genocidal offensive of Ukraine has seen the Western world and particularly NATO members rally together to fight back. The magnitude of heavy sanctions applied to Russia, the weaponry and other support supplied by the Americans and other NATO nations to Ukraine have been unprecedented. As a result, Ukrainian refugees have been welcomed in their millions by Poland and other Eastern European countries primarily as well as parts of the Western world. Globalization has been thrown into disarray for 2022: trade has been disrupted, staple grain foods are in short supply considering Ukraine and Russia have been main suppliers, causing increased hunger and increased inflation.

Climate change, a reality that still is not perceived as a threat by some, has already had devastating effects in several countries around the world, specifically in the last three years. The IPCC Sixth Assessment Report (February 28, 2022) indicates that "increased heat waves, droughts, and floods are already exceeding plants' and animals' tolerance thresholds, driving mass mortalities in species such as trees and corals. These weather extremes are occurring simultaneously, causing cascading impacts that are getting increasingly difficult to manage. Climate change has exposed millions of people to acute food and water insecurity, especially in Africa, Asia, Central and South America, on small islands, and in the Arctic." It is only going to get worse if we make no effort to change our behavior toward respecting our planet. Scientists and activists' endeavor to convince and cajole the nonbelievers or those that are selfish enough not to care about the future world and the legacy left behind. I heard a scientist indicate in an interview on the radio that if scientists and activists give too much of a desperate plea to change our harmful polluting habits and paint a picture of a polluted world in 2050, many people will bemoan overexaggeration and unnecessary doom and gloom. The other concern is that sometimes we have good intentions. For example, India has planted millions of trees in good faith, but in scientific terms, it would appear we still have a lot to learn about reforestation, deforestation, afforestation, agroforestry, and so forth. Are we doing the right thing for specific areas?

In a Sheffield Political Economy Research Institute (SPERI) publication dated January 27, 2020, Jeremy Green, a lecturer in international political economy at the University of Cambridge and SPERI honorary research fellow, said, "We cannot simply reboot the global economy to deliver more carbon-intensive economic growth and restore the legitimacy of global capitalism—because it is our pursuit of limitless growth that is driving the climate crisis."

Jeremy went on to say, "We will need to transform the balance and purpose of the cross-border flows of goods, capital, people, and ideas that have propelled globalization. Some of those cross-border flows, like unsustainable trade practices and fossil fuel sector capital flows, will have to stop. While others, like aid transfers from the Global North to the Global South and flows of climate-related expertise and investment towards the worst affected regions, will have to grow rapidly."

We have plenty of evidence that technology and, specifically, artificial intelligence have benefits such as performing simple to complex tasks quickly and with ease, particularly enhancing food production, which can benefit society. Its co-attraction is cybercrime performed by outsiders on corporations. Corporates contend with formal, documented processes, monitoring, and control issues, none of which applies to cybercrime; hence, cybercrime is agile. Our digital world is enveloping poorer nations and giving them access; this will no doubt facilitate more opportunities to access global legal and illegal markets.

For example, the 2019 democratic presidential campaign debates in America centered on taxing more from the rich, giving middle-class tax cuts, cutting the costs of education generally, giving more for the poor and less privileged, addressing the gender and racial pay gaps, introducing financial transaction taxes, free health care, and closing the gap between the pay of CEOs and their employees. These initiatives are designed to reshape the economy to bring about a more equal society. They have a long way to go.

The World Inequality Lab indicates that it aims to promote research on global inequality dynamics. Its core mission is to maintain and expand the World Inequality Database. It is going to expand, all right: google inequality now and learn what it is predicted to be in 2050.

The hairy question is, How much of this is illegal money? Inequality is almost always a result of laundered money earned through crime and corruption and, importantly, the evasion and avoidance of paying taxes. Multinational corporations can exploit tax laws and tax havens in other countries to avoid paying taxes as well as increase their influence over political decisions.

Because globalization represents an overarching international phenomenon, you would think that the international community's response to the challenge posed by money laundering would have to address the financial, legal, and enforcement issues universally, through a collaborative medley of remedies, much like the protesting Americans and supporting sympathizers in June 2020 agitated for change to police brutality and racialism, known as #BlackLivesMatter.

The 2020 COVID-19 pandemic has proved that globalization is a reality in the way that the pandemic showed its proclivity for rampant transmission across borders and highlighted the inequalities of many societies affected around the world.

Both #BlackLivesMatter and the COVID pandemic have brought inequality to the attention of the world so much better than all the figures and data quoted here could.

Commercial activities are increasingly influencing political decisions as many governments become weaker. Many think that there is a threat of corporations ruling the world because they are gaining so much power, due to globalization.

Statistics show that global trade and investments in the years from 1960 to 1998 worsened inequality both internationally and within countries. It has been predicted by scientists that globalization is also leading to the intrusion of communicable diseases, and as of May 2021, here we are with many countries facing a third and fourth wave of COVID-19.

Sadly, both the advantages of globalization and the disadvantages of inequality raise opportunities for money laundering. This is a powerful driver of global economic inequality and weakened governments who do not, or cannot, care sufficiently for their people. It was past president Obama who described rising inequality and declining mobility as the "defining challenge of our time." Angel Gurría, former secretary-general of the Organization for Economic Co-operation and Development, warned that "high levels of inequality generate high costs for society, dampening social mobility, undermining the labor market prospects of vulnerable social groups, and creating social unrest."

There are many more reasons given that contribute to an unequal society, and they may be reasons for exploitation. For example, we know that salaries and wages discrepancies between the mighty companies' top executives and the day-to-day mundane contributors that keep the wheels turning are unethical. We know that black people generally have fewer opportunities than white people. We know that women are paid less than men. We know that opportunities favor the rich and powerful, and we know that politicians are more likely to engage with the wealthy than the poor and hungry.

But more than any other reason, I believe that the value of money being laundered and the ease with which billions are earned illegally all over the world are the main reasons why the gap is widening between the haves and have-nots. And it is based on greed.

CHAPTER 7

The Birth of the Anti-Money-Laundering Industry (AML)

T HERE HAS NOT been a lack of effort to stem the tide of money laundering activity internationally.

From a global perspective, even thirty years ago, the activities of criminal organizations proved difficult to control; whether applied domestically or internationally, any efforts at control proved fruitless. It became a growing reality in many parts of the world that the money laundering tide had to be stemmed.

Something had to be done.

Transnational organized crime, illegal markets, and money laundering posed serious challenges to international security, economies, and morality; no longer was it an isolated domestic issue for a few cities and coastal towns.

Another concern was that some governments provided transactional crime syndicates with opportunities to expand their activities and enhance their profits. The illegal markets and the powerful criminal networks cleverly reached into weak or vulnerable governments and controlled and used their staff who were amenable to bribery or easily made fearful of losing their job or safety.

It could be said the fight back started with one of the earliest responses authorized by the United States Treasury: the Bank

Secrecy Act of 1970, which established regulatory measures to require banks to file currency transaction reports.

But another change was also taking place. The 1970s started the first waves of deregulation. This was the process of removing or reducing government regulations, specifically to benefit the economic sphere because it was believed that government legislation was inefficient and hurt the economy. It meant that transportation, telecommunications, and banking succeeded in increasing competition as a result. This lowered consumer prices, increased choices, and allowed for product innovation, much to the delight of consumers.

The 1980s saw a further rise in deregulation. The dollarization (i.e. the use of the United States dollar in transactions) found its way into black markets, the Euromarkets, and the financial secrecy havens. Therefore, the finding, freezing, and forfeiting of criminally derived income and assets by authorities became more difficult to implement.

And because it did, the idea of deregulation began to fade.

The United States enacted the Money Laundering Control Act in 1986, making the laundering of proceeds derived from any one of the long lists of offenses a crime. Congress made civil and criminal procedures available to forfeit property involved in a laundering offense.

The extent of money laundering and its negative effect on the world economies attracted the attention of the Group of Seven (G7). This unofficial forum brought together the heads of the richest industrialized countries: France, Germany, Italy, Japan, the United Kingdom, the United States, Canada, and a little later, the president of the European Commission. While it was clear to the forum that illicit activities dampened foreign investment and distorted international capital flows, the consequences, in the longer term, were unpredictable. What did become clear, though, is that in an increasingly interconnected and sophisticated world, money laundering was becoming equally interconnected and sophisticated. Greed, power, and influence grew in tandem.

The G7 took the initiative to set up an intergovernmental organization in 1989—and its mandate was to develop policies to combat money laundering. The Financial Action Task Force (on Money Laundering), or FATF, also known by its French name, Groupe d'action financière (GAFI), was formed. Its mission was to devise international standards to prevent money laundering and to promote the implementation of those standards.

The FATF comprised twenty-six member countries and two regional organizations and included the major financial centers of Europe, North America, and Asia. The participants agreed to work both independently and in cooperation with other organizations such as financial institution officers and regulators to establish and strengthen member and nonmember anti-laundering measures.

FATF recognized that money laundering was constituted of a complex web of economic crimes, thus making conventional law enforcement efforts ineffective.

In April 1990, FATF issued a report containing recommended countermeasures to money laundering. Commonly known as the Forty Recommendations, these countermeasures were designed to provide governments with a comprehensive framework for anti-money-laundering action. The Forty Recommendations, revised and updated twice thereafter, encouraged the full implementation of the Vienna and Strasbourg Conventions and the lifting of bank secrecy laws. FATF, therefore, became (and still is) the center for the criminalization of the laundering of the proceeds derived from all serious crimes, the forfeiture of property connected with a laundering offense or its corresponding value, the establishment of customer identification and recordkeeping rules by accountable institutions, and the creation of financial intelligence units.

Countries were encouraged to become members of FATF and to adopt these recommendations in their legal toolbox. So while many countries had laws that regulated criminality, new laws were required by them to deal with the proceeds of that criminality.

FATF's first policy issued set out these Forty Recommendations for countries to adopt. These were principles for action and allowed countries flexibility in implementing these principles, depending on their circumstances, resources, and constitutional frameworks. The result was to have these recommendations included in the legislation.

At the same time, the Council of Europe wanted to strengthen democracy, human rights, and the rule of law in its member states, in part, by harmonizing its policies and encouraging the adoption of common practices and standards. It adopted the Strasbourg Convention in November 1990, which, like the Vienna Convention, required each party to adopt legislation that criminalizes money laundering.

The First Directive by the European Union for AML was adopted in 1990 to prevent the misuse of the financial system for money laundering. It mandated that financial institutions apply customer due diligence requirements when entering a business relationship (i.e., identify and verify the identity of clients, monitor their transactions, and report suspicious transactions). It became commonly known as KYC—know your customer.

The United States, in the meantime, also followed up on its Money Laundering Control Act with its Financial Crimes Strategy Act of 1998, which called for a strategy to combat money laundering and related crimes. This strategy called for the recognition of high-risk money-laundering zones, greater scrutiny of suspicious transactions, creating new legislation, and putting pressure on nations that have little or no anti-money-laundering controls. This led to multinational agreements and treaties and increased international efforts on the forfeiture of property, thereby promoting international collaboration.

While the above is law, the Vienna Convention of 1998 represented the first concerted effort to influence the international community's response to drug money laundering. It required the signatory jurisdictions to take specific actions, including steps to enact domestic laws criminalizing the laundering of money derived from drug trafficking and to provide for the forfeiture of property derived from such offenses. The convention also promoted international cooperation as an important first step to reducing the global threat of money laundering. States were required to assist in obtaining relevant financial records when requested to do so, ignoring domestic bank secrecy laws. It was not successful, however, and many parties to the convention failed to participate meaningfully. Whereas laws are enforced by courts with legal sanctions following any breach of the law, a convention is different as it is only enforced by political pressure. Also, laws are systemic in that rules are mostly bound by other rules; constitutional conventions stand on their own.

In December 1999, twenty-seven of forty-one member states and one nonmember state (Australia) ratified the Strasbourg Convention. Unlike the Vienna Convention, this treaty did not limit the offense to drug trafficking only and required members to adopt laws criminalizing the laundering of the proceeds derived from any serious crime. The treaty also required signatories to adopt laws authorizing the forfeiture of the proceeds of serious offenses, as well as other aspects related to the crime, or the value of such property. Members were also required to assist foreign jurisdictions regarding forfeiture cases and do the necessary to prevent the disposal of the property before confiscation.

Given the extent of the problem, economists, law enforcement executives, and policymakers agreed on the need to develop an acceptable means of identifying the scope of the laundering problem. The international response to laundering took many forms, including multilateral treaties, regional agreements, international organizations, and the identification of universal counter-laundering measures.

Further EU directives were given. The Third Directive contained details on due diligence, which are the requirements to identify the individual customer, or the beneficial owner (that is, the ultimate owner of a business), to obtain information on the business relationship, and to monitor the associated transactions. It also covered terrorist financing.

By the time the Fourth Directive was implemented by the European Union, the assessment was conducted within the framework of a contract between the European Union and the Council of Europe with the inclusion of reviewing all EU member states.

This Fourth Directive, interestingly, indicated that financial institutions and other obliged entities could apply a risk-based approach. It came into force on June 25, 2015, with the requirement that the member states implement it fully into their domestic legislation by June 26, 2017. It replaced the Third Anti-Money Laundering Directive of 2005, which was repealed.

This was a substantial move in the right direction since the AML/CFT rules, before this directive, mandated a strict application of the same checks and balances that had to be considered for each client and each business client. But with the risk-based approach, any financial institution or relevant business is accredited with the necessary savvy and knowledge about their client base. They know which clients are stable and transparent in terms of their profile, and which type of client could represent a money-laundering or terrorist-funding risk.

For example, Brian Jones, a bank account holder who has worked for one organization for thirty years with a regular salary, has two loans that are dutifully paid off regularly, has lived at the same address for twenty years, and regularly takes a holiday once a year to family in New Zealand, is likely to be ranked as a low-risk customer and therefore very little attention is given to that customer. It is likely the institution will only seek to renew his ID documents and contact details every four years.

But if an account holder represents the profile of someone such as Erin Benarhi, who does not reside in her own home and moves around a lot, travels overseas frequently, works independently and therefore her earnings are erratic and from different countries (even if they are good earnings), then Erin may be categorized as a high-risk customer and the financial institution may want to renew her ID documentation and other relevant information every year.

The above are merely examples, but they do illustrate that a financial institution has the liberty to determine its money-laundering risks. This makes a lot of sense because in the past I have had the experience of regulators undertaking an audit and not understanding the AML risk attached to the client base they are auditing, which is understandable. However, these high, medium, low, or anything in-between risk ratings of customers, whether it be for individuals, sole proprietors, small businesses, commercial companies, or big corporations, need to be carefully assessed, categorized, and documented by the institution in a document referred to as a risk-management and compliance program, a risk evaluation return, a customer identification program, or some similar name, which differs from country to country. Regulators tend to use this document when conducting AML audits to ensure the institution is following its own rules. It may be that regulators make recommendations for improvement or tightening of these rules, especially if the audit reveals serious breaches in its AML application of KYC and other AML initiatives.

Another important condition in the Fourth Directive along with the risk-based approach is that the member states are required to hold information on the beneficial owners of all corporate and other legal entities within their territory in a national central register. Competent authorities and entities have access to it, as well as any person or organization demonstrating a legitimate interest.

In many countries, establishing the details of ultimate beneficial ownership can be quite challenging. Many countries (especially developing countries) have not set up a national central register (as the European Union has), and financial institutions are to make their own inquiries and seek proof of ultimate beneficial ownership.

This is not about ownership of a business, but merely its registration. It does, however, speak to government databases. For example, the Companies and Intellectual Property Commission (CIPC) is a registry of all businesses, local and foreign, operating in South Africa. All foreign banking branches required the directors of the main foreign bank to be listed as directors and can involve some twenty directors. A newly appointed compliance officer discovered that the directors listed were seriously out of date. Directors had resigned, retired, or died in the last few years. Of course, the head office of the foreign bank was contacted for the details, not only of the new directors, but also the reasons for the removal of the old directors. The latter was not available. Eventually, the list of new directors was duly sent to CIPC for updating. However, CIPC insisted that the "current" directors could only be removed based on why they had to be removed and the date of removal. To obtain information from a big foreign bank's head office so many years later was challenging, and eventually, it became clear that the details were obviously never going to be forthcoming. CIPC was informed of the situation. They retained their stance: the names could not be removed until there were concrete reasons to remove them, e.g., date of retirement, date of death, etc. Eventually, the compliance officer made the dates up, and their reasons for leaving (pronounced somebody dead when they may not have been) and sent in the forms to have the names removed. The information was accepted and, of course, makes a mockery of what any type of registry is trying to achieve. As with many instances of information gathering for regulatory purposes, it results in a triumph of box-ticking over reasoned thinking.

This fourth directive was only transposed by the member states on June 26, 2017, but was again revised on June 19, 2018, as the fifth AML directive.

The financial system would not be complete without FATF recommending countries to widen their reporting obligation beyond purely financial institutions to casinos, real estate agents, dealers in precious metals and precious stones, and lawyers, notaries, and accountants. These sectors, although required to apply the AML legislation, tend to be less monitored, supervised, and audited.

Of course, any reference to the banking system only is outdated. Today there are thousands of fintech (financial technology) companies, payment systems (to promote financial inclusion) and cryptocurrencies, cryptocurrency exchanges (more than 500), either regulated by some market conduct authority or not, that facilitate the movement of money, making it more complicated than ever to trace the proceeds of crime.

The International Monetary Fund (IMF) has always been especially concerned about the possible consequences of money laundering, terrorist financing, and related crimes to the integrity and stability of the financial sector and the broader economy. The IMF has therefore been a staunch supporter of this new global regulatory regime.

There is no doubt that money laundering and terrorist financing can threaten a country's economic stability, which is why the IMF has become increasingly active in supporting and promoting the AML/CFT efforts of our member countries, based on the [Financial Action Task Force] standard. What started as a small endeavor some twenty years ago has become part of our core work—from analysis and policy advice, to assessing the health and integrity of financial sectors, to providing financial assistance when needed, to helping countries build institutions and increase operational effectiveness. (Christine Lagarde, managing director of the IMF, March 8, 2018)

The United Nations Drugs and Crime Office (UNDCO) indicated the following on their website (2020):

Developments in financial information, technology, and communication allow money to move anywhere in the world with speed and ease. This makes the task of combating money laundering more urgent than ever.

The deeper "dirty money" gets into the international banking system, the more difficult it is to identify its origin. Because of the clandestine nature of money laundering, it is difficult to estimate the total amount of money that goes through the laundry cycle.

Worldbank.org also fights dirty money and its website indicates that "financial integrity and good governance are essential aspects of the World Bank Group's role in assisting the economic development of developing countries. The World Bank's effort to combat corruption and illicit financial flows is the focus of its Stolen Asset Recovery (StAR) Initiative and its Financial Market Integrity (FMI) teams. StAR and FMI have intensified their activities to help developing countries regain their legitimate assets."

In 2001, the FBI Law Enforcement Bulletin estimated that the amount of money laundering occurring on an annual basis probably ranged between 2 and 5 percent of the world's gross domestic product (GDP).

After twenty years, the annual money laundering estimates persist at 2–5 percent of the world's GDP (see UNDCO quote above). But what has changed is the value of GDP globally, and it must be appreciated that GDP figures in most countries are rebased every few years or so because of obvious changes and new developments taking place within economies.

Stated in hard currency, in 2000, money laundering was estimated at US$33.57 trillion per annum. In 2020, that annual figure increased to $84.56 trillion, some $3 trillion less than in 2019. (Did COVID-19 temporarily disrupt the money launderers?)

Illicit activities dampen foreign investment and distort international capital flows, and the consequences are unpredictable. But what is clear is that in an increasingly interconnected and sophisticated world, money laundering is becoming equally interconnected and sophisticated too.

Greed, power, and influence grow in tandem.

CHAPTER 8

FATF in Slow Motion

CONCEPTUALLY, MONEY LAUNDERING is the effort to conceal the origins of illegally obtained funds that have been converted for legitimate purposes; the banks (as an example) are the facilitators. The source of the funds could seldom be traced to illegal activity. Dirty money was washed clean through the banking system, accountants, lawyers, car dealers, estate agents, etc., and became a legitimate source of funds for any further purchases or deals.

In later years, after 9/11, the financing of terrorism was also included as a money-laundering offense. Terrorism requires inverting the money laundering definition as it could more typically involve money from legal pursuits that are converted into forms that facilitate acts of violence for political purposes.

Based on the many examples that can be researched, laundered money (including terrorist funding) *must be* the biggest industry in the world today.

Money laundering offers so many varied and exciting opportunities. Financial systems, in addition to facilitating legitimate commerce, allow criminals to order the transfer of millions of dollars instantly using personal computers and satellite dishes. Because money laundering relies to some extent on existing financial systems and operations, the criminals' choice of money laundering vehicles is limited only by their creativity. Money is laundered through currency exchange houses, stock brokerage houses, gold dealers, casinos, automobile dealerships, insurance companies, cryptocurrency exchanges, and trading companies. Private banking facilities, offshore tax havens and banking, shell corporations, free trade zones, wire systems, and trade financing all can mask illegal activities.

It is no wonder then, that at that time, governments were concerned about the negative effects on the world economy.

FATF was its new hope.

The latest Forty Recommendations update at the time of writing was June 2019, and details can be accessed quite freely on the FATF website. These recommendations essentially focus on aspects to be adopted by a compliant accountable institution, such as assessing the AML risks, cooperating nationally, managing the confiscation of property, assessing and managing terrorist financing, applying targeted financial sanctions related thereto, the management of customer due diligence (which includes extensive preventive measures and ultimate beneficial ownership), the management of all third parties such as correspondent banks, and the establishment and management of financial intelligence units.

These recommendations have been endorsed by over 180 countries (most of the world) and are universally recognized as the international standard for anti-money-laundering and countering the financing of terrorism (AML/CFT). FATF worked with its regional bodies and other organizations such as the International Monetary Fund, the World Bank, and the United Nations.

Countries are encouraged to first identify, assess, and understand the risks of money laundering and terrorist financing that they face or are likely to face, and then adopt appropriate measures to mitigate the risk. The risk-based approach allows financial institutions, within the framework of the FATF requirements, to adopt appropriate measures at countering money laundering and terrorist financing.

Combating terrorist financing is challenging given that it is different from the laundering of money. Financing could be provided by legally earned money donated to be used for terrorist purposes. While the added nine recommendations on terrorist financing were initially added to the Forty Recommendations (making them forty-nine), they are now integrated throughout the Forty Recommendations. Those that are unique to terrorist financing include the criminalization of terrorist financing, targeted financial sanctions related to terrorism and terrorist financing, and measures to prevent the misuse of nonprofit organizations.

The proliferation of weapons of mass destruction is an added security concern, and in 2008, the FATF's mandate was expanded to include the financing of these. To combat this threat, the recommendations also set out to ensure consistent and effective implementation of targeted financial sanctions when these are called for by the UN Security Council. Interpretive notes (which include examples) are provided with the recommendations, which illustrate how the requirements could be applied. The FATF also produces guidance, best-practice papers, and other advice to assist countries with the implementation of the FATF standards—these are all available on the FATF website https://www.fatf-gafi.org/media/fatf/documents/recommendations/pdfs/.

Countries, therefore, adopt these recommendations and translate them into legislation. As each country assesses its resources and capacity, the legislative outcome is different from one country to another; developed countries usually adopt more of the recommendations than developing countries in a shorter period.

Hence, FATF conducts peer reviews (called mutual evaluations) of each member to assess levels of implementation of these recommendations, providing an in-depth description and analysis of each country's system for preventing criminal abuse of the financial system. This is done approximately every five years for each member state.

A complete mutual evaluation takes up to eighteen months. The stages in this process include training on FATF's recommendations and assessment methodology as well as training for representatives of the assessed country so that they know what they will need to provide and demonstrate during the process. FATF chooses the assessment team relevant to what will be required by them to undertake the assessment. The first aspect to be analyzed is the AML legislation of the country, and this analysis could take up to four months. Ratings are then applied to the forty recommendations.

Assessors undertake a preliminary scoping exercise to include the types of threats, vulnerabilities, and risks the country faces relative to its economic and political reality, and that is aligned to the rule of law and the country's level of maturity in combatting money laundering and terrorist financing.

The onsite visit, up until COVID-19, has been a physical one to the country being assessed. The assessors travel to the country for the onsite visit. In an assessment of this nature, the country must provide information regarding the effectiveness of its processes and systems in all eleven areas that are covered by the FATF methodology.

The assessors provide a mutual evaluation report based on their findings: the effectiveness and technical compliance assessment. The assessed country is given the opportunity to comment on the draft report and has a face-to-face meeting with the assessors. Independent reviewers also review the report. But the assessors are the only ones who decide on the text of the report and the final proposed ratings for effectiveness and technical compliance. This draft report is presented at a FATF plenary, which is held three times a year. A consensus among members overrules the draft findings and ratings by the assessors. Following plenary approval, all countries within the FATF Global Network will review the report for technical quality and consistency before it is published on the website, which is usually two months after plenary approval.

Obviously, for a country that has been identified as largely compliant, the country needs to address its shortcomings; for other countries that are not, FATF issues public warnings for those countries to address their deficiencies.

On the FATF website, a list is available of all the countries rating their effectiveness on eleven preordained outcomes or key goals that must be achieved by the country. It also indicates whether it is a mutual evaluation report (MER) or a follow-up report (FUR). It lists the body that is responsible for the evaluation, for example, the Asia/Pacific Group (ASG) on Money Laundering, the Council of Europe Committee of Experts on the evaluation of AML Measures and the Financing of Terrorism (MONEYVAL), or the Word Bank (WB). From an effectiveness point of view, the ratings for each immediate outcome (IO) are highly effective (HE), substantially effective (SE), moderately effective (ME), and low-level effectiveness (LE). The technical compliance is rated as compliant (C), largely compliant (LC), partially compliant (LC), and noncompliant (NC). Recommendations (R1, R2, etc.) are also tabled.

It is interesting, though, to run your eye over all the color coding and it is clear there are hardly any outcomes that are rated highly effective (HE) for any county. Yet FATF members (since most countries in the world are FATF members) continue to pose great money-laundering and terrorism-financing risks to the global financial system. The examples given in this book expose these member states quite dramatically, e.g., Denmark and the scandal involving the Danish bank Danske AG.

In December 2018, Botswana's 2016 FATF mutual evaluation report drew criticism. It was rated as a high-risk country because it was found to have strategic deficiencies in its AML/CFT framework. While it was conceded that Botswana had national deficiencies, the report lacked balance in the opinion of Chris Douglas, a director of Africa AML and Financial Services (Botswana), because it failed to "put significant weight on the low corruption risk of Botswana, the highly educated and professional nonfinancial and business sector, particularly among the legal, accounting, and investment communities. And the strong implementation of the rule of law in the country. Its listing by the FATF is overkill."

He contended that Botswana had been listed alongside the Bahamas, Ghana, Tunisia, Ethiopia, Trinidad and Tobago, Pakistan, Yemen, Syria, and Sri Lanka—countries listed because of the serious corruption, unstable government, war-torn with internal risks, or serious drug issues. None of these applied to Botswana.

To put it into context, Denmark, a wealthy European country, was compliant with only four of the forty FATF recommendations during its 2016 evaluation, while Botswana was found compliant with none.

Yet Denmark was not listed as a high-risk country by the FATF even though the laundered money leached into the global financial system. Denmark is also a high risk of terrorism financing because, as Chris contends, "since 2012, more than 150 Danish citizens have joined militant religious movements in Syria and Iraq—some of those militants have returned to Denmark—while in Botswana the risk from terrorist activities would be regarded as very low."

The question he posed is "If Botswana was a European country and a FATF member with a large financial services industry, would it have been listed as being of high risk to money laundering and terrorism financing?"

This smacks a lot like the criticism placed at the door of the International Criminal Court of Justice (ICC) a few years ago by members of the African Union at the time of the warrant for the arrest in 2011 of Libyan leader Moammar Gadhafi. It is always contended that the ICC goes after crimes committed in Africa, yet it overlooks crimes caused by countries such as Iraq, Afghanistan, and Pakistan. Similarly, in 2013, several members of the African Union expressed anger at the ICC, calling it racist for failing to file charges against Western leaders or Western allies while prosecuting only African suspects up to that point.

Another criticism leveled at FATF by UCI Law on December 12, 2017, titled "Can the AML system be evaluated without better data?" the following was mooted: There is a minimal effort at evaluation by FATF of how well any AML intervention does in achieving its goals, and this is evident because there are no credible estimates of the amount of money laundered globally or nationally, nor much information on serious harms that AML aims to avert. There are long gaps of about eight years between evaluations (it is supposed to be five years), which tend to rely more on third-round evaluations where the use of the data is more likely to be minimal and inconsistent.

The fourth round (2014–2022), they say, may be improved, but this is the start of the third quarter of 2020 and the COVID-19 pandemic, which will not only delay evaluations but may well change the anti-money-laundering landscape for many of the countries around the world.

Countries have tried their best to implement the FATF recommendations. It takes many years for countries to pass laws. It also means that each country is drafting laws and implementing them at different times within different circumstances. AML recommendations are complicated to apply and even more complicated for FATF to monitor. These recommendations are not always accepted in full, given each country's political appetite, resources and capacity, and law enforcement inadequacies.

The threat of money laundering is challenging to law enforcement. To pursue the trail of evidence of a money launderer, law enforcement agencies must identify and use tools and techniques that can help them, especially when crossing international boundaries. Multilateral agreements among regional and world organizations designed to encourage a standardized approach to money laundering all have contributed to the strides made in addressing the challenges. Unfortunately, efforts by nations independent of the international community result in significant variations from the accepted standard; this facilitates money-laundering activity rather than combats it.

For example, the government of Antigua and Barbuda weakened its laws relating to money laundering, resulting in the US Department of the Treasury issuing an advisory warning to banks and other financial institutions to be wary of all financial transactions routed into, or out of, those jurisdictions. The changes in the law strengthened bank secrecy, inhibited the scope of laundering investigation, and impeded international cooperation. An unharmonized approach among jurisdictions allows launderers to use the different laws and practices to their advantage both at the expense of and disadvantage to the countries interested in pursuing them. This makes it even more difficult for enforcement agencies because already they struggle to work together with financial institution administrators and regulators.

FATF and supporting agencies are well-intentioned. Most countries around the world have supported its anti-money-laundering (AML) initiatives; not being a FATF member signals to investors, "Keep away, your money is not safe here."

The FATF blacklist (referred to as the OECD* blacklist) is a list of countries that the intragovernmental organization considers noncooperative in the global effort to combat money laundering and the financing of terrorism. By issuing the list, FATF hopes to encourage countries to improve their regulatory regimes and establish a global set of AML/CFT standards and norms.

*The OECD stands for the Organization for Economic Cooperation and Development. Its mission is to recommend policies that will improve the economic and social well-being of people around the world. The OECD, as stated on its website, provides a forum in which governments can work together to share experiences and seek solutions to common problems. They work with governments to understand what drives economic, social, and environmental change, measure, analyze productivity and global flows of trade and investment, and analyze and compare data to predict future trends. Based on that, the OECD sets international standards on a wide range of things, from agriculture and tax to the safety of chemicals. There is a personal element too as it includes issues that directly affect everyone's daily life: how much people pay in taxes and social security, how much leisure time they can take, the school systems and their impact on the young, and pension regimes for the old.

The OECD has put twenty-one jurisdictions offering "golden passport" or visa schemes on a blacklist stating that those specific schemes threaten international efforts to combat tax evasion. These schemes give wealthy individuals access to low-income tax on their global assets but do not require them to spend much time in the jurisdiction. Three European countries—Malta, Monaco, and Cyprus—are among those nations flagged as operating these high-risk schemes that sell either residency or citizenship.

Officially known as high-risk jurisdictions subject to a call for action, this list sets out the countries that are considered deficient in their anti-money-laundering and counter financing of terrorism regulatory regimes. The list alerts other member countries, financial institutions particularly, and the public, that the countries listed represent high money laundering and terror financing risk. Usually, a blacklisted country is subject to economic sanctions and other prohibitive measures by FATF member states and other international organizations.

The FATF blacklist is a dynamic one in that countries are added and withdrawn from the blacklist as their AML and CFT regulatory regimes are adjusted to meet the relevant FATF standards. The first FATF blacklist was issued in 2000 with an initial list of fifteen countries. The lists are updated as part of the official FATF statements and reports on a yearly, and sometimes twice-yearly, basis. The current FATF blacklist as of August 3, 2020, is North Korea and Iran.

The world, of course, is not black or white but in between, so the FATF has gray lists too, officially referred to as jurisdictions under increased monitoring. Countries on the FATF gray list represent a much higher risk of money laundering and terrorism financing but have formally committed to working with the FATF to develop action plans that will address their deficiencies. While gray-list classification is not as negative as the blacklist, countries on the list may still face economic sanctions from institutions like the International Monetary Fund and the World Bank and experience adverse effects on trade.

The gray list is updated regularly as new countries are added or as countries that complete their action plans are removed. The current FATF gray list, issued on February 21, 2020, includes the following countries: Albania, the Bahamas, Barbados, Botswana, Cambodia, Ghana, Iceland, Jamaica, Mauritius, Mongolia, Myanmar, Nicaragua, Pakistan, Panama, Syria, Uganda, Yemen, and Zimbabwe.

On a day-to-day basis, financial institutions around the world that have adopted the FATF recommendations are impacted by these lists because their internal regulations require them to have suitable risk-based AML/CFT protections in place to mitigate that threat.

The techniques used by money launderers and financial criminals mean that they bypass these restrictions and turn to the nonfinancial sector to conceal illegal earnings. In response to this trend, FATF released guidelines on designated nonfinancial businesses and professions (DNFBPs) that have similar potential to financial institutions to be used for money laundering. In many countries, this is likely to have been included in the AML/CFT legislation. These industries would include companies or independents offering auditing, accounting, and legal services including trusts, dealers in precious stones and metals, real estate agents, and casinos.

The day-to-day requirements of applying AML/CFT for these industries can be painful and expensive, especially if the company or financial institution is dealing in big volumes or high-value transactions.

CHAPTER 9

Working Hard at Being Ineffective

A LL INSTITUTIONS THAT assist customers with money, transactions, or investments are referred to as accountable institutions and undertake more duties than others in terms of what they are accountable to the regulator for.

Accountable institutions include banks, fintech, money remitters, other forex services, attorneys, trustees and executors, estate agents, financial instrument traders, stockbrokers, management companies, gambling institutions, accountants, auditors, car dealers, and coin exchanges; each country will have identified these institutions in their respective legislation. Some of these institutions, such as a coin exchange, may be regulated as a reporting institution that lifts some of the most onerous regulatory requirements.

Know your customer (KYC)

Every customer (whether it be a one-off purchase or a long-term relationship) must be identified and verified at the time of onboarding and, over time and from time to time, reverification needs to be undertaken from a KYC maintenance point of view. The extent and the time of such maintenance undertaken depend on how the financial institution has risk-rated its customer. In the earlier days of AML rules and regulations, it was a tick-a-box routine and ranged from having a suitable unexpired identity document or passport, a photograph (selfie), the residential address and (for example) a utility bill to prove it, the phone number, proof (for an individual) of the source of income being used for a transaction or a pay slip, and a tax number (with proof). Businesses had to prove their companies were registered with the regulatory authorities as required, and directors had to provide their personal information and documents (shareholders too), as did a key contact or compliance officer representing the company. This resulted in all companies being subject to the same level of KYC, whether the information and transaction were a money-laundering risk to the company or not.

The introduction of the risk-based approach meant that institutions could risk-rate their clients in terms of whether they are high risk, medium risk, low risk, or anything in between, from an AML perspective, and implement the level of KYC requirements accordingly. The management of this risk must be documented in the financial institution's risk management and compliance program/compliance manual/or similar name. This document then becomes the bible by which the institution lives and dies in terms of its anti-money-laundering initiatives. So while it is a risk-based document, there are still many aspects of the legislation that are not risk-based such as sanctions screening of all customers, record keeping, suspicion-based reporting to the local financial intelligence unit, and these aspects are usually included in this document for the sake of completeness to the KYC process. It would appear, then, that regulators do an AML audit against the institution's own risk-and-compliance assessment and, of course, the legislation.

This amendment to a risk-based approach has extended the KYC obligations, particularly where trusts, partnerships, and juristic persons such as a corporation, a partnership, an estate, or any other legal entity recognized by law as having rights and duties are concerned. Accountable Institutions must dig deeper and enquire into matters such as the nature of the client's business operations and the identity of its ultimate beneficial owners (UBOs), being the natural person who benefits from the client's assets and profits.

Depending on the legislation of the country, the documents issued by the country, the target market the financial institution is offering the products to, and the potential customers who fall outside of their target market, KYC is not as easy as one would think.

On fourthline.com, in a white paper dated May 22, 2020, titled *Glocal KYC: Not all EU countries are created equal*, the following example is given:

> The best-known example is the German implementation of 5AML (also known as the GwG), which requires an onerous video KYC process that prescribes in detail what a customer must do to pass identification and verification. While this process works well in the German market, it hurts conversion in other European markets. Other examples of additional requirements imposed by national law include Spain (requires enhanced liveliness detection), France (requires a secondary ID document), and Italy (requires seven additional risk checks).
>
> If a financial institution passports its license to all EU member states, the regulations of its home country apply. In practice, this creates a plaid of regulatory standards within one market. For example, a German bank onboarding customers in Germany will be bound by video KYC, whereas

a Dutch bank onboarding customers in Germany using a passported license will be bound by Dutch regulations—and not video KYC.

A fintech (or any non-EU financial institution) seeking to be regulated in Europe should take this into account when selecting its headquarters. However, the reputation of the national regulator also needs to be considered. When Fourthline* was planning its post-Brexit regulatory strategy, the reputation of the Dutch Central Bank as a strict, trustworthy, and fintech-minded regulator was one of the key reasons for selecting Amsterdam.

*Fourthline verifies millions of identities for banks and fintech, insurers, brokers, and more, across Europe.

Cultural differences only exacerbate the nuances of KYC and enhanced due diligence (EDD). Further examples quoted by fourthline.com include that up to 70 percent of Italian customers use a paper ID to pass KYC, which requires a different authenticity check than the latest-generation passports with a machine-readable zone. Also, municipalities have their version, which means paper documents vary, putting pressure on the banker to know whether the document is indeed correct. Many sign-ups are done with a smartphone these days; iPhones versus older versions of Androids can pose clarity problems with pictures of identity documents or selfies. Not all customers, specifically those that fall in the financial inclusion regulatory proposals such as migrant workers, will have a fixed address, may live on a piece of land in a shack, or only have a place to stay provided cash for the rent is paid every Friday. No cash, no bed.

With technology, KYC can be a more seamless process, but there will always be a subset of clients who need help and support to comply. Assisting them requires an understanding of sign-up patterns across different markets relative to the financial institution's risk appetite. Mostly, sanctions screening is applied to all customers.

Records of all the information discussed in this chapter usually must be kept for about five years from the date of the last transaction or date of termination of the account—for fraud investigation purposes. It is a lot of archiving, which must be done in such a way as to be easily retrievable when the regulators or other law enforcement officials need to investigate suspected money laundering.

Sanctions Screening

KYC includes mandatory sanction screening of the client at the time of onboarding and preferably every day and every time a transaction is performed. It may depend on the resources of the company and the client risk profiles.

The term *politically exposed person*, which is the most familiar description in the industry, was a further check introduced because of the Sani Abacha corruption story. Abacha became Nigeria's head of state because of a military coup in late 1993. Despite serious human rights violations, Abacha stole billions of dollars but died suddenly under suspicious circumstances at the age of fifty-four before he was able to spend it. Some of the money—over the decades—has been retrieved and returned to Nigeria.

Sanctions screening is a control used in the detection, prevention, and disruption of financial crime and in particular, sanctions risk. It involves specialized searches against national and global databases to identify individuals, entities, or countries prohibited from performing certain business activities or transactions. Sanctions are aimed to curb illegal activities, terror financing, nuclear and arms proliferation, and activities considered a threat to the security of a nation, generally.

It is the comparison of one string of text against another to detect similarities that would suggest a match. It compares data sourced from a financial institution's operations, such as customer and transactional records, against lists of names and other indicators of sanctioned parties or locations. These lists typically come from regulatory sources and are supplied, updated, and maintained through external vendors specializing in the consolidation, enhancement, and delivery of these lists. Financial institutions also augment these with other local lists of sanctions, relevant terms, names, or phrases, identified through their operations, research, or intelligence.

As a regulated business, the financial institution is responsible for the risk assessment of its clients based on geography, industry, nature of business, type of clients, country of transaction and operation, size or pattern of transactions, and business relationships.

Each financial institution must check against multiple databases of sanction lists and watch lists maintained by the United Nations, country regulators, and law enforcement agencies. Both politically exposed people (PEP) lists and sanctions lists are periodically updated, so a financial institution is almost forced to do daily checks to protect itself from money-laundering abuse. Smaller financial institutions may indeed do it less or manually but at their peril. Screening solutions also help the financial institution to understand the risk potential of a customer and assign a risk rating for ongoing customer due diligence.

Legal professionals and accounting firms may be at risk of this kind of activity because they act on behalf of domestic or foreign clients and receive payments, manage client funds, or purchase real estate on their behalf. They therefore also require an effective PEP and sanctions screening program to mitigate the risk of potential fraud.

However, for sanctions screening, the rules may differ. If a client fails in a sanctions review, the financial institution must follow the rules of its country. Some countries, like the USA, do not allow you to onboard a client that is found sanctioned under any of its lists.

The challenges of the high number of false-positive alerts and dynamic databases make compliance a cumbersome process even though it may be automated. For example, some lists may have many names that are similar but spelled differently, such as Muhammad, Mohammed, Mohammad, Muhammed, Mohamed, Mohamad, Muhamad, Muhamed, Mohamud, Mohummad, Mohummed, Mouhamed, Mohammod, and Mouhamad.

By following a system of compliance according to the laws of the country, and checking for PEPs and sanctions as mandated, the financial institution can prove compliance and waive any potential penalty if the customer is found guilty of malpractices. Unfortunately, this only encourages suspicion-based reporting: it is easier to report on a high-value transaction than to find out what it is for (an internal investigation can only go so far).

In a sanction's context, some data elements are more relevant when found in combination with other attributes or references. Many controls may not be capable of detecting both factors simultaneously and, therefore, may not be effective.

Some of the most common transactional attributes screened include parties involved in a transaction, such as a remitter and beneficiary, agents, intermediaries, and financial institutions, importers and exporters for trade finance, geography including ports and airports, manufacturers, drawees, drawers, the destination or the country of origin of goods and services, and many more.

In a white paper produced by Ho Kok Yong, SEA financial services leader, Deloitte, it is mooted that artificial intelligence (AI) and machine learning (ML) can substantially improve the sanctions screening scenario because "traditional technological approaches to combat these evolving threats are meeting with less success resulting in large numbers of false positives (95 percent of false positives in some organizations where 98 percent do not result in a suspicious activity report (SAR) or a suspicious transaction report (STR) and an army of resources to tediously dispose of these. Undoubtedly, using limited resources to close off non-material and unimportant alerts is manual and onerous. Furthermore, the ballooning costs of anti-money-laundering compliance (of more than US$25 billion in the United States alone) coupled with the high volume of backlog alerts swamp compliance teams and potentially distract them from 'true' high-risk events and customer circumstances."

The white paper does, however, highlight the risks of AI and ML. Input data is vulnerable to data being outdated, false, irrelevant, and based on initially false information; algorithm design is vulnerable to risks such as biased logic, flawed assumptions or judgments, inappropriate modeling techniques, coding errors, and identifying bogus, spurious patterns in the training data; and output decisions are vulnerable to risks such as incorrect interpretation of the output, inappropriate use of the output, and disregard of the underlying assumptions.

Nevertheless, a case study done with United Overseas Bank (UOB), a leading bank in Asia with a global network of more than five hundred offices and territories in the Asia Pacific, Europe, and North America, yielded positive results. Given the volume and velocity of transactions that flow through the Bank, UOB needed to optimize its alerts management, to reduce the false positives and close alerts more efficiently.

The results achieved proved to be a significant step forward with a 5 percent increase in true positives and 40 percent drop in false positives. The name screening module also saw similar positive results. To enhance the name screening process and to improve detection, the module was designed to manage a wider range of complex name permutations. At the same time, the module was also designed to reduce the number of undetermined hits through enriched "inference" features and the inclusion of additional customer profile identifiers. For its name screening alerts, there was a 60 percent and 50 percent reduction in false positives for individual names and corporate names, respectively.

Sanction screening is improved, and it may reduce the number of STRs, but even then, the FIUs are inundated with STRs and SARs, many of them unnecessary or never to be investigated, and this is unlikely to change. With the trajectory the world is on now regarding AML as more people use digitized financial services, the more likely the number of suspicion-based reports will increase.

Would it make a difference to the FIU? And at what cost to the financial institution? And how much does it contribute to catching the money launderers and the money?

Enhanced Due Diligence (EDD)

EDD is a more detailed standard than KYC and is required for high-value customers and transactions or identified and verified high-risk customers before they can be onboarded. In some countries, laws dictate that institutions establish appropriate, specific, and where necessary, enhanced due diligence policies, procedures, and controls that are designed to detect and report instances of money laundering through those accounts. In addition, they often require that EDD measures be applied to account types such as private banking, correspondent accounts, and offshore banking institutions.

Because regulatory definitions are neither globally consistent nor prescriptive, financial institutions are held to different standards depending on their jurisdiction and regulatory environment. EDD intends to follow a rigorous and robust process of investigation over and above the usual KYC requirements. The financial institution needs to assure itself as to the customers' or businesses' identities and the reasons for the transactions.

EDD, therefore, also includes sanctions screening against sanctions lists and the PEP's list, checking the media for any blight on that person's or company's profile; checking whether any individual is a PEP or linked to one; monitoring the transactions, renewing the documents more frequently, understanding and testing the customer's profile, business and account activity; identifying relevant adverse information and media, and risk; assessing the potential for money laundering and/or terrorist financing to support actionable decisions to mitigate against financial, regulatory and reputational risk and ensure regulatory compliance.

FATF's definitions categorize PEPs as all government officials, political party officials, senior executives and relatives, and close associates such as parents, siblings, children, and the spouse and his or her parents and siblings. Of course, that also includes any adverse media. That takes care of the government, but there are the PIPS too. This abbreviation stands for prominent influential persons, their families, and their cohorts that are required to be checked out.

Robert Mugabe's name was infamously listed on the PEPS list and often used as an example for training purposes on the African continent; the reality is that it did nothing to change the rape of Zimbabwe by Mugabe during his presidency. In 2002, Transparency International reported that Mugabe stood out among the politically corrupt. Did anything change? His name on the PEP list just became an amusing sanction screening example.

It is not that PEPS or PIPS are suspects (we all hasten to add), but it is the extent of their power and influence that makes these categories of persons high risk. These lists are fine to identify wrongdoers. The difficulty comes in when the compliance officer may not tip the client off, but as diplomatically as possible, the officer needs to terminate the relationship with the client or continue to process the transactions and send a suspicious transaction report to the financial intelligence unit. The reality is that the power government officials have, and the influence prominent persons have, means that little happens in any case. I am sure there have been many suspicious transactions completed (and not identified or reported as suspicious) by many past presidents (as an example) over many years when they were a PIP rather than a PEP.

Refer to chapter 2 (South Africa) to read about the state capture of South Africa by the Indian-born Gupta brothers Rajesh, Ajay, and Atul. Five years after revelations, the Guptas and their close collaborator Salim Essa were sanctioned under the Magnitsky Act in the US. Rajesh and Atul are under an Interpol red notice. And a few second-tier lieutenants and enablers were arrested.

Did anyone ever report any of the Gupta brothers in South Africa? Had they not done any suspicious transactions or activity until the whistle was blown on them? That is just one example of many high-profile and powerful individuals. Do they get reported, and if they have, has it brought them to book?

KYC and EDD Maintenance

Once a client is onboarded, regular reviews of client information help a company to keep up to date with changes during the life cycle of a customer relationship that a financial institution maintains. It is tricky to decide how and when to review clients, and depending on the client's lifestyle and technology available, this could change. While linked analysis supports a financial institution to better understand all the connections and hidden links a customer might have with business partners, family members, legal arrangements, or even with employees, media research is still required to stay alert in case a customer's reputation deteriorates overnight or over time.

Around the world, including Africa, the financial sector continues to embrace more technological aids such as biometric applications to assist in ensuring effective and accurate due diligence processes. Whatever systems and platforms are used, they can also be misused or manipulated, which is just another compliance headache.

In some countries, privacy laws have become high-profile and seriously restrictive to all businesses and specifically financial institutions; an example is the General Data Protection Regulation 2016/679 (GDPR), which is a regulation on data protection and privacy in the European Union (EU) and the European Economic Area (EEA) and pulls through to all aspects of the business, from handling prospective curriculum vitae of hopeful applicants to passing client information for marketing purposes to the department down the passage. KYC-regulated requirements strictly applied usually supersede these privacy laws.

Reporting to the Financial Intelligence Unit (FIU)

The anti-money-laundering regime, following preventive logic, is primarily built on the obligation for the so-called accountable and reporting institutions to report suspicious activity and suspicious transactions. Recommendation 32 of FATF requires that competent authorities should maintain comprehensive statistics on matters relevant to the effectiveness and efficiency of the AML/CFT system, including statistics on the suspicious-transaction reports (STRs) received and disseminated; on money laundering and terrorist financing investigations, prosecutions, and convictions; on property frozen, seized, and confiscated; and on mutual legal assistance or other international requests for cooperation.

We know that banks especially deal in big money and the digital trails are complex. To find one transaction among the thousands conducted daily is not something easily done. Transactions and transaction trails can be convoluted, and the beneficiaries spread around the globe mean that compliance officers have little to go on to determine what is suspicious. If in doubt, suspicions are reported to the regulators; the reporting of thousands and thousands of suspicious transactions means that the compliance officers are vindicated (you know, just report it, then you will be off the hook).

This is not meant to suggest that there is no vigilance carried out. There definitely is, but with the many ways of moving money around the world, alerts will be included in digital monitoring systems, which help, of course. But initial vigilance and investigation can go only so far, and if a suspicion remains, it needs to be reported to the regulators. What more can they do?

It is up to the regulatory financial intelligence units (which are not named the same in different countries necessarily) to follow through on these suspicions, depending on what is revealed by their data from other banks and fintech. Not only are their resources usually inadequate for these thousands of transactions, but many investigations require a serious understanding of the movement of money, financial corridors between countries, global financial regimes, access to good partnerships, and good digital platforms to serve as national centers for the collection, analysis, and dissemination of information regarding money laundering and the financing of terrorism.

Experience in reporting feedback indicates that the hundreds of thousands of reports worldwide being sent to these FIUs regularly simply remain there. The statistics may be analyzed, and much of the analysis is interesting but contributes very little to further preventive measures or investigation.

The objective of the FIUs would have, over time, proved to have been effective in significantly assisting in the reduction of the occurrences of money laundering and the financing of terrorism. We know that is not the case. They are simply overwhelmed.

In the IMF eLibrary on FIUs, "Enhancing the Effectiveness of FIUs" reports that it "is not an easy task, given the linkages between its operations and those of the other elements in the AML/CFT system. For example, deficiencies of FIU intelligence might not be attributable to the FIU itself, but to weaknesses in other parts of the system. Similarly, the FIU's output depends, in large part, on the quality of information it receives from reporting institutions, and the FIU can influence such quality only to a limited extent, through training, feedback, and guidance to reporting institutions. Also, any bottlenecks at later stages of the process, such as a lack of expertise on financial operations on the part of law-enforcement agencies or the judiciary, may limit the impact of the FIU's work. An additional source of difficulty in many countries is the lack of a coherent statistical framework covering the various parts of the system."

The banker or person representing the financial institution is also regulated not to raise any query with the customer since that is seen as tipping off the customer if any suspicious activity or transaction is detected. The transaction should still be concluded and reported to the FIU thereafter.

Rather report than not report: the maxim in the compliance world is CYA, which stands for "cover your ass." But it blocks up the AML industry with an incredible amount of data that swells the statistics and has little other value.

The *Economist*, April 12, 2021: "Many crime-fighting agencies lack the funding to properly analyse the torrent of suspicious-activity reports that banks file when they spot potentially dodgy transactions. These reports are a cornerstone of the system. But banks file too many low-quality or unnecessary reports because they are incentivised to cover their backs rather than to apply sensible risk criteria. Globally they file millions of these reports a year; in America alone, about 1.2 million were submitted by deposit-takers last year."

Another reportable obligation is to report all cash transactions more than a stated threshold (determined by each member state). If the bank is offered cash for depositing, the bank must automatically report that client's deposit of any amount that is more than a defined threshold (called cash threshold reporting) to the FIU. The reason is to identify somebody who is depositing cash from unknown sources. The FIU pulls information from all local financial institutions to identify persons who have been making these multiple cash deposits over the threshold at multiple financial institutions. Depending on the outcome, those persons will be investigated. Cash threshold reporting may well have limited the depositing of cash over the years; it just means the cash sloshes around elsewhere and it is not as if the criminals do not know to deposit cash over the threshold amount. However, if I sell my old car for a few thousand dollars over a limit imposed and deposit the money, I will automatically get reported to the local FIU.

An example of a waste of time and effort and movement of unnecessary data in respect of cash threshold reporting is where a fintech acts as an intermediary for a bank to encourage its clients to open a bank account, an FIU has ruled that because each entity is an accountable institution, both must produce a CTR report with the same information—a good example of bureaucracy.

The Wolfsberg Questionnaire

The intentions of the AML industry are noble, but the Wolfsberg Questionnaire is curious given the proponents of this initiative.

The Wolfsberg Group, a cozy association of global banks with a wealth of experience in misdemeanors, published a series of materials supporting the implementation of the Correspondent Banking Due Diligence Questionnaire (CBDDQ). The CBDDQ was launched in 2018 as a significant update to the original Wolfsberg AML Questionnaire covering the major aspects of banks' financial crime programs (such as AML and sanctions). It is designed to be an enhanced and reasonable standard for cross-border and/or other higher risk Correspondent Banking Due Diligence because it reduces to a minimum any additional data requirement, as per the Wolfsberg definition and FATF guidance.

The thirteen global banks of the Wolfsberg Group are Bank of America, Banco Santander, Barclays, Citigroup, Credit Suisse, Deutsche Bank, Goldman Sachs, HSBC, JPMorgan Chase, MUFG Bank, Société Générale, Standard Chartered Bank, and UBS.

So thirteen of the big, powerful banks become the godfathers of one of the most time-consuming and useless processes used as an anti-money-laundering initiative.

They have reason to be concerned as they cannot even trust themselves.

Bank of America was fined $17 billion precipitated by its unlawful conduct during the financial crisis of 2008/2009. This was a historic settlement for financial fraud leading up to and during the financial crisis and is probably still the largest civil settlement with a single entity in American history.

Banco Santander was fined $5.6 million by the Supreme Court, which analyzed 143 segregated securities accounts in 2013 and found that the bank had breached the obligation to identify the beneficial owner, had not obtained information on the purpose and nature of business relationships attached to those accounts, and had not complied with the obligation to communicate possible indications of money laundering.

Barclays Bank opened an account for a company called Advantage Alliance. Leaked documents showed the company moved £60 million between 2012 and 2016. Many of these transactions occurred after the United States imposed sanctions on two Russian brothers, one of them being Arkady Rotenberg, a lifelong friend of Putin. He is a billionaire, no doubt through that association, which has brought him and his brother many contracts for Gazprom and the Sochi Winter Olympics. An investigation by the US Senate accused the Rotenbergs of using secretive purchases of expensive art to evade sanctions—one of the companies involved in the scheme was Advantage Alliance. A FinCEN files reporting team was quoted in BBC News on September 20, 2020 that "secrecy, anonymity, and a lack of regulation create an environment ripe for laundering money and evading sanctions." Auction houses in the US and UK "failed to ask basic questions about the buyers of the art." Despite the sanctions, Ayrton Development Limited, one of many companies within a group, appeared to have paid $7.5 million to acquire the René Magritte painting *La Poitrine* in 2017.

MUFG Bank, Japan's biggest bank in the United States, has been warned several times by the United States banking regulator (Office of the Comptroller of the Currency) that serious problems have been uncovered in its many branches. For years, regulators have complained that MUFG "failed to properly monitor who its customers were and where their money came from." The problems were so severe that one former employee likened the bank's anti-money-laundering program to a dumpster fire. It doesn't matter anymore anyway; in September 2021, MUFG pulled back from US retail banking with the $8 billion sale of MUFG Union Bank (MUB) to US Bancorp (USB.N).

Citigroup, Credit Suisse, Deutsche Bank, Goldman Sachs, HSBC, Société Générale, JPMorgan Chase, Standard Chartered Bank, and UBS have all been fined for money laundering felonies already indicated in earlier chapters.

It is perfectly reasonable if a bank that intends to work with a corresponding bank or any other financial institution, whether locally or internationally, determines whether it is indeed a regulated entity.

Every financial institution must be registered to operate legally. Usually, it is a license or registration certificate that is issued, and this can be checked at any time with the regulator; usually, it is public information available on the official website of the regulator. If a financial institution can provide proof of license or registration with the central bank or another applicable financial regulator, why does the Wolfsberg questionnaire ask for information that, with respect, is of absolutely no consequence to the inquirer, nor is it ever likely to be acted upon?

The effect is that one regulated bank that has dealings with another regulated bank requires that it answers the questions to the satisfaction of the requesting bank: the official due diligence questionnaire (CBDDQ version) has some 150 questions for the responding bank or other financial institution (e.g., a cross-border remitter) to complete.

Different versions have materialized over time by the banks or other financial institutions themselves, designed for customization. Below are random examples of questions that need to be answered. (Alongside I attach my facetious remarks in parentheses, assuming the bank being questioned is in South Africa):

Does the Entity offer correspondent banking services to Foreign Banks?

(Would we be in touch if we didn't?)

Does this South African Entity have a program that sets minimum AML, CTF, and Sanctions standards regarding the following components? [a list is given]

(Of course, we do; we are regulated by the Financial Intelligence Centre in accordance with the Financial Intelligence Centre Act No. 38 of 2001, by the South African Reserve Bank in accordance with the Banks Act No. 94 of 1990, the Protection of Constitutional Democracy Against Terrorist and Related Activities Act No. 33 of 2004, and the Director of Prosecutions Protection of Organised Crime Act No. 121 of 1998—related to money laundering. Isn't that enough proof? Had you bothered to check?)

Have you an Appointed Officer with sufficient experience/expertise?

(Of course, we do. Somebody with experience must be in charge as with any other business or regulatory issue.)

Does the Entity maintain and report metrics on current and past periodic or trigger event due diligence reviews?

(Why do you need to know this? If we said yes, how would you know if we do or do not? And if we said no, would you not want to do business with us?)

Does the Entity have risk-based policies, procedures, and monitoring processes for the identification and reporting of suspicious activity?

(That is the whole point about the AML initiatives.)

Does the Entity have policies, procedures, or other controls designed to prevent the use of another entity's accounts or services in a manner causing the other entity to violate sanctions prohibitions applicable to the other entity (including prohibitions within the other entity's local jurisdiction)?

(I have no idea what this is about.)

Does the Entity provide mandatory training (to its staff), which includes: [seventeen questions related to training follow]?

(Surely every staff member is given training relative to the job they must perform, and especially if it is regulated?)

Compliance officers, who are ever innovative, will have their versions of this questionnaire. Further examples of questions include

Is there a documented and approved exit process for clients where it is agreed the business relationship must be terminated?

(Why do you need to know about this process?)

Does your institution accept clients' introductions (and thus establish a business relationship with an introduced client) from other institutions?

(Is this legally forbidden?)

In accepting these introduced clients, is full reliance placed on the CDD (Customer Due Diligence) of the institution introducing the client? Are these introduced clients risk-rated by your institution's methodology and or risk rating algorithm?

(What would you do if we said no? Or will the questionnaire just be filed away as usual, duly answered?)

And yet other examples of questions:

Does your institution have a requirement to collect valid work permits for wage earners?

(Are you now controlling who we employ?)

Does your institution retain customers' information? If yes, please mention how many years.

(We do what is required by our legislation. Surely if we have the appropriate license and we are regularly inspected by our regulators and we have never had a fine, is that not good enough for you?)

Then there are annual or biannual renewals of these questionnaires. The control of this information—without reading any of it—is mammoth in terms of transferring information and attachments, digital filing, renewals, completing these forms for different banks with many different questions, and diary notes to call for further information. Sophisticated digital and security systems do not necessarily make it easier to work with, just easier to ask more questions and archive until next year.

What does this process achieve? Should there be a money-laundering investigation, the requesting bank can say to the investigators that their partner bank XYZ Bank declared that they trained their thirty-two staff on money laundering: "Of course, in the last six months they may have had new staff and we only request that information annually."

The bottom line is that the Wolfsberg Questionnaire and the many versions thereof made up by compliance officers around the world ask for more questions of their partners/correspondent banks than regulators undertaking an audit or inspection of a financial institution on AML.

Because financial institutions must continue to assess the risk of their partners (other banks), it results in an ongoing movement of financial statements, AML and anti-bribery policies, template questionnaires, completed questionnaires, and audited financial statements being sent back and forth mostly annually. Some banks and fintech could have a hundred partners or correspondent banks that they deal with; why are they shunting these documents from one to another? A compliance officer will tick a box: "Yes, I have AB Bank's annual financial statements. Yes (tick) I have their anti-bribery policy. Oops, I forgot to ask for the sanctions screening process."

What do the financials tell the compliance officers? Many of the financial statements produced by big banks are extraordinarily complex anyway. What is the point of a compliance officer collecting them? Do they read the policies requested and received? No. Even if the compliance officer did read any of these documents, how could he or she determine the effectiveness of the AML policy in terms of implementation? Regulators, of course, also require a copy of the financial statements.

If all the boxes are ticked, the role of compliance has played its part. If there is an investigation by the regulators, it is doubtful if any of the policies are of value—maybe just for the bank being investigated to be able to say to the regulator: "Well, that's what Bank ABC said, so you cannot blame us. Please go ask that bank." And usually, it is a cross-border scenario, which has a host of other connotations attached.

An authenticated license or registration certificate from the regulator/s, a company registration document, and a copy of the anti-money-laundering risk-based document required by FATF to be sent to the local regulator are surely more than sufficient and will tell the requester everything they need to know in order to decide whether they should partner with the institution or not.

The country's AML legislation can be assessed by another financial institution's compliance department from across the oceans together with the FATF's assessment regarding the country's AML efforts (that is, the mutual reports). Any financial institution that is registered (which can be checked with the local regulatory authority) will incorporate the same AML laws. Therefore, if a bank in France wishes to form a relationship with a corresponding bank or banks in South Africa, it would have all the regulatory requirements of what the compliance framework for AML is and the regulators' assessment of the country. The financial institution must comply; the country's laws, however, may not be aggressive enough for the inquirer and the inquirer will then simply refrain from forming a relationship with that financial institution in that country.

To boot, every legitimate fintech and bank has a website where financials are posted as well as many of the main policies, and their license or registration can be checked on applicable regulatory websites.

The Wolfsberg questionnaire should be thrown away. Even better, create a bank/fintech/crypto exchange database where all licensed and regulated financial institutions per country around the world can register themselves and keep their data up to date under the form of a declaration. Rather let the compliance teams around the world concentrate on following the money trails.

Financial Inclusion And Microlending

Banks and fintech also function as money transfer operators and provide payment services. Much of their services focus on volume rather than value and provide a valuable service to the unbanked. IT Online on November 5, 2020, reported, "COVID-19 is catapulting financial services into convergence as the key for the future of payment services." This disruption will also give rise to new market entrants and changing customer expectations as indicated in an analysis released by PwC's strategy division on the convergence of payments, which forms part of a report, "Convergence of Payments—PwC Payment Trend Series # 1." Popular examples include the use of social media platforms for online retail, e-commerce, and retailers offering consumers "buy now, pay later" solutions, mobile banking, and online payment gateways. Emerging markets are currently driving the growth of digital payments and widespread adoption of digital wallets, with countries such as China and South Korea leading the charge globally with mobile payments adoption rates of 32.7 percent and 24.4 percent respectively.

Cybercriminals are therefore increasingly using sites like PayPal, Stripe, Skrill, and Square (sounds like a jingle). Cybercriminals have ways of avoiding detection by using, for example, job advertising sites, and this makes it possible to launder lots of money in insignificant amounts through thousands of electronic transactions.

Chantal Maritz, strategy and payments transformation lead at PwC, comments: "The timing and approach for payment convergence will however differ across the world, with emerging markets showing rapid change relative to mature markets due to the increased rate of mobile and digital adoption based on population and the availability of infrastructure."

The global payments industry is adapting to the changing world, but it comes with challenges. As some countries try to strive toward a cashless economy, some of the problems that they face include additional fraud and cyber risks and the complexity of regulation that tries to create stability and security in an environment of extraordinary growth in this industry.

In terms of cross-border money transfers, there are unique issues too, especially in Africa and other developing countries. There is concern that there are many small businesses that spring up all around the cities and operate in cash only. This is understandable and inevitable given that may be the only way people can survive and make a living. It is also true that some of these businesses make way beyond tax-exempted earnings. Because it is cash that is earned, the business owner certainly does not offer to register for tax, and if it is never queried, the business owner will never pay.

There are spaza shop owners that earn taxable income (the meaning of the Zulu word *spaza* is "hidden"). Statistics of the FIU South Africa report that small business owners are sending their earnings home or outside the country to escape paying income tax in South Africa. There is no pressure to register for tax purposes in these circumstances in South Africa; the South African Revenue Services do not appear to have any plans to improve tax registrations from small businesses. But at the same time, regulation gets ever stricter for AML. There is a disconnect somewhere: tax evasion is a money-laundering offense. However, there are now so many ways in which cash can be sent out of a country legitimately, which facilitates the movement of money, and it is getting easier by the day.

Evidence from some Financial Intelligence Units shows statistics of cash outflows that are quite significant—even though in some countries, exchange control regulations restrict the flow of money out of the country. This means that a Malawian migrant worker in South Africa with a valid passport can send money to a family member in Malawi. This beneficiary is, therefore, able to collect cash at the preferred payout provider after showing proof of identity. This is good from a financial inclusion perspective, but to allow the payment, the migrant worker, before they can send the money, will have to provide a full name, proof of address, proof of source of funds, and a valid unexpired passport. Proof of source of funds and proof of address can sometimes be problematic, especially for the relatively insignificant amounts of money (probably less than US$333 per month) remitted cross-border.

KYC is the first line of defense as per the FATF recommendations. As money laundering is about the proceeds of crime, where else could the governments go but to banks and other financial institutions to police the flow of money and hold the banks to ransom with fines and penalties?

Where there is an affluent customer, the operational cost of KYC and AML allows for profitability, but it is quite different to perform the same checks and balances for the poorer members of society. In many countries, most of the population are low-income earners or are unbanked. Fintech has taken up that space, but they are also required to apply AML. So while it has been fashionable of late to include the concept of financial inclusion in legislation or regulatory guidance notes, the reality of making that inclusion possible requires more time and effort.

For example, some fintech companies in South Africa offer a person the opportunity to open a remittance account with no documents, but just to provide the information requirements such as name, identity number, address, etc., on a mobile app. Because of this concession of not having to provide documents, the customer is restricted to one remittance per month of approximately US$134. The only reason the regulator conceded that no documents were required to substantiate the information provided on the app was that the company had to include, in the process of onboarding, a phone call to the customer to perform a verbal verification. The reality, of course, is that the attempts of verification phone calls meant processing delays as customers are not always available. For that amount of money, the company should be able to decide if it wants to take the risk (of being used for money-laundering purposes). US$134 per month is hardly money laundering or terrorist financing. Even if it is, let compliance focus on the millions and billions. There is plenty there to keep them busy.

Payhawk.com, August 1, 2019, "Why banks should not be responsible for KYC and anti-money-laundering," indicated the following: "Unknown to posh regulators, most South African truck drivers live either on the road or in a slum. Neither place of living comes with the luxury of running water or electricity for which utility bills could be sent."

The author, Tobias Baer, continues with his contention that the stricter the regulations, the more likely a bank will experience a penalty to be larger than the transactions involved in value. He recounts of two large Western European banks that were threatened by the regulator to have their banking license revoked if there are any regulatory breaches on KYC detected. Banks, as a result, become more cautious, compromising innocent customers. "Just read the negative reviews of Revolut on Trustpilot.com to hear the tales of many small businesses who found their entire working capital frozen for weeks on end because Revolut's AML scoring system—a probabilistic estimate—had flagged them as potentially engaging in money laundering."

The article further refers to the process that if a citizen directly deals with a government official, there are the necessary regulations to take the government to court if unfairly or illegally denied freedom. Should any financial institution suspect a customer of money laundering, there are three aspects that need to be strictly applied in terms of AML rules: one, if the financial institution suspects a customer of laundering money, the customer is to be left uninformed of those suspicions and a suspicious transaction report is to be submitted to its FIU; two, the financial institution can end the banking relationship, making use of its contractual right to do so even for the sake of convenience; three, as a private sector institution there is the contradiction that "either they have government-enabled access to such a wealth of information that a customer's privacy is violated, or their efforts to identify criminals are stunted by a lack of information."

With an increasing myriad of ways in which to forge documents, including something simple like a utility bill, there are very few financial institutions that have the capacity, the will, and the expertise to recognize fraudulent documentation. A local identity card is typically easy to verify against a government database, which has to be paid for; to identify a passport can also be done—a paid-for system can provide verification in real time. In some cases, such as needing to verify a work permit or asylum documents, compliance teams must rely on experience to detect imperceptible differences such as the size of the font or the width of a border around the work permit. It all depends on resources and application.

Are Financial Institutions the Right Protectors for Money Laundering?

In this world now, we are characterized by our rights to privacy, but at the same time, we are also characterized by our right to freely access the management of our money. Government databases are already used for the issuing of identity documents, passports, and gun licenses; why can't governments manage this for access by financial institutions, not only in our home country but internationally?

Unfortunately, the trajectory the world is on increases the AML role for banks, and fintech is morphing from the sublime to the ridiculous. There is a compliance officer or compliance team that solely focuses on KYC. All customers are only onboarded if their information has been verified by the documentation received. But behind this requirement is the risk-based approach, which means that depending on the customer's assessed risk profile in terms of financial transactional behavior, customers must get risk-rated. Are they high-risk customers or low-risk customers (and everything in between, depending on the financial institution's risk ratings)? A risk register needs to be available listing every risk—rated as indicated—and should there be any residual risk (risk leftover), that needs to be documented and approved.

This may be the time to say that financial institutions (which are all about money) are regulated to function as protectors of the economies against money laundering. Governments are the protectors of people's money too, but they are not regulated from a money laundering standpoint where corruption, money laundering, and looting take place with impunity in almost every country around the world.

Over and above all the checks and balances, financial institutions have to perform internal audits on their anti-money-laundering processes and procedures, as well as external audits from their independent and external auditors and from their AML regulator too. AML is high-profile in all countries that have agreed to adopt such legislation, and there is this rumor that if our country has good anti-money-laundering legislation, then we will attract investors. Investors are willing to pay more for financial services because of a robust uptake of AML. It sounds reasonable, and in surveys, people are bound to tick *yes*, but the reality is that money laundering strikes anywhere and is ever-present in financial institutions around the world and ever-present in the economies. That is the first reality; the second reality is that the trail of money laundering is less about the person than it is about following the money and suspicious transactions. There is always more than one person involved; it's a web of people, and everyone plays a role and gets paid for it.

As if the regulatory checks and balances are not enough, the article on July 1, 2020, *Financial Management* magazine, "CFOs' growing role in anti-money-laundering and counterterrorist financing," reflects on the following: "The last two years have seen a spate of high-profile CFO resignations following failures in their companies' anti-money-laundering (AML) regimes.

"This global cull has caused finance leaders around the world to reassess their AML and counterterrorist financing (CTF) programmes urgently. But even without it, the recent issuance of new regulations and guidance on AML and CTF is making such reviews necessary."

The above relates to FATF's Terrorist Financing Risk Assessment Guide. The EU's Fifth Money Laundering Directive came into force in January 2020 and served as an update to the Fourth Directive to the European Union's AML legal framework. All twenty-eight of the bloc's member countries had to put these requirements into their domestic laws. New levels of sophisticated money laundering and the advent of cryptocurrency money laundering opportunities prompted the necessary update, including the introduction of UBO registers. Similarly, the Sixth Directive updated the previous two directives, broadening the scope of criminal liability to legal professionals. It also included an update of the list of predicate offenses and provides for tougher penalties of AML transgressors.

In terms of the Terrorist Financing Risk Assessment, the Guide highlights risks associated products such as prepaid cards, money or value transfer services, money remittances, correspondent bank services, hawalas, charities, and precious metals or stones. It calls for closer monitoring and sets standards for both quantitative and qualitative data, which is inclusive of domestic and foreign intelligence information, sources of funding, channels, and financial corridors engaged.

There has been criticism on the above, especially where many of its offerings are low-value products aimed at a mass market with no bank accounts, which is typical of South Africa as an example. It defies the requirement in the legislation to promote financial inclusion. This does not mean that these requirements are not tricky even for countries where most people have bank accounts. It would appear then, that application of these guidelines will have to be organization specific. Will this not increase queries cross-border? Each corridor may have different requirements between sender and beneficiary.

Each business has responsibility for ensuring senior oversight of AML/CTF processes. This oversight role does not necessarily fall to the CFO. But when it does, finance chiefs must ensure they are aware of the risks and have adequate procedures for mitigation.

Easier said than done.

A War Being Lost Despite More Controls

As indicated above, the Fifth and Sixth Money Laundering Directive extend existing customer due-diligence obligations, increase reporting requirements for many businesses, and introduce new risk-assessment duties. It also adds a regulatory imperative that individual senior managers ensure compliance. The earlier directives, therefore, fade into insignificance.

CFOs already have huge responsibilities in bigger organizations, but now they must meet these new requirements overtly and confidently and have sufficient knowledge of customer mechanisms.

To adapt to the changing nature of the potential risks identified, it is a no-brainer that offenses added include cybercrime and environmental crime. Insufficient or insignificant compliance resources or processes to prevent money laundering and terrorist funding could subject senior employees to legal proceedings. It will, of course, still take many countries outside the European Union and USA to fully absorb the requirements of these directives.

Money launderers, if they bothered to follow this legislation, would jump for joy—yet more burden to be carried on the weary shoulders of the compliance regime. The article indicates that companies must understand the origin of inbound money flows. Most of the time they do not know, and these flows are getting ever more complicated, no less from the growth of cryptocurrencies and their usage.

There is also the suggestion that "banks need to play a bigger role in tackling the growing threat of terrorist financing by collaborating with public bodies such as government and regulators, law enforcement bodies, and finance, and trade centers." Unfortunately, in the main, most governments have no interest in money laundering from a practical application perspective, and regulators have little experience in banking and fintech.

The complexity and magnitude of the AML and CFT legislation against a fast-paced uptake of digital movement of money all around the world (including to and from blacklisted countries such as North Korea), using hundreds of different channels and facilitators, prompts the thought that our money laundering legislation is getting us nowhere fast.

An article contributed by David G. W. Birch, who is an author, advisor, and global commentator on digital financial services, to *Forbes*, May 3, 2021 ("The Case Against the Anti-Money Laundering Rules"), is subtitled "If There's a War on Money Laundering, We Are Losing It." He refers to a profound tweet by Paul Graham wherein he asked what the ratio is between "trouble caused for the innocent to the trouble caused for the guilty by KYC regulation."

It is the same type of question one wants to ask the Republican Party in America regarding their gun laws. The contenders indicate that it is their constitutional right to own guns. While all the gun purchases statistics, daily shootings statistics, and mass shootings statistics (where four people are killed in one incident) are carefully counted daily, how many Americans have had to use a gun (honestly) to save their lives? Do we know?

It is interesting that the article also suggests that the more financial institutions open to allow more people into its fold, the more likely cash might disappear. Let artificial intelligence perform digital due diligence.

The *Economist* of April 12, 2021, reported that yet another bank was preparing to face the music over "alleged failings in its efforts to curb flows of dirty money." NatWest is, at the time of writing, the latest lender to be accused of falling short in the fight against dirty money. NatWest was likely to be fined up to £340 million after admitting three counts of failing to properly monitor £365 million deposited into the account of a Bradford jeweler over a few years, £264 million of that representing cash.

"These cases imply that banks remain the Achilles heel in the global war on money-laundering, despite the reams of regulations aimed at turning them into frontline soldiers in that conflict. However, closer examination suggests that the global anti-money-laundering system has serious structural flaws, largely because governments have outsourced to the private sector much of the policing they should have been doing themselves."

A study published by Ronald Pol, a financial-crime expert (reported by the *Economist*, April 17, 2021), concluded that the global AML system could be "the world's least effective policy experiment" and that compliance costs for banks and other businesses could be more than one hundred times higher than the amount of money laundered. Audits on financial institutions sway heavily in favor of AML, and in some countries, it links to two or more regulators. Because of this, it is not unusual for firms such as HSBC or JPMorgan Chase to have 3,000–5,000 specialists focused on fighting financial crime, and more than 20,000 overall in risk and compliance.

Maybe the effort into AML has stamped out some malicious practices, but the reality is that criminals have not even been forced to get innovative or creative about laundering money; it is not much more difficult today than it was twenty years ago to "rinse dirty money by setting up a shell company, disguising the loot flowing through it as legitimate revenue, and persuading an established bank to process it."

The numbers tell of a war being lost. *The Global Threat Assessment*, a report by John Cusack, an ex-chair of the Wolfsberg Group, estimates that $5.8 trillion worth of financial crime was perpetrated in 2018—equivalent at the time to 6.7 percent of global GDP, which is higher than previously estimated from other sources quoted in this book. But how much is intercepted by authorities remains far less than a paltry 1.1 percent.

Also, some experts are of the opinion that the success rate is even less in later years with some of the blame falling on the increase in trade-based money laundering (TBML), meaning it is legitimized by creative paperwork for cross-border trade. Marcus Pleyer (referred to below) reported in December 2020 that creative work includes multiple invoicing of foodstuffs such as highly perishable goods, which are ripe for multiple invoicing.

Some examples include a professional money-laundering network that uses food import/export companies to clean a drug cartel's dirty money as the money launderers could ship fewer goods than stated in a contract or they could price the goods above their market value, or they do not send the goods at all but supply invoices. A popular variation is overpaying massively for a product by providing a falsified invoice. These may be a little easier to detect, but as soon as shell companies and third-party bank accounts are used, it becomes much more complex to detect until a full investigation is undertaken by the experienced. It is clear from this that professional money launderers use international trade to disguise dirty money. This fuels corruption and terrorism and hampers competition.

A concrete example referenced in the report suggests that one criminal network—just one—using trade-based money laundering and other techniques, was able to move US$400 million over several years.

Shell shock

Marcus Pleyer of Germany assumed the position of president of FATF on July 1, 2020, and during his term of office accused most countries of failing to tackle money laundering. Some countries have been able to achieve solid marks in the organization's assessments "by passing nice-looking AML laws, only to water them down later or fail to implement key provisions."

Global efforts to stamp out money laundering have waned, if anything, over the past five years, says Robert Barrington of the University of Sussex. He reported that in 2016, David Cameron, Britain's then prime minister, hosted a global anticorruption summit, and other governments queued up to back the cause. But it proved a false dawn. Britain became distracted by Brexit. In America, President Donald Trump showed scant leadership on the issue. China and Russia have stymied attempts to coordinate action against corruption.

To carry out the AML regulatory requirements, financial institutions and investigative authorities are hampered by issues related to transparency, especially related to business ownership, a lack of collaboration, and a lack of resources.

Investigators struggle to identify the beneficial owners of shell companies, who hide behind legal shell companies and nominees. There have been moves to build public registers of company owners. Britain launched one in 2016, and its offshore satellites, such as the British Virgin Islands and Jersey, have been compelled to set up registers or strengthen existing ones. America recently passed a law requiring ownership data on firms registered at state level, including in Delaware's incorporation factories, to be held in a federal register.

According to https://researchbriefings.files.parliament.uk/documents/CBP-8259/CBP-8259.pdf, an analysis of EU member state compliance with this requirement in March 2020 by Global Witness, found that seventeen of twenty-seven EU member countries still had not introduced a publicly available register of company beneficial ownership (including France and Spain), five countries had introduced such registers but with significant restrictions that hinder its usefulness (including Germany and Ireland), and only five had implemented public registers that are free to access (including Denmark).

However, many countries still eschew registers, and those that have them have already faced problems. In Britain, criminals have been willing to risk filing false information or none at all, given the modest penalties for doing so. Hong Kong, meanwhile, plans to scale back the details company owners must disclose on its register.

The FATF is seeking to toughen its standard on beneficial-ownership transparency; the current version says merely that "competent authorities" should have access to such information timeously. It is reported that getting its core members—from America and the EU to China and Russia—to agree on a new text will be difficult.

The *Economist*, April 17, 2021, indicates that while financial intelligence units do collaborate, big money-laundering schemes are so sophisticated and transnational that their efforts "remain balkanized," and the "mutual legal assistance" system, which countries investigating crimes use to request information from each other, is "clunky."

As for data flowing to and from banks, the benefits of sharing are indisputable. "The value of information coming from a network of banks is thousands of times higher than the information any one bank has, because you can see not just where the money came from, but where it went, and where it went from there, and so on," says the head of a large international bank. But in this context, the level of collaboration is "terrible." America does best, thanks to the Patriot Act, but even their information-sharing is "on a tiny scale." Anything more requires a warrant from a judge, "which is hard if you don't know what the crime is yet." Britain is in second place, he says, with "about 30 percent" of the data-sharing done in America. And in third place? "No one."

A daunting obstacle to sharing information is data-privacy laws, which in many places prevent banks from passing information to authorities, particularly foreign ones. Some big banks have lobbied for exceptions to be made for AML, but governments, it is retorted by one bank, don't see it as a legislative priority.

Another difficulty, which is a dearth of resources, stems from the white-collar crime, which is less visible than violent crime. Spending on curbing the latter goes down better with the public. In Britain, fraud makes up more than a third of reported crime yet gets less than 1 percent of police resources in terms of officers. Banks can spend all they like on AML, but the criminals won't end up in court if governments fail to invest in policing and prosecution.

Red-Tape Revolution

If the AML system is to be fit for purpose, then governments must work harder together. "Blaming banks for not properly implementing [AML] laws is a convenient fiction. Mr. Pol's report (as referred to earlier) also gives an unfair pass to the nonbank actors that enable corruption. "While fines for banks with poor AML controls have risen relentlessly, lawyers who set up dodgy shell companies, accountants who sign off on their fishy filings, and the like have been getting away with slaps on the wrist. Britain's revenues and customs agency, for instance, supervises more than 30,000 accountants, estate agents, and other businesses for money-laundering purposes; in the 2019–20 financial year, it issued just thirty-one fines, averaging £290,000. Governments also need to get to grips with the AML implications of cryptocurrencies and the firms and exchanges that hawk them."

The Cleaning Of Criminals' Money

The whole point of AML legislation is that banks should not have been used as anchorages to hold illegally earned money for criminals, and then, when the money was withdrawn, it was used for legitimate purposes.

An article by Prof. Prem Sikka (professor of accounting at the University of Sheffield), "We must stop British banks from cleaning criminals' money," in Left Foot Forward, initially written on April 9, 2019 and updated on September 24, 2020, is recounted by me. Although the article refers only to British banks, I have generalized this by referring to all banks (especially big banks) around the world because this is relevant to my misgivings about the anti-money-laundering initiatives we implement in banks.

For some fifty years, financial institutions have been the epicenter of global corruption and fraud. There are many examples, such as rigged interest rates (the Libor scandal of 2012), facilitating tax evasion, and mis-sold financial products.

Banks have rigged interest rates and exchange rates. They have engaged in fraud, tax avoidance, money laundering, and mis-sold numerous financial products.

Despite the billions of dollars in fines in 2019 charged to financial institutions for noncompliance, it has not checked their bad behavior and nefarious deeds.

At the time of writing this article, the number of suspicious activity reports filed by banks in the United States with FinCEN, namely 2,100 indicate that more than $2 trillion of potentially corrupt transactions passed through the books of global banks, already named many times aiding and abetting money laundering.

The money was moved through shell companies, often registered in secretive offshore tax havens. Entities registered in the US, Cyprus, Hong Kong, the United Arab Emirates, Russia, and Switzerland were also used. The FinCEN leaks refer to the UK as a higher-risk jurisdiction because it included the names of over 3,000 UK-registered companies, more than any other country reported.

Despite the requirements of banks to extensively check customers before onboarding them or performing even a single transaction, the International Consortium of Investigative Journalists' analysis of the FinCEN files proved that companies were registered in offshore jurisdictions and did so without knowing who the ultimate owner of the account was.

HSBC is a good example of a bank not learning any lessons from past misdemeanors. In 2012, a US Senate Committee report identified numerous anti-money-laundering failures by HSBC and its subsidiaries, including a failure to monitor $60 trillion in wire transfers and account activity, which HSBC was fined $1.9 billion for. Included in the fine was proof that the bank had facilitated narcotics traffickers to launder hundreds of millions of dollars through its subsidiaries and sanctioned countries.

As part of a deferred prosecution agreement so that the bank did not lose its license, HSBC admitted to charges. This resulted, instead, in a five-year probation under the supervision of New York state financial crimes prosecutor Michael Cherkasky.

HSBC has its headquarters in the UK, so it was surprising that the UK did not mount an inquiry. It is revealed in the article that the then-chancellor George Osborne secretly wrote to the US authorities and urged them not to prosecute HSBC as the bank was too big to fail.

Even after the scrutiny of the FinCEN links, the silence of the regulators and protection from politicians erodes incentives to curb antisocial practices. After scrutiny of the FinCEN leaks, the investigative journalists alleged that HSBC continued the same trajectory of improper and devious transactions even while under probation.

Obviously, it should not be forgotten that all of the above cannot be possible without the cooperation of lawyers, accountants, and financial experts.

Banks have little, if any, economic incentive to behave honorably. Profits from illicit practices boost the share price, dividends, and executive pay. Fines become part of business costs and are passed on to customers at higher charges. This article contends that if banks fall on tough times, central banks bail them out (prevalent during the 2008 financial crises). Seldom do directors bear any personal cost, and shareholders remain happy as a result.

Substantial amounts of money are moved usually without much ado (unless not permitted by exchange control regulations which most countries do not have).

Professor Sikka believes the "too big to fail" syndrome needs to be tackled by breaking up banks so that the closure of corrupt institutions causes less economic turbulence. Directors of such institutions need to be prosecuted and held personally accountable. Big banks are probably well beyond this point. It is true that a big bank cannot afford to fail because of the effect it could have on one or more economies. They know that only too well; fines do not seem to dampen their performance or their spirit.

It is mooted that "too many regulators sympathize with the industry instead of protecting the people." To check this cognitive capture, regulators need to be overseen by a supervisory board consisting of diverse stakeholders.

"The UK has twenty-five overlapping anti-money-laundering regulators, which include trade associations representing accountants, lawyers, and financial experts. This needs to be replaced by a single independent body with some teeth."

When questioned by the BBC about its alleged money laundering failures, HSBC said, "Starting in 2012, HSBC embarked on a multiyear journey to overhaul its ability to combat financial crime across more than sixty jurisdictions . . . HSBC is a much safer institution than it was in 2012."

Sadly, the *Guardian*, July 21, 2021, reported the following: "HSBC discovered a suspected money-laundering network that received $4.2 billion (£3 billion) worth of payments, it has emerged, raising questions over whether it disclosed the information to US monitors who at the time were ensuring the bank cleaned up its act."

Money laundering just carries on.

CHAPTER 10

The Legalizing of
Money Laundering

BELOW ARE ALL the ways in which we legalize money laundering. That is why it is so pervasive and relatively easy for the rich and powerful to do so.

Corporate Governance Loses to Profits

Those who have been in business for the last three decades will know that the objective of companies was to make a profit and to keep shareholders happy.

Things are different today. In the last few years, an understanding of ethics and good corporate governance have dominated corporate corridors and pushed at the job descriptions of compliance officers and risk officers and introduced ethics and governance departments and officers. Larger companies specifically disavow the view of profit as a business's only responsibility and use their money and influence to back movements pushing for racial and gender equality, giving more than legally required toward social responsibility (usually including volunteers from their own employees), addressing climate change, or even taking overtly political positions. Just as important is the inclusion of all stakeholders; not just with the focus on customers, but also on suppliers, partners, their own employees, and affected communities.

Is it that sweet?

In an article written by Andrew Ross Sorkin for the *New York Times* (September 13, 2020), Sorkin says, "There remains an inconvenient truth for everyone seeking a cuddlier version of capitalism: If a company isn't making profits for shareholders, it is very hard to take care of its other constituents. Profits and growth must come first." But it is something "that in this age of heightened scrutiny, many CEOs are reluctant to say out loud."

The *Harvard Business Review* provided a discussion document, "Big Ideas and Debates in Corporate Governance" (October 14, 2019), written by Lynn S. Paine (Baker Foundation professor, John G. McLean Professor of Business Administration Emerita, and senior associate dean for International Development at Harvard Business School) and Suraj Srinivasan (Philip J. Stemberg, Professor of Business Administration at Harvard Business School).

It indicates that some authorities give primacy to shareholders' interest in maximizing their financial returns and others argue that shareholders' other interests—in corporate strategy, executive compensation, and environmental policies, for example—and the interests of other parties, must be respected as well.

"These debates have taken on a new intensity in the face of changing capital markets and mega-forces such as climate change, income inequality, digitalization, and rising populism sweeping the globe."

There are many governance codes out there such as the New Paradigm, the Common Sense Principles, the King IV Report, and the 2018 UK Corporate Governance Code, which indicate followers for the conventional practices and followers of other efforts to align their activities with society's interest in building a more inclusive, equitable, and sustainable economy.

"Overall, the rise of ownership concentration, greater shareholder engagement, and hedge-fund activism point to an era of greater shareholder influence over companies. These developments raise questions about the accountability of shareholders, particularly those who seek to influence corporate actions, and about the prevalent model of shareholder value maximization as the goal of good corporate governance."

Since the 1990s, the powers and rights of shareholders have increased considerably in many countries. The questions the authors pose are just how much power should be in the hands of shareholders, how that power would be shared among the different types of shareholders, and how companies should decide what a reasonable balance of power is among shareholders, boards, and management.

Corporations are more complex than they have ever been. The structure and leadership of boards, like the processes for selecting their members, vary widely by law and custom across jurisdictions. This brings about questions in terms of understanding corporate governance: how can transparency and reporting be enhanced without compromising competitively valuable information or creating unfairness in the market?

Research has been done in different parts of the world on the relationship between profit and governance, but the results have been mixed and inconclusive. There is skepticism on my part, despite surveys that may indicate that investors, customers, analysts, and climate activists want and appreciate good governance and are willing to pay for it, that such surveys are seldom an accurate reflection of the board and senior executive members. My skepticism is based on experience. Delving deeper into survey feedback using one-on-one interviews or small group workshops paints a vastly different picture of corporate governance and ethics in the workplace.

DAWN PRETORIUS

Some big companies have fallen from grace—ostensibly from failure in corporate governance; sometimes, it is blatant dishonesty and downright criminality. Corporate governance is about a vision, values, frameworks, and policies, all easily framed in beautiful language but not easily implemented, tangible, or even understood by those who work for these companies. Simplistically, corporate governance is about doing the right thing. The difficulty in this complex world of ours is, what is the right thing?

Intouchnetworks.com, on July 22, 2020, "Businesses Behaving Badly," gave one example—that of Volkswagen. In September 2015, a paper referred to as the "diesel dupe" was published by the Environmental Protection Agency, which revealed that many models of Volkswagen cars that were being sold in the United States contained a "defeat device." This device had been specially installed to detect when a car was being evaluated for emissions. This clever device is designed to change a car's performance to improve its emissions results when undergoing emission tests. When this was discovered, the German car giant admitted to cheating on its emissions tests in the US. Obviously Volkswagen had to pay a fine of $18 billion to the Environmental Protection Agency. This is not failed governance; this is criminal intent.

One of the top corporate scandals in 2018 was the collapse of Carillion, reported by the *Financial Director* on March 19, 2019.

Carillion was a British multinational facilities management and construction giant and the United Kingdom's second-largest building and outsourcing provider prior to its fall (since liquidated). It was listed on the FTSE 250, had earned an annual £5 billion worth in revenues, and employed 43,000 workers across the world. The article titled "Not too big to fail" indicates that "unfortunately, things looked a lot healthier for the construction giant from the outside looking in."

The UK's Financial Reporting Council had raised concerns about the future of the company as early as 2015. Banks saw warning signs, and investors were warned too, but big tenders continued to go to Carillion, despite accounting delays, profit warnings, write-downs, a share price drop of 39 percent, and the loss of its CEO. "On January 15, 2018, Carillion was pushed into compulsory liquidation—by which time the company had racked up debts of £1.5 billion with less than £30 million left in the bank."

The board obviously did not manage the company's risk adequately, but why? It was not about having no skills; it was about managing a razor-thin risk-reward equation because the company continued to take on high debt while trading on low margins. The article goes on to say, "In terms of viability, authorities have since particularly called into question the company's stress-testing procedures of cash flows to demonstrate viability.

"More crucial was the board's insufficient handling of annual reporting and accounts—including revenue recognition on significant contracts, the massive carrying value of goodwill and alternative performance measures."

Are these examples of failed governance (which is the role of oversight in doing the right thing) or a deliberate attempt to con the stakeholders while they took risks to get the company back on track? And what was their real purpose of profitability?

One of South Africa's top companies on its stock exchange was Steinhoff (Steinhoff International Holdings NV). Although incorporated in the Netherlands, the company's head office is in South Africa. With the resignation of its CEO Markus Jooste, the failure of the company was cemented. He admitted that some mistakes were made. That was a euphemistic rendition of reality when it became clear that the company's external auditors were not prepared to sign off the 2017 annual financial statements. These shenanigans had been performed for many years; why did previous auditors not recognize what was happening?

Despite the information on ethics and corporate governance and the adoption of corporate governance frameworks by corporations, how much of an effect does it really have? Profits are seldom, if ever, invested in society unless a percentage is mandated by company law for social responsibility purposes.

In the *Harvard Business Review*, I was pleased to see King IV (fourth version) Code on corporate governance highlighted. It was drafted in South Africa by a retired judge of the (previous) Supreme Court of South Africa, Mervyn E. King. This code is applicable to all entities including all nonprofit and government institutions. A code is not law; it is a statement of what should be done, and King IV is an "apply and explain" document, meaning that King IV

> encourages organizations to move beyond compliance to crafting actions that are appropriate to the organizations' context, and which will move them closer to achieving the goals enshrined in its seventeen principles. In so doing, King IV is helping organizations realize the benefits of corporate governance. (Institute of Directors, February 2019: *Why King IV's "apply and explain" is so important*)

It is a good document; it is a wise document. But does it change the behavior of a board of directors? This code (which includes all juristic entities including government and nonprofit institutions) is considered one of the best in the world. Sadly, its efficacy is questionable, especially in the hands of the ruling ANC government institutions. Imagine a scenario in the boardroom:

would somebody say, "Stop! This is not ethical. This goes against the King Code. Do we need to admit failure?"

When there is intent to hide what is really happening in a company or making a profit even though it compromises the ethics of a company, corporate governance is easily pushed aside. Even for concerned employees, whistleblowing is a risky thing; turning a blind eye is simpler (*maybe I will get a piece of the pie*). Sadly, corporate governance is just one more tool ineffective against the laundering of money.

> A plethora of corporate governance codes have been written across the world, and in spite of their recommendations which inter alia seek to protect stakeholder interests and shareholder value, many governance failures and organisational collapses continue seemingly unabated. To use the Eskom debacle in South Africa as a recent example; notwithstanding their public claims of being compliant with numerous legislation—including the provisions of the King Code for Corporate Governance for South Africa, 2016 ("King IV")—it is alarming that this organisation is ostensibly at polar opposite sides to good governance. Despite scooping a number of awards for its annual integrated reporting in 2015, the ongoing revelations of poor governance at the organisation appear to indicate that the information disclosed in its annual report was either misleading, inaccurate, or incomplete. It has become clear that the integrity of the organisation's external reporting cannot be relied on by stakeholders. In the absence of accountability, this situation is unlikely to improve.

(August 5, 2019, CGF Research Institute Pty. Ltd., Johannesburg)

The Wicked Web Of Company Structures

It is a known fact that companies and trusts (and similar structures) are misused globally for money laundering.

There is insufficient evidence to quantify the exact extent of money laundering through corporate structures, partnerships, and trusts. A few countries have been implementing a series of reforms to increase the transparency of incorporated legal persons and arrangements and to prevent their misuse for illicit purposes. These reforms include, but are not limited to, the introduction of publicly accessible registers, e.g., in the UK known as the PSC (People with Significant Control) register; the abolition of bearer shares, the introduction of a register of trusts with tax consequences, and the introduction of Unexplained Wealth Orders. Vulnerabilities "include the ability for criminals to create complex and opaque structures, comprising multiple legal entities and arrangements across multiple jurisdictions, which can be used to obscure who really owns and controls assets. Companies, partnerships, and trusts can be set up and dissolved with relative ease and low cost and used to transfer large sums of money at less risk of detection from law enforcement or the regulated sector" (National Risk Assessment UK 2015).

Corporate structures are created by criminals or on their behalf, whether locally or overseas, frequently using the services of regulated professionals, with the intention of subsequently using the structure to hide wealth or enable money laundering. The incorporation of the company may be done in a way that conforms to the applicable legal requirements and minimizes suspicion. In general, companies and partnerships are particularly attractive to criminals because of their separate legal personalities, the relative ease and low cost with which they can be incorporated and dissolved (intended to fulfill the needs of a wide range of legitimate businesses), and the ability to use business accounts to merge legitimate and illegitimate funds.

An interesting example was given in *Capitalism and Greed* (Tim Wu's book *The Curse of Bigness: Antitrust in the New Gilded Age*, 2018): "An investigative report into high-end real estate purchases in Canada gives valuable insight into money-laundering activities. The 'No Reason to Hide' report reveals that 50 percent of the high-value property purchased had no transparency regarding ownership. Holding companies (or unlikely nominees) owned the property, including students and homemakers. Further investigations traced many of the purchases to China and criminal gangs operating out of Guangdong province. The gangs were shipping various narcotics into Canada and were using high-end property purchases to 'clean' their money. Although many trusts and shell companies are operating within the law, their anonymity is attractive to criminals seeking to launder the proceeds of crime."

The *Times* UK reported that Britain is one of the easiest places in the world to set up a new company. Because of that, it has led to an "explosion of start-ups," as well as an escalation in ghost companies used to move cash and avoid tax. Almost 3,000 companies listed their beneficial owners as a company in a tax haven in 2018, according to the campaign group Global Witness.

Many of these features are common to companies and company incorporation systems around the world. The fact that companies or partnerships can easily be terminated is attractive to criminals and money launderers. The other attractive option to them is the set-up sequences of limited companies for illicit purposes, then winding them down before being required to submit accounts (this is known as phoenix companies). The Australian Securities and Investment Commission describes that illegal phoenix activity occurs when a new company, for little or no value, continues the business of an existing company that has been liquidated or otherwise abandoned to avoid paying outstanding debts, which can include taxes, creditors, and employee entitlements. Also, financial centers allow complex and layered ownership structures to be created quickly, for little cost and minimal requirements of transparency. Money flows therefore become difficult to trace, depending on where these phoenix companies are registered; some jurisdictions do not need the identity of officers and directors, nor do they need to appoint a locally resident director.

Some new regulations in different parts of the world have created an inconsistency in this regard. Although the requirement for identification and verification has intensified, access to information is still limited, and "legal concealment strategies are multilayered and complex. Indeed, beneficial ownership and UBO (ultimate beneficial owner)* rely heavily on customer self-certification, as well as information held in company registries and financial institutions, trusts, regulatory bodies, or authorities" (Dun and Bradstreet: *Understanding Beneficial Ownership*, 2017).

According to the World Bank, even when public registries do exist, such as the UK's Persons of Significant Control register, detailed information on UBO is very rarely included because it is not mandatory. Despite the efforts by governments and regulators to increase transparency and disclosure, information on the UBO of offshore corporate vehicles will not be included in anti-money-laundering/terrorism funding central registries.

However the explanations of complex legal structures are described, the challenge is to identify them. The unraveling of these structures, which are specifically designed to conceal the desired information, takes time, knowledge, and patience. In the AML space, there is still confusion over the many varied definitions of beneficial ownership; there is a lack of ownership registries, and accurate ones at that. There are many hurdles attached to getting cooperation from the companies, and finally, there is what in the industry is indicated as disclosure fatigue.

*An ultimate beneficial owner is defined as the natural person(s) who ultimately owns or controls a customer and/or the natural person on whose behalf a transaction is being conducted. It also includes those persons who exercise ultimate effective control over a legal person or arrangement. The article goes on to say that it becomes more complex when ownership is obscured by layers of indirect ownership. Convoluted ownership structures are considered high-risk in terms of trying to determine ultimate beneficial ownership just because the identification calls for greater scrutiny to be carried out by compliance. Greater scrutiny, and the time taken to undertake such scrutiny, does not necessarily result in a satisfactory outcome.

The United States has drafted a new act called the Corporate Transparency Act to take effect in 2022/2023. This means that US companies will have to report their UBO information to the Financial Crimes Enforcement Network (FinCEN). The information is quite simple: full legal name of the beneficial owner, date of birth, residential or business address, and proof of identity.

There are buts: But the registry will not be publicly available, only to law enforcement or financial institutions with customers' consent. But not all companies will be required to report their UBO information to FinCEN, and exemptions include companies with more than twenty employees and gross receipts or sales of more than $5 million; a physical presence in the US; reporting companies like banks, credit unions, and registered brokers or dealers, dormant companies and unregistered foreign entities (i.e. not registered with a state). But the FATF notes that it is up to the registry to actively verify and monitor the UBO information for this approach to be successful. But how will the act deal with trusts, estates, and other complex financial structures?

While passing the law is an essential first step, the details of the regulations to come and how FinCEN operates the registry will tell how successful the Corporate Transparency Act is. FinCEN issued an advance notice of proposed rulemaking to gather feedback before giving final rules.

An article (Trulioo, October 13, 2021) says that some of the questions are potential game-changers. "For example, the definition of beneficial ownership; should it be the same as has been used previously under customer due diligence requirements? Does the definition of 'own' and 'control' need to be precisely defined? And should substantial control be limited to one beneficial owner?"

The article goes on to question what precise information is needed when undertaking regulatory reporting about a company's corporate affiliates, parents, and subsidiaries. How will it be reported in the first place, and in the second place, how are companies going to provide helpful information to regulators at minimal cost?

Convoluted corporate structures (especially ones with lots of money) are deliberately designed to confuse inquirers, investigators, and the tax authorities and will seek the assistance of highly paid and, therefore, highly motivated lawyers, accountants, and auditors to circumvent complex tax laws both domestically and internationally.

Below are a few randomly chosen links to examples of company structures taken from the Internet. They are so convoluted that one image cannot provide the detail but just the overview of the complexity. (The detail is not needed to make my point.)

The first image is that of Samsung's corporate structure (2014), followed by Trump's business interests, Jeff Bezos's empire Amazon, and the last example is Naspers Limited, a multinational consumer

Internet company headquartered in South Africa. Naspers's principal operations include online classified advertising, fintech, payments, and food delivery. Naspers owns, or has controlling interests in, various businesses, including Prosus, Media24, and Takealot. As of 2018, Naspers has a 31 percent stake in Tencent, becoming its largest shareholder, and Africa's biggest public company. In recent years, Naspers has continued to build substantial holdings in consumer internet companies around the world, with a particular focus on India.

The web of Trump business interests

Visual by The Washington Post from Trump's 2018 financial disclosure.

● OWNERSHIP INCLUDES A TRUMP ORGANIZATION   ● NO IDENTIFIED TRUMP ORGANIZATIONAL OWNER

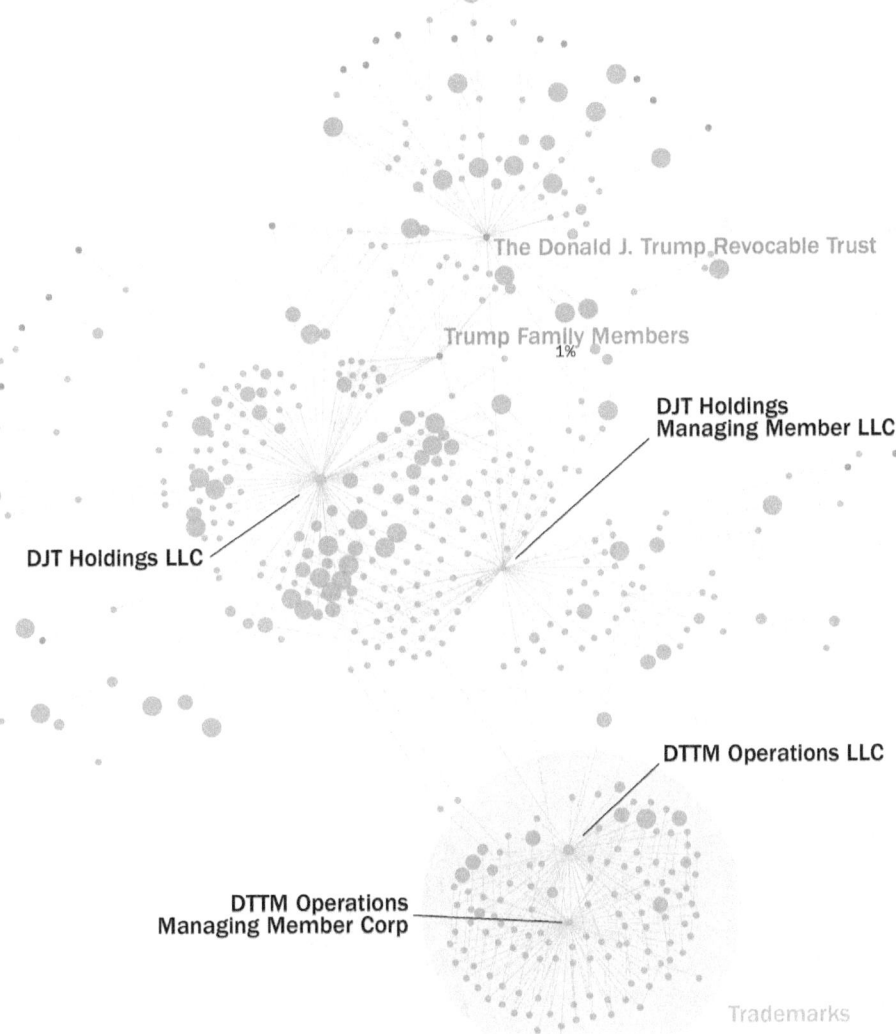

The Donald J. Trump Revocable Trust

Trump Family Members
1%

DJT Holdings
Managing Member LLC

DJT Holdings LLC

DTTM Operations LLC

DTTM Operations
Managing Member Corp

Trademarks

THE BEZOS EMPIRE

Acquisitions

Investments

BLUE ORIGIN

The Washington Post
Nash Holdings LLC

*Denotes successful IPO exit
†Sold to Google

BEZOS
EXPEDITIONS

NASPERS CONTROL STRUCTURE

Based on Naspers 2016 Annual Financial Statements and on historic share registers of Nasbel and Keerom

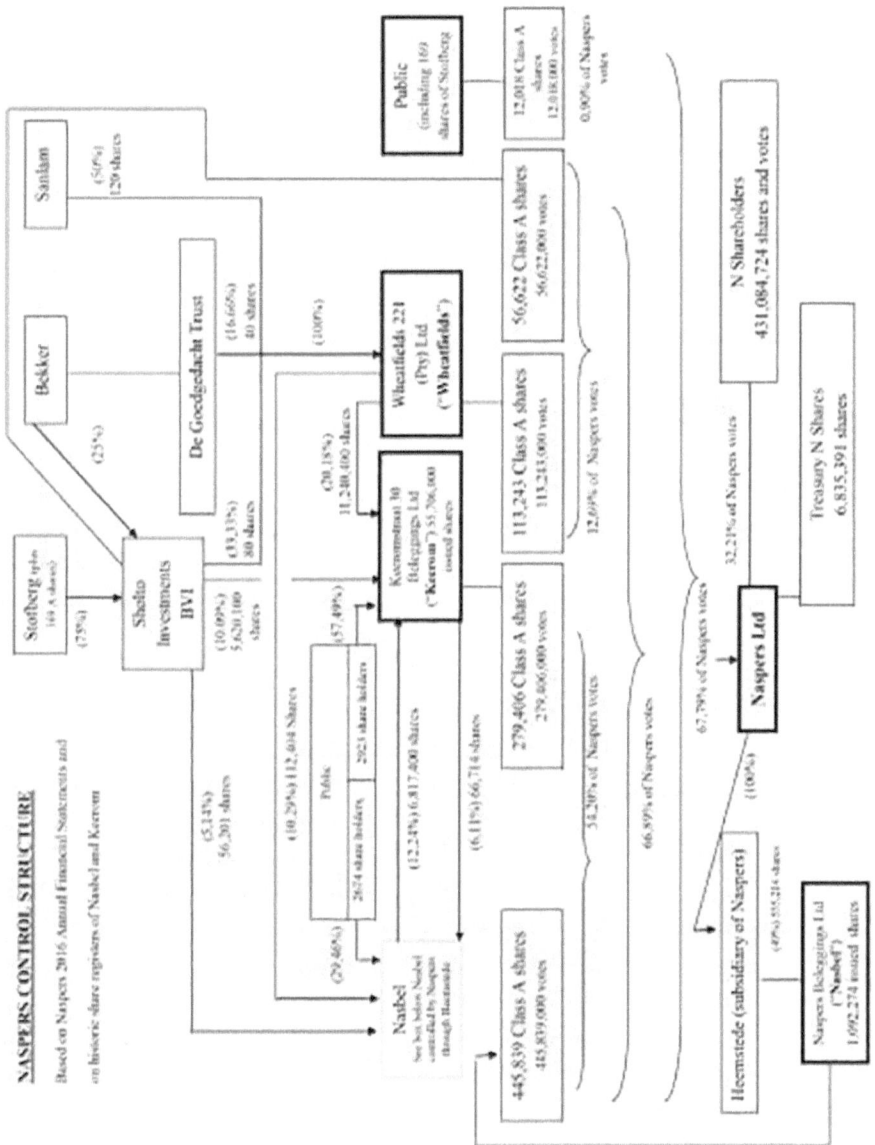

Figure 8: Samsung group ownership structure

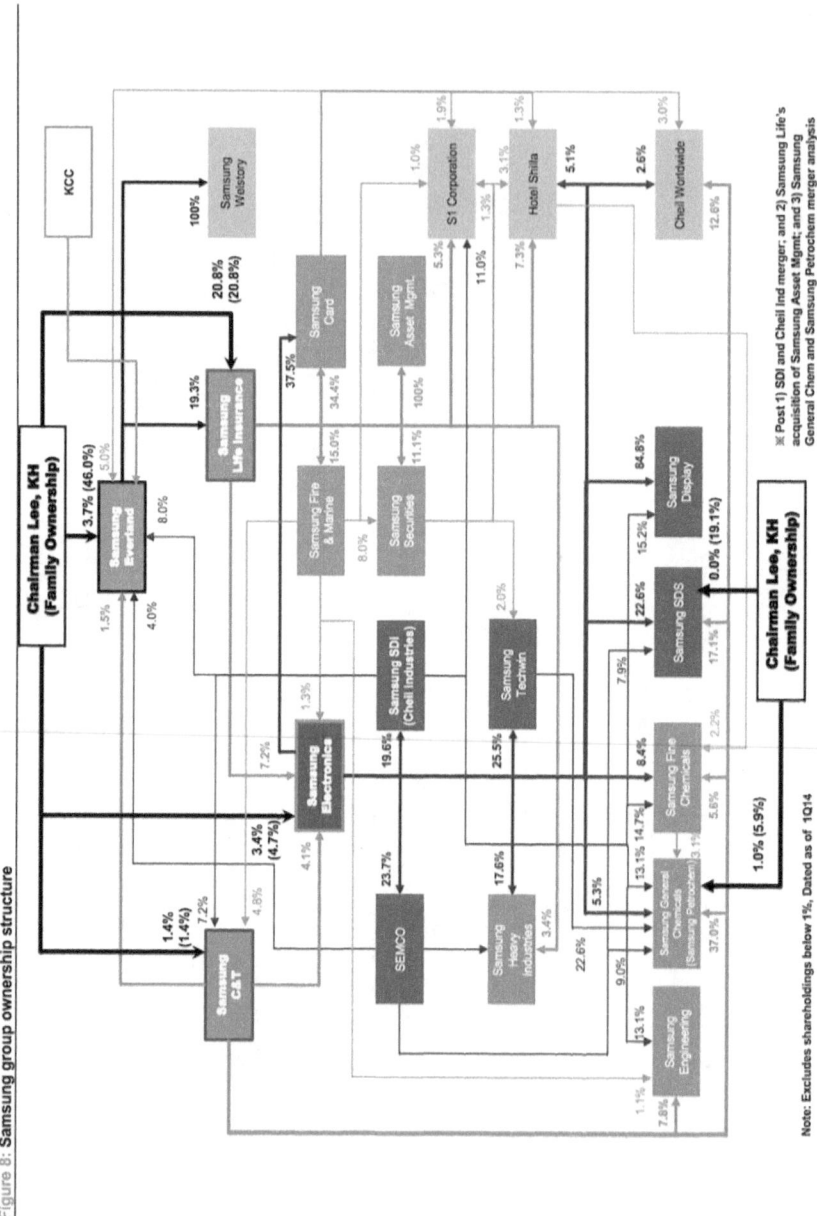

Note: Excludes shareholdings below 1%, Dated as of 1Q14

※ Post 1) SDI and Cheil Ind merger; and 2) Samsung Life's acquisition of Samsung Asset Mgmt; and 3) Samsung General Chem and Samsung Petrochem merger analysis

These corporate structure vehicles exist to enable organizations to create a loop in which they own holdings of other companies in the same loop, as well as potentially shares in themselves and sometimes legitimately benefit from various tax loopholes or incentives.

Getting to the details is not straightforward. Dun and Bradstreet say that "typically, it can take days to manually identify attributes (confirming self-certified information such as company name, address, registration details), verify those attributes (such as ownership levels and financial reports), and if deemed necessary, conduct enhanced due diligence. To calculate ultimate beneficial ownership, compliance teams often working in silos and—in different jurisdictions—must rely on multiple reports and spreadsheets, as well as a range of online business information reports. These reports are inflexible, potentially inaccurate, and do not necessarily integrate with other systems and data sources. And of course, the structure can shift quickly, with small changes in one part affecting the whole."

Why, when company structures grow, do they get so complicated when one company owns another company, and it spreads exponentially over many pages? Why is it necessary to have such convoluted business structures? Exactly what does it facilitate and who ultimately benefits? And if it is for tax benefits, then clearly the tax system is designed to specifically embellish the UBOs.

So that now leads me to tax issues.

Tax Tricks And Gymnastics

Warren Buffett, an American business magnate, investor, and philanthropist, famously acknowledged that he pays less tax on a percentage basis than his secretary.

The top echelon of the wealthy around the world can dodge tax for three reasons. The first reason is that tax laws in most countries around the world are designed to benefit the rich. The second reason is that the rich can employ the best tax minds to find loopholes or cleverly disguise income and capital gains. The third reason is that tax law in most countries is so complicated that very few people fully understand it, especially when it also relates to foreign investment, offshore components and entities. Following the trail of money can be daunting, time-consuming, and frustrating, and then applying all of this to one tax return makes for a huge amount of creative accounting and reporting.

There are other countries that charge no income tax, irrespective of income earned, namely Monaco, Bahamas, Andorra, Bermuda, and the United Arab Emirates. I hasten to add that no tax payable does not necessarily mean that the cost of living in relation to the country's GDP is comfortable.

Paying taxes is either source-based (where the income is sourced from) or residency-based (irrespective of where your income is earned in the world). There are, of course, various international tax agreements that are relevant when calculating tax liability, just to add another level of complexity.

It is a misnomer to say that the more money you earn and accumulate, the more taxes you pay. It is if you simply check the tax tables. But tax laws around most of the world allow for cunning and agile tax gymnastics. Some tricks are called loopholes in the law, which are termed legitimate tax avoidance, but others are termed tax evasion, which is illegitimate. The difference between the two is a fine line, mostly only known to tax magicians.

Why is tax law so complicated? The reason is to protect the rich and powerful. What other reason could there be? It certainly does not help the poor and middle class. In fact, middle-class professionals are the mainstay of the economy, and tax on a salary can be up to 45 to 50 percent. We do know that some countries offer, for example, free medical, free or limited educational fees, housing support, and so on, which, of course, also, as it happens, often benefit the wealthy.

A *CT Mirror* article published on June 12, 2021, "The secret IRS files: A trove of never-before-seen records," reveals how the wealthiest avoid income tax, based on ProPublica investigations, and makes for interesting reading. To refer to the profit saga, many big companies do not pay dividends to their shareholders, thanks to Warren Buffett and his company Berkshire. "Buffett has always argued that it is better to use that money to find investments for Berkshire that will further boost the value of shares held by him and other investors. If Berkshire had offered anywhere close to the average dividend in recent years, Buffett would have received over $1 billion in dividend income and owed hundreds of millions in taxes each year." Many Silicon Valley and infotech companies have emulated Buffett's model. Companies like Microsoft and Oracle offered shareholders in earlier years, rocketing growth and profits, but did not pay dividends. Google, Facebook, Amazon, and Tesla do not pay dividends.

The article goes on to ask, "So how do mega billionaires pay their mega bills while opting for $1 salaries and hanging on to their stock? According to public documents and experts, the answer for some is borrowing money—lots of it . . . for the ultrawealthy, it can be a way to access billions without producing income, and thus, income tax."

The article provides the math behind this statement, and for the wealthy to cough up collateral is no problem. An example is given of Tesla reporting that Elon Musk pledged in 2020 some ninety-two million shares, which were worth about $57.7 billion as of May 29, 2021, as collateral for personal loans. Between the years 2014 and 2018, the article reveals Elon's true tax rate was 3.27 percent.

It also continues with the fact that corporate taxes have fallen in recent decades, resulting in widespread corporate tax avoidance. Companies like Google, Facebook, Microsoft, and Apple have paid little or no United States corporate tax because they send their earnings abroad.

The bottom line is that the very wealthy have a number of tax avoidance options, which include estate planning and using obscure and complicated trust structures to pass the maximum on to their heirs. Nearly a quarter of the top richest Americans have inherited their fortunes in this way.

It is an argument to bring in the charitable donations that the rich may pay out; it is another argument to say that if the Internal Revenue Service had been paid more taxes, it would not be a necessity. It also gives the donating company, aside from tax write-offs, marketing kudos.

The pandemic is purported to have been a rewarding couple of years for billionaires. According to *Forbes*, billionaires accumulated a further $1.2 trillion to their fortunes from January 2020 to the end of April 2021.

"That windfall is among the many factors that have led the country to an inflection point, one that traces back to a half century of growing wealth inequality and the financial crisis of 2008, which left many with lasting economic damage. American history is rich with such turns. There have been famous acts of tax resistance, like the Boston Tea Party, countered by less well-known efforts to have the rich pay more."

The above is a sample of wealth and taxes in America. But other examples around the world also qualify for tax tricks.

There exists the Tax Justice Network, and the following is taken from their website.

The Tax Justice Network on its website https://taxjustice.net (Let's Take Back Control of Our Tax Systems) "believes our tax and financial systems are our most powerful tools for creating a just society that gives equal weight to the needs of everyone. But under pressure from corporate giants and the super-rich, our governments have programmed these systems to prioritize the wealthiest over everybody else, wiring financial secrecy and tax havens into the core of our global economy. This fuels inequality, fosters corruption, and undermines democracy. We work to repair these injustices by inspiring and equipping people and governments to reprogram their tax and financial systems."

An article on March 9, 2021, by the Tax Justice Network titled "Tax haven ranking shows countries setting global tax rules do most to help firms bend them" makes for a fascinating read. It provides for the top ten greatest enablers of corporate tax abuse risks.

A report produced in 2021 by the United Nations' High-Level Panel on International Financial Accountability, Transparency, and Integrity (FACTI) calls for a fundamental overhaul of the global architecture around tax and financial transparency to address these global inequalities in taxing rights between countries because there are countries where companies and individuals go to avoid paying tax. Business Tech, in their article on exactly that dated March 13, 2021, explains that the Corporate Tax Haven Index for 2021 shows countries that are the most complicit in helping multinational corporations underpay corporate income tax and reflects the ease with which tax laws around the world can be abused or misused. The index measures against twenty defined indicators how much scope for corporate tax abuse the jurisdiction's tax and financial systems allow and how much financial activity from multinational corporations the jurisdiction hosts.

For example, a territory like the Bahamas has a high tax haven score (100—the top of the scale), but only accounts for 0.31 percent of global foreign investment flows, so it ranks 12th in the list of biggest tax havens. The Netherlands, meanwhile, has a lower tax haven score (80), but has 11 percent of all foreign investment flows, placing it higher, at 4th. The British Virgin Islands emerged as the biggest tax haven in the world; it does not impose any corporate income tax, making the assessed indicators obsolete, so it is obviously attractive to corporations and accounts for 2.3 percent of all foreign direct investment.

Theconversation.com (October 3, 2019) published "How multinationals continue to avoid paying hundreds of billions of dollars in tax"—as the authors' research reveals. They found that "countries with a higher share of FDI [foreign direct investment] from tax havens report profits that are systematically and significantly lower, suggesting these profits have been shifted to tax havens before being reported in high-tax countries." This, they say, equates to about US$125 billion in lost tax revenue for some seventy-nine countries researched. As a result, government services are underfunded or have to be funded in some other way. Often, however, that simply means the burden falls on lower-income taxpayers. This is a significant contributing factor to rising inequality in most countries around the world.

Although the focus is on companies here, many of the world's wealthiest individuals are rich because of inheriting money or benefitting from corporate success. The Panama and Pandora Papers, touched on in chapter 2, highlighted the fact that individuals with the means to do so actively seek to seriously minimize their tax liability, and therefore, whether it is tax avoidance or tax evasion is of little consequence. The less they understand how it is done, the better.

In most countries, the evasion of tax is a money-laundering offense. There is no doubt that "this fuels inequality, fosters corruption, and undermines democracy." If we want to combat inequality and minimize the laundering of money, bringing about global tax cohesion is a necessity.

The *American Prospect*, October 12, 2021: "Rich Folks' Tax Dodging": The Biden administration has its own calculation. The four hundred richest families only paid an average of 8.2 percent of their income over a period of eight tax years. The administration economists included in their calculations the unrealized capital gains (in run-up in stocks they owned) for each year. The reason for this calculation is that monitors such as *Forbes* and *Fortune* chiefly measure the value of the billionaires' stockholdings. It follows therefore that if the conventional measurement of wealth was calculated that way, then surely their income should be calculated that way too.

An article in *Time*, "The World at a Crossroads: How a New Deal for Global Taxation Might Save Democracy on August 11, 2021, by Malcolm Turnbull, who served as the twenty-ninth prime minister of Australia from 2015 to 2018, has the following to say: "Every year, multinational corporations divert some $1.38 trillion in profits away from the countries where they were made to places with much lower, or even zero, corporate tax rates. And while much of this is strictly legal, that doesn't make it right."

He contends that the combination of complex tax laws and outdated global rules for large multinationals and wealthy individuals means that tax is, as a result, optional because of the money that they can invest in the skills of accountants and lawyers. This has a negative effect on national budgets, creates resentment, and stokes right-wing populism that is shaking the foundations of liberal democracy. "Nothing fuels mistrust in government, or the belief that justice and the rule of law serve only to protect the rich and powerful, more potently than wealthy corporations and individuals not paying their fair share of tax . . . after all, our tax systems were designed not just to fund government services but to redistribute wealth and income, to mitigate inequality, and to ensure a social-welfare safety net for all."

Why indeed, is tax so complicated? It is one of the most discriminatory aspects of our society. We expect everybody to pay taxes if they are earning money, and yet our tax laws are deliberately designed (I disagree with Turnbull that it is outdated global rules) and misused to service wealthy corporations and individuals. Mostly, the wealthiest countries join in on various world proposals (e.g., tax proposals by the OECD and climate change by the United Nations); they know it is going to cost them rather than benefit them (the greed thing again among the rich and powerful because they want to be seen to doing the right thing, and even if some heads of state do, it is a hard sell).

As Turnbull goes on to say, "We can debate whether tax rates should be higher or lower—but not whether taxes are optional. If everybody pays, then everybody can pay less.

"And yes, combatting populism needs more than tax reform. But we need a fair and just tax system to help defuse the gnawing sense of irreversible inequality that is enabling so many illiberal leaders. The future of our liberal democracies depends on it."

Where there is a will, there is a way. This proverb has been with us since 1640, and look where it has gotten us. We have the energy and the skills—it just must be redirected. The first move toward some modicum of fairness is the 136 countries that have agreed to enforce a corporate tax rate of at least 15 percent and a fairer system of taxing profits where they are earned (October 2021).

But it is not going to make an iota of difference to global inequality.

The Money-laundering Facilitators

To undertake these complicated company structures, find tax and other legal loopholes, design complex transaction flows, and have the gumption to do it for great sums of compensation, there are the facilitators. These are experienced lawyers, accountants, money value transfer services, trust service providers, tax advisors, dealers in precious metals/stones, and real estate professionals, to name a few.

Facilitators tend to belong to one of three categories as described by the FATF:

- individual professional money launderer (PML)—specializes in providing money-laundering services while also acting in a legitimate professional occupation
- professional money-laundering organization (PMLO)—a structured group of two or more individuals whose core activity is laundering funds
- professional money-laundering network (PMLN)—usually operates globally as a collection of associates who work together to facilitate money-laundering schemes.

The services provided may verge on legitimate avoidance initially, but with a lot of sways, greed steps in and tax evasion becomes the norm. Facilitators are usually aware that the money they move is not legitimate. Their primary concern is ensuring the proceeds reach the destination by the safest and most efficient route. With this in mind, the PML will use any number of money-laundering tools and techniques to achieve this result, such as international trade, underground banking, account settlement schemes, and cryptocurrencies. Some of the methods used include registering and maintaining juristic entities, providing false documentation, combining legal and illegal proceeds, placing and moving illicit cash, indirectly purchasing and holding assets, and orchestrating lawsuits.

The above suggests that the impact of these facilitators on global money-laundering is significant.

To do anything about the risks presented by PMLs and their networks, authorities must be able to identify who they are. The types of individuals or organizations prone to this activity are entities or individuals that can use their occupation, business infrastructure, and knowledge to facilitate money-laundering activities. Even bank employees can provide certain services to enable money laundering to go undetected, such as monitoring (or not) money flows to and from controlled accounts, coordinating financial transactions, and accepting fictitious client documentation.

The more complex and different company laws are, the more complex and different tax laws are. The more complex company structures are allowed, the longer offshore tax havens linger on hiding anonymity, and while money-laundering facilitators remain accessible, the less likely the world can address the effects of money laundering.

Auditors could be discussed in a category all of their own. There are four major companies operating in several parts of the world, namely PwC, KPMG, EY, and Deloitte. They collectively dominate 97 percent of the FTSE 350 London Stock Exchange audit market, 99.4 percent of the top five hundred publicly traded companies on the New York Stock Exchange and Nasdaq, and as an example, 96 percent of all companies listed on the Johannesburg Stock Exchange.

These firms have been the subject of a number of investigations into the quality of their audits following a series of high-profile company collapses. This prompted a review by Sir Donald Brydon, a British businessman, chairman of the Sage Group and charities Chance to Shine and the Science Museum Foundation.

"The Brydon Report: Industry reacts to findings and audit recommendations," published on December 20, 2019, by AccountancyAge.com, included comments by the auditing industry on the sixty-four recommendations made by Dr. Donald Brydon in response to the criticism of these auditing firms over several years. While his findings applied to the UK, it has resonated with other countries to look to this report for guidance. As Mark Smith, Partner for Innovation Incentives, Ayming, responded to the recommendations in the same article, "However, after a string of investigations and scandals and calls from industry bodies such as the CMA to break up this oligopoly, a perfect storm means the dominance of these are being challenged. There's a serious image problem."

As reported by Daniel Ellis, policy and public affairs manager of the Institute of Chartered Accountants for England and Wales, 2021: "Ultimately, we want to get it right—that has to be the overarching principle. And no one—government, the profession, or investors—wants to be having this debate in ten years' time. We want to get it right this time."

Worldwide, there clearly is still a long way to go for a rethink on auditing and related professional services.

The Big Four has blurred the public's trust in the auditing profession after many scandals. The *Daily Maverick* has said that they all play a systemic role in economic crimes and state capture. The evidence suggests that these firms have prioritized profit over professional duties and the law.

In Germany, the conduct of EY during the $2 billion Wirecard fraud (possibly the largest fraud in that country's history) is still under investigation and has prompted a heated debate about the need for audit reform beyond the mandatory rotation of firms, which continues to be the sole focus of the local regulatory framework.

> "They have expressed amazement at the scale of the Wirecard lobbying operation, with its network of former police chiefs, ministers, and spymasters, and at revelations that BaFin* employees traded Wirecard shares while the company was under investigation." ("Wirecard inquiry: Germany's political and financial elite exposed," April 9, 2021)

*German regulators for financial institutions

Taken from the *Daily Maverick*, February 24, 2021, "VBS liquidator looks to claw back the money by suing KPMG for R864 million."

"VBS Mutual Bank was looted into insolvency by its managers and their sidekicks, notably several politicians, auditors, and businesspeople. The fraud was made public when the South African Reserve Bank put the bank under curatorship and ordered a forensic investigation.

VBS's accounting system allowed for fictitious account entries to be shown as deposits and credits in VBS bank accounts, which specifically paved the way for its managers and their associates to steal money from VBS for themselves and to distribute looted monies to "politicians, fixers, and associates to help keep the secret." This South African bank also filed papers suing KPMG for R864 million, contending that its audit partner Sipho Malaba himself not only stole millions in benefits and cash from VBS but also lied to the Reserve Bank.

KPMG also failed in its audit of the Gupta family company, Linkway Trading. South Africa's government was, for many years, captured by the Gupta family, described as a modern-day coup d'état achieved with bribery instead of bullets. One auditor, the engagement partner for Linkway Trading, took the fall for the audit failure. Among other charges, he failed to investigate some seven unusual transactions reflected in Linkway's financial records, which included accounting records of the Gupta family wedding, which had received a lot of publicity at the time. The Waterkloof military base in Pretoria was used as a landing base for a private plane filled with guests for the wedding of the niece of the politically connected Gupta brothers at Sun City. It was supposed to have been a clandestine operation, but there was a security leak that had diplomatic repercussions and questions asked of President Jacob Zuma's administration. The auditor furthermore restated certain costs related to the wedding as an unspecified tax-deductible, which it was not. This violated the independent Regulatory Board for Auditors in the Auditor's Money Laundering Guide. The Guptas have a convoluted string of businesses; Linkway Trading formed part of a group of companies called the Island Site Group, most of which were also audited by KPMG.

As of June 6, 2022, the Guptas have been arrested in the United Arab Emirates. At this stage, it is unclear whether they will face charges in South Africa. BBC.com reports that the two brothers Atul and Rajesh also face accusations of money laundering in India, where tax officials raided properties belonging to them in 2018 in multiple cities, including their company office in capital Delhi.

Malaysian regulators (2019) fined Deloitte RM2.2 million ($535,000 at the time) for allegedly failing to report irregularities as the auditor of companies linked to the state fund 1Malaysian Development Berhad (1MDB). Deloitte is still to pay $80 million to the Malaysian government because of this corruption saga that involved former Malaysian prime minister Najib Razak, who allegedly used the state fund 1MDB and its SRC International unit to embezzle billions from 2011 to 2014 (see further details in chapter 2).

The *Guardian*, January 23, 2020, refers to PwC being engulfed in a financial scandal with Africa's richest woman, Isabel dos Santos, and auditing the books of Angola's state oil company, Sonangol, during a period that is still under criminal investigation. Sonangol underpins the Angolan economy. Part of the criticism is that PwC did Sonangol's accounts while at the same time collecting fees to advise on a major restructure. PwC has presumably ended all engagements for Dos Santos and members of her family. This scandal is referred to as the Luanda Leaks investigation and reveals extensive use of the biggest global accounting firms by her businesses, with London-headquartered PwC emerging as one of the favored advisers. The Luanda Leaks reveal PwC acted for at least twenty companies owned by Dos Santos, her husband, and their associates. It provided tax advice, consultancy, and auditing services to entities in Malta, Luxembourg, Angola, Portugal, and the Netherlands.

The British apparel retailer BHS collapsed in 2016 despite PwC having signed it off as a going concern. Construction company Carillion, discussed in chapter 9, found that KPMG failed to "exercise professional skepticism."

Critics argue that audits can be compromised if a firm responsible for checking the books of a business is also receiving often much larger fees for advising that business on matters such as tax schemes, cost-cutting, and restructuring.

The above issues have aided and abetted money laundering. While there are sparks of recognition and spats of application to mitigate the risks of money laundering, the power of money for personal gain is intrinsic in all societies around the world.

In India, the government is seeking a five-year ban on the local affiliates of both KPMG and Deloitte for their role in helping hide bad loans at construction firm Infrastructure Leasing and Financial Services. Indian prosecutors claim the auditors "actively connived" with management—similar to the VBS mutual bank debacle in South Africa.

Again, we always thought that if a company is audited, then it is safe to assume all is good about that company's operation. Audited financial statements are passed around from one organization to the next in terms of knowing your (company) client. The fact that auditors sign it renders the outcome of nobody ever bothering to read it for money laundering purposes (granting credit is obviously a different motive). The closest anybody comes to reading these are to check: Do the assets exceed the liabilities? Has the company made a profit?

Are auditors to be added to the queue of professions we thought to be trustworthy but, in fact, are not? Auditing bigwigs use young, inexperienced auditors who are doing their articles to undertake audits. I am not denigrating their abilities, but the creative accounting being conducted by greedy, experienced, and corrupt executives would require time and, yes, a lot of digging. I should imagine that some younger auditors have been intimidated by senior executives during an audit.

Therefore, all eyes are on Sir Donald Brydon, who has been conducting a UK government probe into the profession for many months, seeking to improve the effectiveness of audits. While his findings will apply to the UK, other jurisdictions will be looking to him for guidance, given how these issues resonate beyond borders.

Brydon, however, also has defended the profession against mounting attacks.

"It is not auditors that cause companies to fail, that's the result of the actions of directors," he said. "I'm a little troubled by the current mood that reaches for a shotgun aimed at auditors every time there's a corporate problem."

What Brydon contends is the sort of knee-jerk reaction we've seen in South Africa too, which lets directors, executives, and others off the hook for their role in what happened.

An auditor's role is a difficult one. Auditors have serious issues to grapple with, but the preeminence of professional skepticism in their role is necessary. There needs to be a greater focus on jettisoning the mechanical tick-box approach of auditing and factoring in the bigger picture of nonfinancial factors. Auditors are not unwanted or useless, but care has to be taken and the skepticism referred to earlier: Knowingly or unknowingly, are auditors aiding and abetting money laundering?

Taken from Brydon's final report on the matter, *Report of the Independent Review into the Quality and Effectiveness of Audit*, December 2019: "It is consequently understandable that there is both confusion and a gap between the reality and the expectations of the performance of auditors in this area. If an auditor is giving an unmodified opinion, then they are stating effectively that they have obtained credible assurance that the financial statements are true and fair or phrased as presented fairly in all material respects. But some would ask: how can this be so if there has been a material fraud that the auditor has failed to detect? Relying on users fully understanding that auditors may have done enough work to reach a reasonable expectation of the financial statements being free of material misstatement is not a satisfactory answer.

"Yet, Harry Goddard of Deloitte said recently, 'Statutory auditors, working essentially to a 175-year-old model and a set of responsibilities laid down in law, are not fraud investigators.'"

But reassessing the role of auditors considering the many money laundering breaches can only be a good thing.

The Regulators

By referring to the FATF list on their website, you will know which countries have AML legislation that is designed for the monitoring and tackling of money laundering, terrorist financing, financial fraud, and sanctions, and this is conducted in collaboration with interagency coordination and surveillance.

Each member or associate country adopts the FATF recommendations from time to time appropriate to its resources and political will. Regulatory paths then result in different uptakes as each country decides on the ultimate overseer of money laundering for the country. In Hong Kong, it is the Monetary Authority. In the United States, it is the Financial Crimes Enforcement Network Center (FinCEN). In France, it is the Processing and Action against Clandestine Financial Circuits (TRACFIN). In the United Kingdom, it is the Financial Conduct Authority (FCA). In Germany, it is the Federal Financial Supervisory Authority (BaFin), and in Peru, it is the Financial Intelligence Unit Peru, and so on. The European Commission carries out risk assessments to identify risks affecting the European Union market internally. It also promotes the adoption of global solutions to respond to these threats at the international level.

It seems that for the regulators and regulatory agencies, fines for breach of AML regulations and laws are a big money-spinner. Some examples of banks fined in 2021:

> AMbank—fined $700 million for criminal breach of trust, money laundering, and abuse of power in the 1MDB financial scandal.
> ABN AMRO—fined $574 million as part of a settlement with Dutch prosecutors because of their serious shortcomings in AML.

Capital One—fined $390 million for failure to report suspicious activity despite knowing of criminal charges against specific customers, including an organized crime syndicate, and failure to file currency transaction reports.

Deutsche Bank—fined $130 million for violations of the Foreign Corrupt Practices Act (FCPA), as well as for their involvement in a commodities fraud scheme.

Julius Baer—fined $79 million for facilitating bribes and turning a blind eye to compliance as the bank laundered over $36 million in bribes to FIFA officials through the US.

So, over a billion dollars in fines in one year, and from only five banks. Kyckr is a primary source company intelligence gatherer, and their statistics show that during the first half of 2021, eighty banks were fined an estimated US$2,732,099,008 for AML- and KYC-related violations. Banks undergo long (long means a typical review can last at least six months) and torturous reviews of their anti-money-laundering systems and pay large fines, yet life simply goes on until the next painful review. The fines make big headlines, but little else seems to happen. And clients, in most cases, do not care about the reputational damage; they may say they do in a survey, but they do not necessarily change their bank account, probably because the bank next door is not likely to be much different.

Of course, Global Value reports that fines issued to financial services firms (that is, not just banks) for AML failures reached a low of $1.6 billion in 2021 whereas in 2018 it was at its peak at $3.3 billion. Why is that? According to a study done by reg-tech firm Kroll, the value of AML fines is falling because regulators are turning their attention to cryptocurrencies.

But who else are the regulators looking at? It appears no one else but the cash cows for the regulators. Which brings us to the next question—what happens to all this money? It is ironic that the banks are fined for AML failures and pay large fines with the money that the regulators are implying is tainted money in the first place.

With so many innovative ways in which money can be moved around the world quickly and effectively and the exponential growth in cryptocurrencies and assets, regulatory authorities struggle to keep up with changes and with the technology that facilitates those changes. It is not necessarily a criticism but a concern that authorities tend to focus on the submission of documents to prove all sorts of aspects. Producing compliance manuals, risk assessments, and policies for all aspects of the business, from transaction monitoring, sanctions screening, corporate governance, antifraud and corruption, human trafficking recognition, and privacy, to business continuity and disaster recovery play a big part in determining whether a bank or fintech is savvy in its management of anti-money-laundering. It looks good on paper. Any further queries on these documents usually only prompt the need for another document. There is an unending supply of these.

Financial market conduct regulations also include requirements to be met to ensure individuals are fit and proper to undertake a particular role in a financial institution. Some requirements include examinations and product certification, all of which presuppose that businesses do not know what they are doing and employ useless staff. They do know what they are doing and that is why they are in business, but unnecessary regulatory requirements just become perfunctory tasks, which take a lot of time, pushing a lot of paper around from one entity to another while the laundered billions merely pass through.

Because of the day-to-day requirements to keep regulatory fines at bay, compliance resources are more likely to be swallowed by tick-box routines rather than applying minds and investigative intelligence to high-value transactions. Obviously, we should have information on our client, but is there a case for following transactions more carefully? Sadly, even the risk-based approach is based on the client, and not the transaction. Far more sophisticated monitoring systems need to be designed and, wait for it, managed globally for the movement of high values.

There are plenty of tools against money laundering, but what is lacking is a wider focus from the regulators, coupled with a lack of investment in efficient and qualified investigatory and prosecutorial resources—without effective prosecution and widespread regulatory oversight, any robust gold-standard regulatory framework will be of little avail.

Political Survival And Justice Systems

Taken from knowledgehub.transparency.org, "Transparency Palestine, Political Corruption in the Arab World," June 2014: Abuse of power, being a form of political corruption, is a direct violation of the rule of law, epitomized by placing self-interest before public interest while serving in a public office. A good example is when the judiciary's independence is undermined by being made subordinate to other powers, and it is when public prosecution apparatuses become defenders of the regime rather than the citizens.

Many justice systems around the world can protect their powerful rulers and their families and assist in their political survival, instead of protecting the rape of the world by money launderers. Where does it go wrong?

An example is Equatorial Guinea.

After becoming independent from Spain in 1968, Equatorial Guinea was ruled by president for life Francisco Macías Nguema, until he was overthrown in a coup in 1979 by his nephew Teodoro Obiang Nguema Mbasogo, who has served as the country's president since. Both presidents have been widely characterized as dictators by foreign observers.

Suddenly, in 1995, the Republic of Equatorial Guinea struck oil and became one of the richest countries in Africa, with an impressive GDP. But the population of some one million people never benefited from this discovery. The 2019 World Report on this country indicates that life was not transformed for its average citizens. The country ranks 144th on the 2019 Human Development Index, with less than half the population having access to clean drinking water and around one in twelve children dying before the age of five.

Human Rights Watch (October 17, 2017, "How Equatorial Guinea Turned Corruption into an Art Form") reported as follows:

> It's easy to hide money using infrastructure projects. You bill the government US$50 million for a building that only cost US$10 million. Who's an expert enough to tell if the government overpaid?
>
> We spoke to one Italian businessperson there who explained how simple it is. The government would award contracts to a company owned by the first lady, and the entire project would then be subcontracted to a company partially owned by the president's son.

The president's son just happens to be his vice president too.

Where did the money go? The ruling family flaunted it and spent it, but the son of the president, Teodorin Obiang, appeared to be comfortable with being the most noticeable wealthy member of the ruling clan.

The spending of Teodorin scandalously included a mansion near the Champs-Élysées, which flaunted a hammam, a gym, a disco, a hairdressing studio, and gold-plated taps. Hundreds of artworks and a dozen Fabergé eggs give an indication of the inside of the mansion. Outside the mansion, it was complemented by two Bugatti Veyrons, which are a world first for speed and cost. They were two of a fleet of luxury cars. Bottles of wine found on the estate during an investigation were worth thousands of euros each. Teodorin was given a three-year suspended jail term by a French court and a suspended fine of €30 million for embezzlement, money laundering, corruption, and abuse of trust, which also funded his jet-set lifestyle in Paris. Finally, the French no longer ignored the families of corrupt foreign dictators buying up real estate in Paris.

There was ostentatious spending on infrastructure projects—an example of which included the building of a five-star hotel with fifty-two villas to host an African Union summit in 2011—one villa for every head of state, but to date, it is reported, the villas have remained empty. The project required an enormous six-lane highway to access in Sipopo. The government also built an alternative capital with five major airports.

In the meantime, the US Department of Justice prosecuted Teodorin for money laundering, which cost him $30 million. Switzerland investigated him and seized his $100 million yacht.

All this while two thirds of the country's people live on less than a dollar a day (2021). The French law, UK, and USA froze his assets, sold them, and gave the money as restitution to the people of Equatorial Guinea. In his own country, however, this now fifty-two-year-old vice president still lives in luxury and is waiting to succeed his father, who is about eighty years old. One cannot help but be suspicious about whether the people benefitted from *all* the money returned to the state.

Another example of a warped justice system is that of the United States.

The United States of America has been the accepted leader of justice and human rights in the modern world, but both of those in later years have been exposed, revealing many flaws.

Despite all the legal checks and balances, Donald Trump, during his presidency, was allowed to sail through the impeachment charges by hampering the provision of evidence or witnesses. The constitutional grounds for his presidential impeachment in 2019 included the following introduction:

> Our President holds the ultimate public trust. He is vested with powers so great that they frightened the Framers of our Constitution; in exchange, he swears an oath to faithfully execute the laws that hold those powers in check. This oath is no formality. The Framers foresaw that a faithless President could destroy their experiment in democracy. As George Mason warned at the Constitutional Convention held in Philadelphia in 1787, "if we do not provide against corruption, our government will soon be at an end." Mason evoked a well-known historical truth: when corrupt motives take root, they drive an endless thirst for power and contempt for checks and balances. It is then only the smallest of steps toward acts of oppression and assaults on free and fair elections.

A president faithful only to himself—who will sell out democracy and national security for his own personal advantage—is a danger to every American. Indeed, he threatens America itself.

Seven of the eight charges included in the grounds for impeachment were

- Obstruction of justice

    Some reminders include Trump's endeavors to drop the investigation into his relationship with Russia during the 2016 election. Trump fired James Comey when he refused to drop the investigation. For the same reason, he tried to fire Robert Mueller to no avail. Trump ordered White House counsel Don McGahn to create a false record indicating that no attempts took place, to which McGahn refused. He continued to repeatedly attempt to intimidate or influence witnesses in proceedings against him. Robert Mueller's investigation revealed multiple instances where there was considerable evidence that Trump had committed obstruction of justice.

- Profiting from the presidency

    The Constitution's Foreign Emoluments Clause prohibits the president from accepting personal benefits from any foreign government or official. Trump retained his ownership interests in his family business while in office, hence openly violating the Constitution throughout his presidency, also funneling taxpayers' money into his family business, thereby violating the Domestic Emoluments Clause.

(Trump spent over \$100 million taxpayer dollars to golf and vacation at his own properties.)

He solicited value when he called on Russia (a foreign national) to find Hillary Clinton's missing emails on July 27, 2016. Five hours later, Russian hackers attacked Clinton's personal office. Also, his family members Trump Jr. and Jared Kushner were invited to meet with a Russian national regarding information to incriminate Clinton. Campaign chairman Paul Manafort took the meeting. Paul was charged with a seven-and-a-half-year sentence in jail when he was charged with conspiracy charges that stemmed from a justice department inquiry into Russian election meddling. He and Rick Gates also met with Konstantin Kilimnik, a Russian spy, multiple times in the summer of 2016 to provide him with internal campaign polling data detailing the Trump campaign's Midwestern strategy. Because of the pandemic and underlying health conditions, Paul is serving the rest of his sentence at home.

Trump used US military aid to pressure Ukraine to interfere in the 2020 elections and illegally withheld \$400 million of military aid to Ukraine. In a call with the president of Ukraine, Trump asked Ukraine to do him a favor by investigating Joe Biden's family and a debunked conspiracy theory (that has been pushed by Russian intelligence) alleging Ukraine hacked the Direct Numerical Control computer servers, which, if connected, can distribute programs to different machines as required.

Trump told the press that in addition to Ukraine, China should investigate the Bidens specifically in return for ongoing trading negotiations. As a result, the Chinese reported on Biden's son's business.

- Advocating for political and police violence

    When Trump gave cover to the neo-Nazis who rioted in Charlottesville and murdered a protester, he violated his obligation to protect people against domestic violence and encouraged police officers to rough up people they had under arrest. Trump and his rhetoric have been cited in numerous criminal proceedings as being the inspiration and justification for political violence.

    When faced with impeachment in the House, Trump alluded to his supporters engaging in insurrection to keep him in power—a rallying cry readily picked up by his supporters.

    (And he has done it again with the infamous January 6, 2021, attack on Capitol Hill in Washington.)

- Abuse of power

    Trump abused his presidential power. Furthermore, the Trump administration tried to conceal the whistleblower complaint that brought this corruption to light and label the civil servant who filed it as partisan.

    In addition, Trump's decision to pardon Joe Arpaio (who was convicted for contempt of court after ignoring a court order that he stop detaining and searching people based on the color of their skin) demonstrated his disregard for equal and individual rights and flouted the Fifth Amendment as a result.

- Engaging in reckless conduct

    This ranges from confrontational actions, inflammatory tweets, and unfit behavior as commander in chief.

- Persecuting political opponents

    Trump and Attorney General Barr asked foreign intelligence agencies to assist in an investigation to discredit Robert Mueller, hoping to undermine the credibility of the Mueller Report.

- Attacking the free press

    President Trump repeatedly attacked the concept of an independent press.

    He called critical coverage "fake news" and journalists "the enemy of the American people," made threats to change libel laws and revoke licenses, and his battles with CNN led him to try to interfere in the AT&T/Time Warner merger.

    His administration repeatedly and baselessly revoked press credentials for critical coverage, thereby demonstrating his unwillingness to respect and uphold the Constitution, and his disdain for the foundations of a free society.

    He dismissed the murder of a critical journalist, citing the economic partnership the US has with the offending nation (reference to Jamal Khashoggi, a Saudi dissident, journalist, and columnist for the

Washington Post who was assassinated on October 2, 2018, by agents of the Saudi government at the Saudi consulate in Istanbul, Turkey).

The Free Speech for People white paper *The Legal Case for a Congressional Investigation on Whether to Impeach President Donald J. Trump* served as the basis for this list. Of course, his tax affairs are not transparent to the public; in information revealed in earlier years, there was already suspicion of tax evasion.

Forbes published an article on August 20, 2020, titled "Trump's Business Partners Allegedly Involved in Human Trafficking, Mafia Matters, Probable Money Laundering." It included seven names of Russians with whom he had close associations before and during his presidency.

So many of his allies, business associates, past employees during his presidency have been charged with crimes, viz Steve Bannon, charged with defrauding Trump supporters in a campaign to help build the president's signature wall along the US-Mexico border; Michael Cohen, Trump's former personal lawyer serving a three-year prison sentence (also from home) guilty of crimes including arranging hush-money payments before the 2016 election to women who had said they had sexual encounters with Trump; Paul Manafort, Trump's former campaign chairman, found guilty of tax and bank fraud in a jury trial in August 2018 but his sentence is now resumed from home because of the pandemic; Roger Stone, his longtime friend and adviser convicted of lying under oath to lawmakers investigating Russian interference in the 2016 US election and his sentence subsequently commuted by Trump; Michael Flynn, who served as Trump's national security adviser for less than thirty days in 2017, pleaded guilty to lying to the FBI about his interactions with Russia's ambassador to the US just before Trump took office. Trump pardoned him.

Presently there are still about a dozen investigations against him, and some of them include suspected money laundering and links to the Russian presidency and Russian oligarchs. *Time* on March 24, 2019, gave a list of twelve investigations but indicated that some may not yet have been made public, and there are other loosely connected players also being investigated because of the Mueller investigation. Other investigations include real estate loan transactions through Deutsche Bank, the since-dissolved Donald J. Trump Foundation, and its directors, which has been sued by the New York attorney general's office for what they say is a shocking pattern of illegality and for violating tax laws, for business and personal purposes.

The *New York Times* investigation found that Donald Trump received at least $413 million in today's dollars from his father's real estate empire, much of it through tax dodges in the 1990s. Donald Trump assisted his father in many tax dodges and continued to participate in dubious tax schemes during the 1990s, including instances of outright fraud, which greatly increased the fortune he received from his parents.

In the last couple of days in the office, he hastily pardoned many more of his cohorts for their crimes and had them released from their remaining jail terms. Strange, isn't it, that a sitting president can pardon absolute rogues who aided and abetted his unethical and, in many respects, illegal term of office?

Some names that come to mind: Albert Pirro Jr., an influential Republican businessman convicted of thirty-four felony counts of tax evasion and conspiracy in 2000; former White House chief strategist and former Trump campaign CEO, executive chairman of Breitbart who was awaiting trial on a federal case in which he allegedly defrauded Trump-supporting donors of over $1 million as part of a crowdfunding effort to build that damn border wall; Republican fundraiser—and major Trump campaign backer in 2016—who pleaded guilty in October 2020 to acting as an unregistered foreign agent in a scheme to accept millions of dollars from Malaysian and Chinese interests to lobby the Trump administration, who also commuted the sentence of Kwame Kilpatrick, the former Detroit mayor who was sentenced to some thirty years in prison on corruption charges; controversial figure Paul Erickson, who has close ties to the National Rifle Association, sentenced to seven years in federal prison 2020 on charges of wire fraud and money laundering as part of an effort to defraud investors in an energy scheme in North Dakota and former boyfriend of Russian agent Maria Butina (who was convicted in 2018 of acting as an unregistered foreign agent of Russia within the United States); Rick Renzi, a former Republican representative from Arizona, granted a full pardon following his conviction in 2013 of extortion, bribery, insurance fraud, money laundering, and racketeering in relationship to a land-swap scheme; and former Trump campaign manager Paul Manafort sought early release from prison because of the threat the coronavirus posed to his health, to serve the remainder of his seven-and-a-half-year sentence for a series of convictions on charges of tax evasion, failing to report foreign bank accounts, witness tampering, and engaging in unregistered lobbying for foreign interests. Out of interest, among the luxury goods on display during Manafort's trial for thirty-two counts of financial fraud and money laundering, was a python coat for which he paid $18,500, nearly twice what he paid for an ostrich waistcoat, but a mere fraction of what he spent on clothes, rugs, and garden landscaping—all funded by lobbying for foreign governments.

You get the gist of what Trump considered pardonable reasons. Maybe he believes the next Republican president (investigations and court cases take a long time), four or eight years from now, will pardon him too, or when he runs again for office, he can pardon himself.

Another justice escape artist is past president Jacob Zuma.

Past president Zuma of South Africa is facing one count of racketeering, two counts of corruption, one count of money laundering, and twelve counts of fraud in the Arms Deal case—for the third time. The arms deal took place in 1999 when Zuma moved from being a provincial minister to deputy president. He is accused of accepting 783 illegal payments.

His financial adviser, Schabir Shaik, was found guilty of trying to solicit bribes on his behalf from a French arms firm and was jailed in 2005 and sentenced to two terms of fifteen years for corruption and a three-year term for fraud. The sentences, which ran concurrently, meant Shaik was given a fifteen-year sentence. Two years and four months later, he was released on medical parole because he was terminally ill, so much so that he is still alive and kicking. He flouted his medical parole several times and it just became a news item for a while and then it was forgotten until he was completely exonerated by the current president in January 2020.

The case against Zuma was dropped shortly before he ran for president in 2009. Why were the charges dropped? The National Prosecuting Authority of South Africa announced that it was dropping criminal charges of corruption, fraud, money laundering, and tax evasion against Jacob Zuma, head of the African National Congress at the time, thereby clearing the way for parliament to elect him as president in the vote scheduled in the following weeks.

But this was not Zuma's first experience with the law; Zuma was first charged with corruption in 2005. The case was dismissed then because the prosecution could not provide adequate evidence after the court excluded as inadmissible vital incriminating evidence seized by police in a raid on the defendant's home. The charges were reinstated following a South African appellate court ruling in November 2007 that the incriminating evidence that was once deemed inadmissible is, in fact, legal. Zuma was also tried and acquitted of rape in 2006 (Library of Congress, January 2, 2008).

On a day of high drama, an elite South African police team known as the Hawks raided the luxurious home of the Guptas, who were accused of improper dealings with him. This operation was part of an investigation into allegations of influence-peddling in the government and the misuse of millions of dollars of public funds.

Zuma was forced to resign by his own party as a result in February 2018. The charges were then reinstated for the corruption relating to the £1.8 billion arms deal.

The trial was postponed a couple of times, and the last straw was Zuma's contempt of court.

The constitutional court eventually ordered that if Zuma did not voluntarily hand himself over to the police, then he should be arrested. In a last-minute ditch to save Zuma, his legal team pleaded for him not to be arrested as it would be a "prejudice to his life." Hundreds of Zuma's supporters pledged to prevent attempts to arrest him at his home in Nkandla.

Zuma's compliance with the imprisonment order, after days of refusing to do so, finally meant he was arrested on July 7, 2021. That brought an end to an impasse that had gripped South Africa. His sentence was fifteen months for contempt of court despite legal attempts to avoid imprisonment.

One of the defenses by his legal team argued that the former president would turn eighty on his next birthday, his health was precarious, and he was not a flight risk as he was under the care and security of the state. Of course, he would be eligible for parole after four months. Even that did not stick, and Zuma was released on medical parole September 2021 because of a yet-undisclosed medical condition.

As an update to June 2022, Zuma is still avoiding court days for reasons of medical health. The court case for the $2.5 billion arms corruption deal has been dragging on for years. He is never going to jail.

Lula da Silva is another example of a warped justice at the helm.

The Conversation, March 16, 2021: Ex-president Luiz Inácio "Lula" da Silva, who served as president of Brazil between 2003 and 2010, was jailed in 2018 for twelve years, subsequently reduced to ten years and eight months. He was one of the dozens of politicians and business leaders across the country that were charged for receiving bribes in what became known as Operation Car Wash—a big operation.

A year later, the same prosecutorial team accused the following president, Michel Temer, of accepting millions in bribes. After his term ended in 2019, he was arrested, but his trial was later suspended. He had secured enough votes in the lower house of Congress to avoid facing trial on charges of obstructing justice and racketeering.

In the meantime, Lula was released from jail in the same year, and in March 2021, the Supreme Court annulled his conviction. Because polls showed Lula still had 50 percent public support, he decided (May 2022) to run again for president.

France24.com July 6, 2021, reported that the current Brazilian president, Bolsonaro, was also currently under suspicion for partaking in a scheme called rachadinha: "Rio de Janeiro state prosecutors have formally pressed charges against federal senator Flavio Bolsonaro, the president's eldest son, over his alleged participation in a similar racket when he was a state lawmaker."

The article continues that "while the rachadinha is not directly connected to the Senate inquiry, it adds to recent allegations about irregularities in the government's purchase of vaccines and calls into question Bolsonaro's anticorruption platform."

The above four examples show that you just need to get voted in and be popular; honesty and integrity and caring about people have nothing to do with being the leader of a country. For most of us who try to get a professional job, we have to go through many interviews, psychological testing, credit reviews, aptitude tests, a clean record and qualifications, and previous jobs that are checked for authenticity.

Popularity, power, and money are intertwined into political will and very unjust justice systems.

Whistleblowing—Which Is The Right Direction For It To Blow?

Many employees simply turn a blind eye; they do not want to know, don't want to get involved, don't want to make trouble, and don't want to get fired. Whistleblowing seldom has a good outcome for the whistleblower.

The Open Democracy Advice Centre's Heroes Under Fire are South African whistleblowers' stories that start with the words "These are the stories of whistleblowers. They are all unique, but similarities emerge that paint a picture of struggle and adversity for people seeking to do the right thing in the public interest."

That is true, especially for whistleblowers who do not make headlines; below are three of those stories in brief.

In 2006, a shopkeeper and independent bread distributor complained to the Competition Commission of South Africa about collusion in the baking industry. Bakers had collectively decided to reduce the discount offered to distributors. Big brand names were found guilty of breaching the Competition Act, which drew a collective R90 million fine. He did good for many poor people, but his business eventually failed after producers began withdrawing their business.

Moses was an African National Congress (ANC) municipal councilor who attempted to expose corruption in his municipality. He and a colleague raised their concerns through a variety of political channels in the belief action would be taken. They delivered evidence to the ANC secretary-general and to the Office of the President and a further meeting. Two days later, on March 13, 2009, Moses' body was found slumped over the steering wheel of his car with two bullet wounds. Although a couple of people were arrested, charged, and sentenced for his murder, his dossier was found in the home of a former intelligence boss.

Clinton was a compliance licensing official at the Eastern Cape gambling board. He revealed irregularities in the appointment of the chief executive officer. After an investigation by the Public Protector confirmed his claims, the outcome was that the CEO retained his position and Clinton was forced to resign. Thereafter, the battles with authorities and the loss of income had to be faced.

But when big money-laundering cases are concerned, a different picture of the whistleblower emerges.

Angelo Agrizzi was the former chief operating officer at a South African facilities management company, Bosasa Operations, and he was the whistleblower. (Dynabu Operations was renamed Bosasa Operations in 2000.) *Daily Maverick*, November 19, 2019, "What is going on at the Bosasa-run Lindela Repatriation Centre?" reported on Lindela, west of Johannesburg, which is a name associated with twenty-two years of abuse of its inmates. In 1996 it was converted from a miners' hostel compound into a holding facility for undocumented immigrants awaiting deportation.

Lindela is supported by the South African Police, which arrests irregular immigrants and detains them until their immigration status is determined.

The South African Police Services arrests suspected irregular immigrants and detains them at a police station until their immigration status is determined by the Department of Home Affairs (DHA). The DHA charges those found to be irregular and is legally and administratively responsible for their transport, holding, processing, repatriation, and release. Bosasa, on behalf of the DHA, manages the catering, health, safety, accommodation, and services at Lindela.

Bosasa has never lost the tender for Lindela despite twenty-one deaths reported there in 2015 within an eight-month period. Bosasa runs Lindela to this day.

Up to 2017, human rights groups produced sad reports of Lindela: inadequate medical care and oversight, poor living conditions, instances of abuse of detainees by guards, recurrent detention of minors, neglect of the procedural rights of detainees, illegally long detention periods, and restricted access to Lindela for monitoring purposes.

The Department of Home Affairs continues to pay Bosasa (now renamed African Global Operations) R9.5 million a month to run Lindela. The contract is not publicly available; all queries are passed on to the DHA. Despite overall unsatisfactory conditions in every respect and human rights violations, nothing much happened. In 2014, a high court order assigned the South African Human Rights Commission (SAHRC) to monitor Lindela. But the SAHRC did not respond to any inquiries by the *Daily Maverick* since its 2017 annual report.

And after 2017, there were no monitoring or reports; inquiries made to the SAHRC yielded no results. So much for human rights.

In 2019 at the Zondo Commission (created to deal with state capture), it was revealed that Bosasa bribed government officials for tenders, among other examples, and that funds meant for Lindela were instead put into the executives' pockets during the festive season. The opposition political party also reported the facility to be underutilized, but costs did not reflect this fact. It was also found that the police statistics of suspected irregular immigrants arrested per month were not reconcilable with the DHA's reported deportations in the 2017/18 financial year.

Agrizzi gave damning evidence that implicated many senior government officials associated and other high-profile people with Bosasa: for over twenty years, he and other Bosasa staff members repeatedly bribed officials in return for government tenders worth hundreds of millions of euros. The suspects allegedly received cash gifts, financial assistance to acquire properties and cars, and payments to travel agents to facilitate their trips overseas.

But he failed to divulge his own true position: as of February 6, 2019, the Agrizzis owned movable assets (excluding jewelry, furniture, and art) of R35.6 million, not R2.65 million as previously stated. He had opened bank accounts in Italy with South African money and, in March, bought real estate in Castel Del Piano in Italy for €880,000 and a luxury vehicle. Furthermore, his wife had a bank account of €714,419.50.

Agrizzi also lied at the state capture inquiry where he had made a number of allegations against Bosasa and its late boss Gavin Watson (who is rumored to have committed suicide by crashing his car into a wall outside the OR Tambo International Airport) two days before his scheduled testimony date.

Agrizzi was charged with corruption, money laundering, and fraud as were Bosasa and two of its subsidiaries. However, not all people were implicated, such as former president Zuma and the

South African Revenue Service commissioner, who were called to book.

On August 13, 2021, IOL reported that Agrizzi, who failed to appear in court on three occasions this year because of ill health, would yet again probably not be medically fit to stand trial. The case continued to be postponed to January 2022 (as per News24, October 28, 2021) to deliberate on whether Agrizzi would be fit to stand trial. It is April 2022, and Agrizzi has still complained of ill health and that the state will not send a doctor to examine him. Nothing has changed.

In the example below, the whistleblower remains unknown for good reason. As long ago as 2012, a whistleblower's attorney turned in documents and trading records to regulators regarding the rigging of the interbank offered rate (Libor). The *Wall Street Journal* revealed that the attorney was representing a former Deutsche Bank AG executive—said to be the whistleblower.

"Libor rigging was one of the most sweeping abuses involving Wall Street to emerge in the wake of the 2008 financial crisis. Multiple banks were accused of submitting bogus rates at the direction of traders who had put positions on to profit illicitly."

Libor provides loan issuers with a benchmark for the interest rates they charge on different financial products. Libor is set each day by collecting estimates from up to eighteen global banks on the interest rates they would charge for different loan maturities, given their outlook on local economic conditions. It is hard to overstate the Libor's importance as it was used as a reference rate for trillions of dollars of loans, mortgages, and other financial products.

According to the Commodities Futures Trading Commission (CFTC), which polices the derivatives trading market in the US, the information helped the agency find direct evidence of wrongdoing as part of an already open investigation, and prompted another federal regulator and foreign agency to bring on similar allegations.

> Neither the whistle-blower nor the firm accused of misconduct was identified by the CFTC, in keeping with the federal government's policy of withholding information that could reveal a tipster's identity. (*Daily Maverick*, October 22, 2021, "Tipster Who Got $200 Million Blew Whistle on Benchmark Rigging")

The CFTC, as with other regulatory institutions, gives awards for help in its enforcement actions as well as those brought by other domestic or foreign regulators if certain conditions are met. The CFTC recognized that this whistleblower deserved a substantial reward.

> Whistle-blowers are eligible to receive between 10 percent and 30 percent of the monetary sanctions collected. The CFTC pays for the awards through a fund established by Congress, which is funded by sanctions paid to the agency. No money is taken or withheld from injured customers to fund the program.

This whistleblower was awarded $200 million. Comment by Jane Crankshaw on October 22, 2021, on the article is as follows:

> A whistleblower's fee of between 10–30 percent of the monetary sanctions collected is obviously more valuable than the commission from participating in the scheme! The whistleblower in this case did the math and realized he would make more by being

a whistleblower than sticking to his participating commission AND he would remain anonymous! Not entirely kosher but clever!

However, whistleblowing is considered effective and necessary. On January 1, 2021, the United States Congress enacted the Anti-Money-Laundering Act (AMLA), which establishes new whistleblower protections for employees of financial services institutions. Among other things, the AMLA significantly increases the potential value of awards for whistleblowers under the Bank Secrecy Act as the above example shows. Whistleblowers are also not required to be US citizens or residents.

This just puts the ethical question into whistleblowing.

CHAPTER 11

The Covert Epicenter of Wealth: Shells and Havens

A TAX HAVEN IS not only an island with pretty beaches; it is just another jurisdiction that offers low, or sometimes, no taxes to attract foreign investment.

For a wealthy sun-and-sea worshiper, many of the tax havens are, indeed, lovely. The Cayman Islands in the Caribbean, still a British overseas territory, boast beautiful tropical islands, pristine beaches, great diving sites, and lush tropical forests. It also happens to be one of the world's largest tax havens; it has more registered businesses than it has people. Given that, between the visitors and the registered businesses, the Cayman Islands are self-sufficient.

Tax havens are not illegal. It just means the investment or the earnings of companies, corporations, and individuals are put somewhere else where the tax rate is lower or nonexistent, irrespective of where the money was earned or saved.

A Deloitte article (undated), "Tax havens and the game of hide and seek, Insight into cross border tax practices of multinationals" refers to the concept of using a tax haven with an attractive tax regime and a high degree of secrecy to provide legitimately for tax planning purposes.

"These countries or jurisdictions offer lower tax rates, credit mechanism, or deduction resulting in limited or no tax on certain profits. Also, there is less red tape involved with no complicated exchange controls, labor, and equity."

If a company properly attributes profits to the tax haven and the company is managed and controlled from that jurisdiction with sufficient economic substance—such as operations—to justify tax residency, then that renders a more favorable tax outcome and takes away the complexity of multinational tax reporting because tax is different in every country. For example, the European Union produces an annual list of tax havens that contains no EU member countries, even though many other lists identify Ireland, Luxembourg, and a host of other European countries as tax havens.

The Tax Justice Network has published its Corporate Tax Haven Index for 2021, showing which countries are most complicit in helping multinational corporations underpay corporate income tax.

Countries are ranked by their Corporate Tax Haven Index value, which is calculated by measuring how much scope for corporate tax abuse the jurisdiction's tax and financial systems allow—assessed against twenty indicators—as well as measuring how much financial activity from multinational corporations the jurisdiction hosts.

For example, a territory like the Bahamas has a high tax haven score (100—the top of the scale) but only accounts for 0.31 percent of global foreign investment flows, so it ranks 12th in the list of the biggest tax havens.

Some gaps highlighted include a lack of transparency in some types of contracts (like mining contracts), tax affairs having limited public oversight, and looser rules on controlled foreign companies.

In this measurement, the British Virgin Islands emerged as the biggest tax haven in the world. These islands do not impose any corporate income tax, which makes most of the indicators assessed by the Tax Justice Network obsolete. No tax means there is no need for loopholes. The jurisdiction also accounts for 2.3 percent of all foreign direct investment ($2.2 trillion), making it the go-to for corporations looking to avoid the taxman.

In the second, the third, and fourth place are the Cayman Islands, Bermuda, and believe it or not, the Netherlands. The Netherlands has a lower tax haven score (80) but has 11 percent of all foreign investment flows. Hence, it is fourth place.

The United States is described as a tax haven—*Forbes* even calls it the best in the world (the US government would never do so) because it fits all the key criteria, such as providing legal ways to avoid virtually all taxation and strong taxpayer privacy.

"Tax havens are also used for the protection and exploitation of intellectual property because they can be held offshore and licensed to other group entities in various countries. All foreign sales and licensing fees will then be attributable to the tax haven. In some cases, licensing fees may be subject to royalties' withholding tax at a rate much lower than the corporate tax rate in those jurisdictions. This makes it more tax-efficient to hold and manage the intellectual property centrally via an entity situated in a tax haven. Therefore, tax havens have made efficient tax planning for multinationals achievable with relative ease."

Tax havens offer these benefits as they are not generally industrialized countries; by offering ease of business and minimizing tax to attract foreign investment, they create employment and encourage a transfer of skills to their jurisdiction so that they can become a self-sufficient economy. The privacy of financial information is attractive too.

Leaks such as the infamous Panama Papers and HSBC Swiss leak have served to heighten awareness of what is widely known as base erosion and profit shifting (BEPS). However, what's becoming increasingly clear is that more needs to be done to make offshore tax havens less murky. (SAIPA Tax Professional, *The Secret Underworld of Tax Havens*)

The Panama Papers (and later, the Pandora Papers) leaks have highlighted what is the "complex nature of the structures used to hide the beneficial owners and accrual of taxable income, using these structures to either shift profits to more tax-favorable jurisdictions, or the outright erosion of the tax base."

FinCEN Files investigation (named a Pulitzer Prize finalist, June 11, 2021), was the global exposé by hundreds of journalists from the International Consortium of Investigative Journalists (ICIJ) and BuzzFeed News, the *New York Times*, the *Wall Street Journal*, and hundreds of other media partners in eighty-eight countries, which revealed how a broken US-led enforcement system allowed banks to continue to profit from moving trillions of dollars in dirty money. It exposed too how the mega-wealthy and criminal groups have used the offshore financial system to dodge taxes and launder dirty money.

This exposure revealed the role of some of the world's biggest banks in facilitating "international money laundering, the trafficking of goods and people and corruption that continues to frustrate regulators across the world."

The FinCEN Files investigation found that five global banks—JPMorgan Chase, HSBC, Standard Chartered Bank, Deutsche Bank, and Bank of New York Mellon—continued to profit from suspicious transactions even after they paid fines to US authorities for previous misconduct and signed some deferred-prosecution deals.

In September, the ICIJ, BuzzFeed News, and other partners published hundreds of news stories that were able to provide information on how laws intended to stop financial crime have instead allowed it to flourish. They further revealed how banks that move dirty money protect themselves and the filing of suspicious activity reports to the financial intelligence units that "authorities are unlikely to read, let alone act on."

As a matter of interest, the whistleblower here was Natalie Mayflower Sours Edwards, a US Treasury official who disclosed the financial intelligence documents to BuzzFeed News; she was sentenced to six months in prison. This sentence was generally protested as unjust and unfair because "our criminal justice system must recognize that much of what we know about financial corruption, government surveillance, and corporate crime comes not from reporters working in isolation but from journalists working with people who risk their liberty and livelihood to ensure that the truth comes out."

Journalists across the world contacted thousands of sources ranging from presidential advisers, bankers, police officers, gangsters, and arms dealers and, as a result, also collected some 17,000 additional documents, including audit reports.

New York's top banking regulator, who plays a big role in policing global banks, acknowledged dirty money had metastasized "within the guts of financial institutions."

It was said that the FinCEN Files took financial reporting to new heights; this was a massive reporting effort, which not only exposed major banks profiting from dirty money, but that the US government watched but rarely took action.

The ICIJ also commented (June 1, 2021) on how the world's richest defend their wealth, with help from a dedicated industry, based on a book written by Chick Collins, who offers an insider's account of the "wealth defense industry" and the inequality it perpetuates. In his book *The Wealth Hoarders*, subtitled *How billionaires pay millions to hide trillions*, he offers insiders' accounts of what's described as the wealth defense industry—made up of a coalition of professionals from advisors to lawyers and accountants—and how it deploys anonymous shell companies, family offices, offshore accounts, and trusts to help the world's richest people shield their wealth from tax collectors.

In their interview with Collins, the ICIJ reports that he referred to social scientist Jeffrey Winters, who wrote a book called *Oligarchy*. His idea is that "what distinguishes ordinary rich people from an oligarchy is that all oligarchs invest in wealth defense, they use their wealth to get more power and wealth and defend their wealth and to lobby and rig the rules around them. And I would argue that about the $30 million and up a level, people start to invest in wealth defense."

Winters goes on to write that there are tens of thousands of these wealth defenders who wake up in the morning and are devoted to helping the richest people in the world get richer and pass on their wealth with as little taxes as possible. They are not as wealthy as their clients but are well paid for their expertise.

Russian oligarchs exist at the behest of Vladimir Putin. But the Western and Mid-Eastern world has their own oligarchs. In the *Daily Maverick* of March 27, 2022, author Yanis Varoufakis, former finance minister of Greece, leader of the MeRA25 party, and professor of economics at the University of Greece, asked the question *Why stop at the Russian oligarchs?* The war in Ukraine has highlighted the plight of Russian oligarchs, who are being targeted, and the sanctions imposed on Russian oligarchs. Yanis asks why this is a Russian phenomenon. "US's wealthiest 0.01 percent have taken about $1.2 trillion out of the US, principally to avoid paying taxes."

The *Washington Post* of April 5, 2022, "The Gatekeepers Who Open America to Shell Companies and Secret Owners," indicates that "with scant oversight, registered agents have long been seen as a weak point in the US financial system."

Their data reveals that a number of LLCs' records show that foreign court records have been listed in lawsuits that allege incidents such as medical fraud in Russia, bank theft in Zimbabwe, and tax fraud in Hungary.

Registered agents that were interviewed by the authors acknowledge knowing little or nothing about the owners of companies they are paid to front, or even what function those companies serve. Some agents represent more than 250 companies, and others have owned up to representing 1,200 companies, many of which are linked to foreign owners. One agent, who also had a full-time job elsewhere, shared the information that one of the companies had tried to sell unproven and dangerous medical treatments to patients with incurable diseases. The agent insisted what they were doing was completely legal, namely representing companies without questions or judgment. The agent is quoted as saying, "It's not my responsibility what a business does. It's a fraud-friendly state by the laws that are created. Unless the state changes that, I'm just doing my part."

The irony is that financial institutions are legally required to do a full KYC for their clients—even for a single transaction—whereas registered agents are not uniformly required to do so. In 2021, federal law required LLCs and similar business entities to provide the names and birth dates of their owners to a new government database. "But that registry is not accessible to the public, and transparency advocates argue that the sheer volume of information may leave federal authorities unable to identify many fraudulent entries and the owners behind them. Delaware alone recorded more than 180,000 new LLCs in 2020, records show.

"The proposed Enablers Act would go further, requiring every registered agent not only to identify company owners but also to look for and report red flags."

Another irony is that "Wyoming doesn't keep a comprehensive list of registered agents, and some can be as elusive as the company owners they represent."

An offshore haven is the first line of defense to maintain secrecy. Tax havens offered by elite small countries survive on the earnings from the assets they hold, and of course, these countries are reliant on the offshore tax haven industry. However, tax equality around the world is distorted as a result. To stop the practice would be a huge disruption to economies and the financial legal system. But if you want to curb money laundering, that is a place to start.

The second is multiple-structured and convoluted companies as discussed in the previous chapter. The third and the most secretive of all are shell companies held offshore.

Vice knows she's ugly, so puts on her mask.

—Benjamin Franklin

A shell company is aptly named. The shell is not open for inspection; you must pry it open with difficulty, usually having to apply some nifty tools to assist you.

A shell company is a business entity formed to protect a company's assets, in secrecy legally. Shell companies are non-traded corporations, meaning that they are not listed on any stock exchanges for buying and selling by investors. A shell company can hold or store money when the so-called owner is planning to start a new company, for anonymity purposes from prying partners or spouses, creditors, or government authorities. The assets can also be transferred to another company, leaving the liabilities behind.

Shell companies can undertake common business practices on behalf of shareholders, such as open bank and brokerage accounts, conduct regular financial transactions, may enter into a series of transactions with other shell companies, shift funds inside and outside the company, buy real estate and other companies, and hold copyrights and rake in royalties. They can also be used to stage a hostile takeover of another company or hold assets in preparation for creating a new company. But the best benefit of all, it would seem, is tax avoidance. Provided the assets held in the shell company are earned offshore, they are considered legitimate and cannot be taxed by outside countries.

To sum up the benefits of a shell company, a veil of secrecy for the owner is provided by expert facilitators such as accountants, lawyers, and agents for advice and management, and access to lucrative foreign markets and business opportunities in other countries, as well as establishing holding companies to protect their intellectual property and trade secrets. Operating in secrecy is a business plus.

This is a great recipe for conducting business with more ease; it is also a great recipe to facilitate fraud, corruption, and money laundering.

A shell company, therefore, exists merely on paper or digitally. It is a company without active business operations or activities or significant assets. It has no office and no employees, but likely has a bank account and holds passive investments. It may also be the registered owner of assets such as intellectual property or yachts.

In Latin American countries, for example, wealthy individuals have been using shell companies for years to hide their assets and avoid being targeted by kidnappers. And in the world of high-end art, many large-scale collectors use offshore shell companies to mask the true owners of world masterpieces.

By now we know that tax burdens are reduced significantly because the assets are hidden from the tax authorities. When that happens, not only are tax burdens reduced significantly but these assets are also likely to be insulated from volatile or poorly performing national economies too. The assets are located separately and therefore remain protected from those economies' woes.

As an example, during the financial crisis of 2008, Greece experienced the anger of its people who rioted in the streets over national economic belt-tightening and inflation, and the national deficit skyrocketed. Another example is Venezuela's economy, which fell in 2015, causing citizens to starve and businesses to fail. If a Greek or Venezuelan company had placed assets in an offshore shell company, the capital would have been protected and the company insulated from its home's failing economy.

Large corporations such as Apple have moved jobs and profits offshore, taking advantage of minimal tax payments. This is the process of offshoring or outsourcing work that was once conducted domestically.

Another application is a reverse merger, which is the acquisition of a publicly traded company that has usually lain dormant for several years. Because the shell company is already listed on the public market, purchasing the entity allows an investor to avoid going through the lengthy and expensive process of setting up an initial public offering (IPO).

In this case, buying a shell company is similar to buying a shelf corporation. The company has value because it already exists, and the purchase provides a significant shortcut. For new startups, the reverse merger can present major savings.

A reverse merger comes with possible pitfalls, such as an unclean shell that has a hidden history of lawsuits, fraudulent behavior, or unmet liabilities.

In the *New York Times* article "How to Set Up a Shell Company" on November 7, 2019, the following excerpts are interesting to note: "If you're looking for secrecy, the United States is a far better bet than the classic tropical-island tax haven," says Jason Sharman, a professor of politics and international relations at the University of Cambridge. To study the effectiveness of international rules against anonymous, untraceable shell companies, Sharman and two other researchers impersonated twenty-one different fictitious consultants and sent 7,400 emails to 3,700 so-called corporate service providers (often law or accounting firms) in 182 countries, asking for help setting one up. Half the respondents failed to comply with regulations requiring the collection of identity documents. The conclusion: It is more than three times as hard to put an untraceable shell company in an offshore tax haven than in a developed country.

To me it is possible that fictitious consultants alerted experienced lawyers, accountants, and other shell onboarding agents to false IDs, and they may have rejected some based on being suspicious about investigative journalists.

Some hints from that article:

> For anonymity, set up your company in Nevada, Delaware, or Wyoming; it can be done in ten to forty minutes, and for as little as $200.
>
> Usually, you want the name [of the shell company] that's furthest distant from your own. Go bland: The idea is to be forgettable.
>
> There are effectively no upper limits on the amount of assets a shell company can hold. For really rich people, rather than a single shell company, you have interlocking networks where company A owns company B, which owns company C, which owns an art collection or a big mansion.
>
> Anonymity is akin to legal immunity. Companies can't be chucked in jail.

Structurally, a shell company should register with the country where it is created (e.g., Cayman Islands), but corporations and other entities that create shell companies usually hire a registered agent who is an expert in structuring shell companies in the country where it is being established. However, it is not necessary for an American or an American company to register a shell company offshore or overseas. Americans can simply register in Nevada or Delaware, Wyoming, or any of the other remaining forty-seven states that allow it. Registered agents register their names when opening a shell company, along with the name of a nominal owner or shareholder director to complete the sign-up process. Depending on the country where the shell company is created, the price lawyers charge for establishing the company varies widely, anywhere from a few thousand dollars to several hundred thousand dollars for larger companies. A registered agent will focus on the registration and administration of the shell company.

Some of the tax havens like Panama and the British Virgin Islands have tough laws to protect the identity of owners or beneficiaries of these shell companies. Anonymity can be even further protected by using fake directors and public faces of shell companies.

Of course, the revelations of the Panama Papers in 2016 (a leak of 11.5 million documents to the German newspaper *Süddeutsche Zeitung* revealed information about owners of more than 214,000 shell companies administered by the law firm Mossack Fonseca in Panama) highlighted the illegal use of shell companies and found that not only the rich and famous were involved but also businessmen, autocrats, and terrorists from around the world, especially for the reasons of tax evasion as one of the many illegal activities.

As a comparison in terms of money offshore and government spending on COVID-19 in 2020, Zuza Nazaruk, a

Rotterdam-based journalist who focuses on social inclusion and climate emergency, in her article in the Morocco World News on April 6, 2020, indicated that "the inadequacy of governmental response to the COVID-19 pandemic worldwide is a direct result of putting profits before society. Market deregulation, praised in the neoliberal order as bringing never-ending economic growth, has led to fortunes being stacked offshore at the expense of the public sector." So while the world struggles to mitigate the impact of COVID-19, trillions of dollars lay safely in offshore accounts, protected in shell companies.

It is fair to report that many countries did provide for COVID-19 rescue packages: for example, Donald Trump, on March 27, 2020, signed the largest COVID-19 rescue package in US history, worth $2.2 trillion, but the author indicates that "the numbers look significantly less impressive if compared to the staggering wealth hidden in offshore accounts."

But there has been some serious traction on anonymous shell companies in the US.

In all the reading and research carried out on shell companies and money laundering, there was always a brief reference to shell companies that, although they are legal (and the presumption is that it is by anyone and anywhere), they are also used for illegal purposes. Only a few articles refer to the following legislation of the United States and seldom quote the name of the act:

Rule 12b-2 of the federal regulations issued under the United States Securities Exchange Act of 1934 wherein the US Securities and Exchange Commission defines a shell company as follows:

> Shell company: The term *shell company* means a registrant, other than an asset-backed issuer, that has
>
> (1) No or nominal operations, and

(2) Either
- (i) No or nominal assets
- (ii) Assets consisting solely of cash and cash equivalents, or
- (iii) Assets consisting of any amount of cash and cash equivalents and nominal other assets.

It had no effect. In 2019, in the aftermath of the Panama Papers, financial authorities in the United States were galvanized into introducing the Corporate Transparency Act (CTA) to eliminate the anonymity applied to shell companies and limited liability companies (LLCs). Under the CTA, shell companies and LLCs are required to provide the ultimate beneficial ownership information to the Financial Crimes Enforcement Network (FinCEN) at the time of formation of the shell company. Also, a provision in the National Defense Authorization Act (NDAA), which came into effect on January 1, 2021, is designed to eliminate the anonymity of shell companies for US companies (among other bank secrecy issues) and reporting companies doing business in the United States.

This is said to be a pivotal step forward in the global fight against corruption, and the NDAA law will now require approximately thirty million companies to disclose the identities of their real owners so that law enforcement and banks can monitor abuse.

Sadly, trusts and partnerships are not included. (Why not?) Exemptions include public companies and other private companies that have more than twenty full-time employees, those that report $5 million in annual income to the IRS, and those that have a physical presence (office) in the US. The information in the registry on the beneficial owners will be kept by FinCEN. It will not be publicly available but can be shared with financial institutions and law-enforcement-type authorities as relevant, but only with the reporting company's consent.

That means that now, when someone opens a shell corporation, they'll be required to provide the owner's name and some basic identifying information. This simple step will give law enforcement and national security officials a powerful tool to crack down on corruption.

India has been trying too. After it decided to demonetize on November 8, 2016, shell companies surged, and some 2,000 shell companies were shut down while the Securities and Exchange Board of India imposed trading restrictions on 162 listed entities operating as shell companies. Wikipedia reported that hundreds of shell companies were registered in a few buildings in Kolkata: many of those were found to be locked, with their padlocks coated in dust, and many others had office space the size of cubicles. The following legislation deals with practices related to AML: the Benami Transactions Prohibition (Amendment) Act, 2016, which prohibits anyone from holding assets under a fake name to avoid taxation; the Companies Act of 2013 Rules 2017, which restricts the number of layers of subsidiaries a company can have; the Prevention of Money Laundering Act; the Indian Penal Code if the shell company is engaged in a Ponzi scheme; the Black Money and Imposition of Tax Act; and the Income Tax Act.

A task force on shell corporations was established in 2017 to effectively tackle malpractice by shell companies in a comprehensive manner. One of the major achievements of the task force is the compilation of a database of shell companies by the Serious Fraud Investigation Office. This database comprises three lists, namely the Confirmed List, Derived List, and Suspect List.

Shell companies are intrinsic to the Indian economy, so the task is almost insurmountable. Despite their efforts, though, nowhere is there a definitive and legal definition of a shell company under any law, and there is no specific law to deal with them. The Indian government has been making significant efforts to restrict shell companies from engaging in illegal activities. Complex corporate structures also make it difficult to track transactions from different accounts and to be able to differentiate between illegal and legal shell companies. This poses a challenge for the Indian regulatory authorities. Without a better understanding of their activities and effective oversight, the chances of shell companies being misused are still exceedingly high in India.

The jury is out on whether any initiatives taken so far by governments and law enforcement of most countries in curbing the use of shell companies for holding laundered money are far-reaching enough to stem their use. There are still a lot of assets in shell companies that are protected and held in secrecy for many companies around the world. Further investigation by journalists revealed the Pandora Papers in 2021, which gave the world greater insight into the use of shell companies, this time involving fourteen companies that held the documents of 27,000 shell companies. The problem will persist for many years.

But even after these dramatic revelations, many money launderers are seldom convicted, and they continue unabated, amassing or spending a fortune. If they are investigated (as a start), investigations can take years because of the endless trails of evidence spread around the world, the secrecy of offshore havens encountered, and dealing with the resistance and obfuscation, not only from suspected launderers or people associated with them but also from bankers and other financial institutions who have transactions they know are suspect. (If caught out, of course, they would cooperate with regulators.)

It has been recognized too that financial institution regulators are not keen to be associated with investigating the crime of money laundering because of possible damage to their reputations, which could be tainted with the accusation of nonperformance on their side, i.e. how did they not know this was happening in the first place?

In terms of the business world order for corporate governance, transparency, and disclosure, corporations have a long way to go. The irony of the last few decades: "How is it that a country that targets terrorist financing and banks that evade economic sanctions also allows the creation of anonymous entities that can hide the true source of funds?" (White Collar Watch, *New York Times*, July 11, 2019).

Shell companies, therefore, remain a great place to keep laundered money and avoid paying taxes. Until shell companies are off the world financial agenda, they will always provide an easy roadmap for illegal use.

CHAPTER 12

Greed, the Basis of
Money Laundering

I S GREED GOOD or bad? In chapter 5, I indicated the following: We become greedy, but being greedy is difficult to define.

The American Psychological Association (APA PsychNet), in a journal article in 2012, "The good and bad about greed: How the manifestations of greed can be used to improve organizational and individual behavior and performance," points out that greed is so much part of human history because there is the ongoing need to serve powerful egos that are championed and rewarded in all levels of society. The contention is that greed is not all bad. It could just be the result of "overzealousness in organizations in which the rules about ambition and competition are unclear and excess is encouraged." The article goes on to say that, of course, it becomes problematic when it leads to illegal or criminal actions. While it cannot be eliminated from our human social systems, it can have a positive influence on the behavior and performance of organizations.

But in January 2009 the same association referred to how greed in America outstripped need and that its culture had set up its citizens for economic fall (note that the financial crisis had started to take hold in America and most of the world at that time). "As the world slipped into economic meltdown, the nation started talking about greed: greedy lenders, greedy Wall Street executives, greedy CEOs, and greedy Americans who used credit to finance untenable lifestyles."

We cannot just fault American culture. Most countries display this materialistic type of culture and economic system. Capitalism, as we know it today, encourages materialistic values and research shows that people high on materialism are "more likely to engage in unethical business behaviors and manipulate people for their own purposes."

Further, the APA research showed that people who live in competitive free market systems cared more about money, power, and achievement than people who live under more cooperative systems. It also revealed that the more people who cared about money and power, the less they cared about community and relationships.

In that article, University of Rochester social psychologist Richard Ryan, Ph.D., was quoted for his profound comment: "Rather than rewarding good practices, we've been rewarding outcomes, however they're attained. And that's driven a lot of greedy behavior from folks who wouldn't normally act that way."

This greed is reflected in our economies, in our businesses, in our daily lives, and in our aspirational values. In fact, "the love of money for money's sake is the social disease of our time. We see it all around us: in the celebration of ill-gotten stock gains, public admiration for the heads of criminal banks, the words of Kanye West, in the commercialization of charity and even spirituality" (R. J. Eskow, "Six Signs Our Culture Is Sick with Greed," Salon. com December 2, 2013).

In chapter 4, I spoke about global inequality, which has intensified over the years; two years and more of economic lockdown due to COVID-19 has added to that inequality.

It is fair to say that, worldwide, we have supported, allowed, and nurtured a culture of laundering money, because the laundering of money has not abated despite intensive and applied legislation and resources worldwide; in fact, money laundering has become a matter of ingenuity. Technology will only exacerbate the difficulties encountered in investigating possible money laundering, following the money, and engaging with international law enforcement and other investigative authorities. While technology can and does provide enhanced protection, we are seeing that the many options offered to perform financial transactions both nationally and internationally, particularly cross-border, facilitate the movement of money, which may or may not include cash and crypto or a mixture of these options, add complexity to the "follow the money" trail.

Conferences to which wealthy corporate CEOs go for better insights and to experience a comingling of the search for individual and collective insights increasingly identify with the desire to accumulate wealth. "You can have it all," these events seem to say. "You can gain peace of mind, unlock the mysteries of human existence, and become a billionaire at the same time."

This is not a twenty-first-century phenomenon. In the last century, in the 1987 movie *Wall Street*, Gordon Gekko, a fictional character played by Michael Douglas, was depicted as a rogue who became a cultural symbol of greed. Gordon Gekko, as a corporate trader and wealthy investor, gave an insightful speech where he said, "Greed, for lack of a better word, is good" and made the point that greed is a clean drive that "captures the essence of the evolutionary spirit."

In a book written by Lisa Duggan (*The Mean Girl*), which tells the story of the famous author Ayn Rand, Duggan refers to Rand's ideologies, which purport that "being selfish and greedy are not only desirable qualities but necessary in order to succeed."

Ayn Rand coined the phrase "rational egoism," which she defined as "a practical intention of self-interest condoned as the natural thing to do" in her book *The Virtue of Selfishness*.

The relevance is about every man for himself, but it is not just to meet life's challenges. A little success and it becomes a driving force to exceed and use whoever you can and whatever you can to climb the staircase to excessive wealth and power.

Back to R. J. Eskow: He indicates that "we can't afford to live in a world where our only aspiration is to accumulate wealth, irrespective of how it's accumulated while ignoring the flourishing of the human spirit in its artistic, idealistic, and intellectual aspects." But does the average person care about this in a competitive world?

Once the taste of a richer life is within reach, the love of possessions and the money spent on the self-satisfying use of unnecessary resources greedily extends to be an all-encompassing goal. This leads to a throwaway culture, which is now so much part of who we are that the sea, soil, and snow have become our waste bins. The planet has finite resources, and we are fast taking away more than the earth can replenish, resulting in loss of biodiversity, deforestation, and soil erosion. Even though scientists and extreme climate experiences have already alerted us that we must save our planet or else millions of people will be displaced, and society and economics will be disrupted (all of which is happening already), there is plenty of evidence that the richest care the least because they are affected the least. And they are living in the now.

As quoted by Sofo Archon in his article "Economic System Creates Poverty, Greed, Violence, Disease, and Environmental Destruction," "Only when the last tree has been cut down, the last fish has been caught, and the last stream has been poisoned, will we realize that we cannot eat money" (Cree Indian proverb).

On November 24, 2013, in the Huffington Post, "Reversing the Culture of Greed" by Jung-kyu Kim, the author tells us that "a culture of extreme individualism and profit-seeking has frayed our social fabric. To reverse the decline, we must discard the notion that greed is good."

He further indicates that "the single-minded pursuit of profit is a dangerous phenomenon which can dull our sensitivities and gradually obliterate all other social and human considerations. While Confucians did not deny the validity of the profit motive per se, they held that it should be brought under control by a spirit of compassion, aesthetic sensibility, and humaneness—what Confucius called ren."

I am not sure that resonates in our world of greed. Of course, there are people in this world who are good citizens, caring citizens, and good contributors to society and taking on incredible projects to sustain the beauty of our earth, improve our lives and our health. Many of these people are unsung heroes and are sometimes unnoticed and seldom applauded. Rather, it is the brash, the greedy, the wealthy, and the powerful that are idolized.

The world has made great strides in eradicating poverty in the last fifty years. But in 2021, poverty is on the rise; the pandemic no doubt has a lot to do with it, but the real reason, in my opinion, is the growing inequality: big companies earning more than the GDP of some countries, more individuals on the same trajectory, and through excessive corruption and money laundering, the growing weakness of government resources to care for its people.

The World Bank indicated that as of October 14, 2021, more than 40 percent of the global poor live in economies affected by fragility, conflict, and violence, and the number is expected to rise to 67 percent in the next decade. About 70 percent of the global poor aged fifteen and older have no schooling or only some basic education. The World Bank goes on to say that the new poor will be more urban than the chronic poor, be more engaged in informal services and manufacturing and less in agriculture, and live in congested urban settings and work sectors most affected by lockdowns and mobility restrictions. The prediction is that under these conditions, the global objective of bringing the global absolute poverty rate to 3 percent or less, which was already at risk before the crisis, is now beyond reach without swift, significant, and substantial policy action. A wonderful recipe to enhance crime and its result: money laundering.

Why are money laundering, global inequality, and corrupt governments not to blame here? All three factors are growing exponentially. Money not invested in climate change will only exacerbate poverty and migration, money not invested in education will add to more criminal activities (you have to live somehow), and corrupt governments with their leanings toward more authoritarian rule, failing justice, denial of wrongdoings, and determination to not stand down just show the extent to which the hold on power is the holy grail.

The World Bank's stated goal to end poverty works hand in hand with its goal to promote shared prosperity, focused on increasing income growth among the bottom 40 percent in every country. Boosting shared prosperity broadly translates into improving the welfare of the least well-off in each country and includes a strong emphasis on tackling persistent inequalities that keep people in poverty from generation to generation.

Just to end extreme poverty, the United Nations estimates that the total cost per year would be about $175 billion, which represents less than 1 percent of the combined income of the richest countries in the world. Obviously, poverty rates in different countries differ from the average; in sub-Saharan Africa and South Asia, 40 percent of the region's people live on less than $1.90 per year. In the Middle East and North Africa, poverty figures have doubled because of the crises such as those experienced in Syria,

Yemen, and Afghanistan. Already the war in Ukraine (as of June 2022) only exacerbates the above figures.

The following are just reminders of the other consequences of laundering money:

The role of governments is one serious factor; the role of conglomerates is another.

An article in the *Daily Maverick* of November 28, 2021, was written by Trevor Shaku, who is the national spokesperson for the South African Federation of Trade Unions but wrote in his personal capacity as follows: "Despite the development of regulations to try to monitor the activities of imperial conglomerates, the tendency of these multinational and transnational corporations to cheat the public continues." He contends that history shows that foreign direct investment intended particularly for developing countries from multinational corporations and transnational corporations is concerned with exporting capital and finding natural resources to exploit cheap labor in order to multiply their profits, rather than expanding production and creating jobs per se.

Nevertheless, these countries continue to seek foreign investment and often must make conditions ripe for the maximization of profits for these companies.

Many such direct investment interventions exploited the developing world by relaxing capital and exchange controls in the 1990s to enable companies to embark on capital flight and steal monies through illicit financial flows. This developed by the way in which the concentration of production fused with banks, created big multinationals that exercised more power over their governments, and led to the exportation of capital (not goods) via mis-invoicing, transfer pricing, and base erosion and profit shifting into tax havens. These illicit flows still continue today. What is revealing is the value these illicit financial flows have cost South Africa as an example. Oxfam South Africa reported that between 2010 and 2014, the government potentially lost $7.4 billion annually.

The Alternative Information and Development Center reported that global export mis-invoicing between 2000 and 2014 was estimated at $385.1 billion (more than R2 trillion). Global Financial Integrity estimated in 2017 that the value of illicit financial flows was 7 percent to 8 percent annually (between R200 billion and R400 billion). The economy, the author indicates, is losing gross domestic product while the government is losing tax collections.

These illicit flows, which shrink South Africa's GDP, make its debt-to-GDP ratio widen, giving the government the excuse to cut government expenditure on public goods and services to contain debt and consolidate the tax revenue. That inevitably leads to budget cuts on education, health care, correctional services, and social developments—all of which affect human rights, which are enshrined in the South African Constitution.

The case of Elizabeth Holmes is another example of deliberate deception, extracting money from just as greedy investors. Theranos, an American company, was founded in 2003 by nineteen-year-old Elizabeth Holmes. The product on offer was a specific automated device that could perform blood tests quickly and with only a little blood required. The company raised US$700 million from venture capitalists and private high-profile investors. At its peak in 2013/14, the valuation of the company was worth $10 billion. Because Theranos never went public, it was not under public scrutiny. That gave investors an opportunity to get in while it was on the rise, but you would have thought that it also put the burden on them to vet the blood-testing startup independently.

A year later, medical research professors along with an investigative journalist from the *Wall Street Journal* questioned the validity of its technology. The company began to face many legal and commercial inquiries from medical authorities, regulators, investors, partners, and patients. The company was finally dissolved in September 2018 after Theranos, Holmes, and its former company president were charged with fraud.

Holmes's trial was delayed because of her pregnancy and COVID-19. In January 2022, she was found guilty of conspiracy to commit fraud against investors and three charges of wire fraud. The charges, when Holmes is sentenced, carry a maximum prison term of twenty years each. She denied the charges and embellished her defense by citing that her onetime partner and clandestine lover, Sunny Balwani, who was twenty years her senior, controlled and abused her during their relationship. Sunny Balwani will face trial in the same court for similar charges. This adds a complication as Sunny will no doubt return the compliment in his trial. Holmes's sentencing may be delayed until after the Sunny case has been concluded.

Wire fraud can include charges of money laundering. It involves the use of some form of telecommunications or the Internet, where a person has voluntarily and intentionally devised or participated in a scheme to defraud another out of money. But when a company is run in this way, one wonders whether there were any accounting irregularities too.

The above is by no means an isolated case—just the latest example of another bad apple.

The invasive attribute of money laundering is not difficult to see and understand.

On May 30, 2021, hackers performed the world's largest (at the time) organized cyberattack on the Brazil-based JBS in its North American and Australian systems and affected a fifth of the United States' beef production, thereby highlighting the vulnerability to economic insecurity in sectors such as agriculture, transportation, and energy. It created chaos and huge concern because it followed on from the previous month's ransomware attack on the US oil production's Colonial Pipeline. These companies were held hostage by their balls. JBS's chief executive officer paid $11 million "to prevent potential risk to customers." Colonial Pipeline paid a $4.4 million ransom to the Russian-based criminal gang to unlock its systems and data.

Money was earned outside the country of the hackers, tax-free, with little risk, and security of economic vulnerabilities disincentivized. Most markets around the world are not mandated to counter cyberattacks. The *Washington Post*'s Cybersecurity 202 of June 2, 2021, reported that "a one-size-fits-all regulatory approach probably is not the right model for an industry that is as complex as the food and agriculture industry," according to Scott Algeier, executive director of the Information Technology–Information Sharing and Analysis Center. "The adversaries attacking the networks are creative and agile. Regulations tend to be stagnant and often produce a climate of compliance rather than creative and innovative solutions."

Just another way to make it big in the money-laundering world.

The world as we know it continues to protect the greedy and the powerful. In South Africa, we have become a well-known example of state capture. Wikipedia defines state capture as the following: "The classical definition of state capture refers to the way formal procedures (such as laws and social norms) and government bureaucracy are manipulated by government officials, state-backed companies, private companies, or private individuals so as to influence state policies and laws in their favor.

"State capture seeks to influence the formation of laws, to protect and promote influential actors and their interests. In this way it differs from most other forms of corruption, which instead seek selective enforcement of already existing laws."

During the presidency of Jacob Zuma, it became very clear that, as Abby Innes, assistant professor of political economy at the London School of Economics, told the BBC, "it's also about strategically weakening that part of the state's law enforcement mechanism that might crack down on corruption."

South Africa's State Capture Commission, chaired by deputy chief justice Raymond Zondo, released part 1 of its inquiry report. The process has taken four years.

Part 1 of the report recounts the fascinating account of three public entities, namely South African Airways, the South African Revenue Services, and the South African government's information arm. These companies were "systematically captured with criminal intent." The South African public was misinformed by the *New Age*, a puppet media organization funded by the diversion of public funds. Simply, the *New Age* covered up the true story.

"Notorious ringmasters" are named in the report: past president Zuma, former SAA chair Dudu Myeni, Zuma's present spokesperson Mzwanele Manyi, and a man who took over from Themba Maseko, who was dismissed at the bidding of the Gupta family.

The recommendations of this report are typical: laws and ethical codes need to be strengthened, institutional gaps in corporate governance require stronger codes of ethics, inexperienced or ineffective staff need to be replaced, some traced monies must be repaid, and of course, many investigations and prosecutions were recommended.

Sadly, will this report lie in dusty splendor along with some others such as has happened with similar reports in the past, such as the Asmal report on Chapter Nine institutions* as well as the Farlam report on Marikana massacre"?**

*South Africa's criminal justice and chapter 9 institutions, which were created by the architects of the country's constitution for the purpose of preventing abuses of power, are either under attack or, in the case of the criminal justice system, in a state of disarray. This is a huge price for South Africa to pay so that a clique of highly placed individuals can be allowed to act with impunity to advance their own material interests above those of the country. (Institute of Security Studies, November 19, 2013, on the attacks on South African public protector Thuli Madonsela in relation to her report on the investigation into the R210 million upgrade to President Jacob Zuma's private Nkandla homestead).

**The Marikana massacre refers to the killing of 34 miners at a strike of rightfully disgruntled workers on the Lonmin platinum mines in August 2012 by the South African security forces. While compensation has been paid to the victim's relatives, the "Government has only made a partial payment for the 279 wrongly arrested mine workers. Not even one of the injured mine workers has been compensated a cent by the state, nine years on." (News24, 18 August 2021).

Given the mostly weak and under-resourced government institutions, there is currently little evidence that the government has the technical ability, the money, and importantly, the political will to implement the recommendations. As The Conversation purports, the commission is merely an exercise in catharsis and not the first step to delivering justice and accountability.

Zondo's report captures the extent of corruption by the Guptas and the government in South Africa. Former president Jacob Zuma and his diverse network of exploited and exploitative allies were responsible.

> But there will be many more twists in the plot.
> There will be lawfare, and attempts to subvert the
> criminal justice system, which is still recovering
> from state capture. The power struggle within the
> governing African National Congress in the run-up

to its five-yearly national elective conference at the end of this year will be even more bloody as a result.

The Zondo Commission and all the hype about state capture did not make any difference. A new president promising to fight corruption (as they all do in every country and fail to effectively implement in most cases) faces the Pandemic Feeding Frenzy, an aptly named article by the *Daily Maverick* of January 26, 2022. It sets out the details of the final and sixth report at the end of an eighteen-month investigation. It paints a picture of how "corruption and corrupt practices have become an almost impenetrable web. Its sticky edges are held up by dirty officials and politicians, from those in senior positions to paper-pushers."

It refers to the deliberate flouting of rules, turning a blind eye, ignoring accountability and oversight and deals for pals, which reverberated throughout South Africa's provinces, municipalities, and other government departments in deals compromising protection and fumigation equipment, catering, water supply, field hospitals, and even temporary homeless shelters.

The Special Investigating Unit (SIU) found companies that were awarded contracts that were not tax-compliant, splitting the bids to meet quotation thresholds, using suppliers not registered on the government's central supplier database, and the South African Health Product Regulatory Authority supplying medical equipment and product specifications, ignored.

Obstacles faced by the unit included the absence of paper trails, lost or deleted files, whistleblower intimidation, deliberate noncooperation by officials, and reluctance to sign statements. Even more concerning is "seemingly no consequences for ignoring the SIU recommendations."

What is the point of all this legislation when it is so easy to ignore (never mind circumvent) and there are no fines for flouting the law? 5,467 contracts were awarded to 3,066 service providers, of which 62 percent were found to be irregular. Two hundred twenty-four government officials were referred for disciplinary action, 386 were referred for prosecution by the National Prosecuting Authority, and 330 companies were recommended for blacklisting.

The sad part is that these examples relegate themselves to the possible demise of places like South Africa's flagship Kruger National Park, which was one of the most profitable parks in the world and attracted more than a million visitors a year pre-pandemic. But now there are dwindling resources—not enough to sustain or protect the Big Five, especially the rhinos, which are still being targeted by international criminal networks. This also means that many owners are running out of private funds to look after their animals. Sadly too, there are some two million poor people who live on the borders of the Kruger, and killing animals to eat is now a desperate attempt to stave off hunger (*Daily Maverick*, January 25, 2022, "Beyond its exceptional beauty, Kruger National Park is on the ropes and hurting").

The government has nothing to offer its marginalized people because the greedy and powerful have taken it all, with no consequences to them or their families.

Where does all this money go?

Of course, laundered money can be used for anything, anywhere in the world. It can be invested in legitimate start-up companies; it may be used by somebody who has a passion to support a cause that could be philanthropic or selfish or invested in further illegal activity such as drug trafficking, or it can be invested outside of the country it was earned in for pure self-indulgence such as property, yachts, and art; and those aspects too can be fraught with corruption. Of course, that simply spurs the promotion and consumption of luxury goods, and the money-laundering cycle continues.

CHAPTER 13

What Needs to Change?

WHAT ARE THE downsides of money laundering except for the persons, companies, gangs, or networks that are successfully engaging in it?

In terms of the inequality that is now very prevalent in most countries around the world, there is no doubt that there are negative effects on our world economies. Money laundering is invasive and pervasive in all types of economies, be they developed, emerging, or underdeveloped.

I defy the good old maxims about money laundering:

Maxim 1: Emerging or underdeveloped markets attract money launderers because their resources to fight money laundering are inadequate, particularly when it comes to experienced investigators and law enforcement capabilities. It is indeed, but the sophisticated or developed markets attract the more sophisticated money launderers with lots more money. It is just that in developed countries, the damage money laundering does to the economy is less obvious.

Maxim 2: Money laundering creates unpredictable changes in money demand, causes large fluctuations in international exchange rates and capital flow. We have learned to live with this and account for this economically over the last few decades because it has become the norm. It is an accepted way of life.

Maxim 3: False signals of laundered money affect monetary policies related to inflation, GDP, interest rates, exports and imports, and currency exchange. Yes, but central banks have been managing this for years when devising their monetary policies. The longer-term effect is the growing inequality of income distribution in the world and weaker governments (financially).

Maxim 4: Foreign investors are not attracted to countries that have a reputation for money laundering. Tell me, which country is not defiled by money laundering? In underdeveloped countries or emerging markets, how money is laundered is just easier to see, and it is easier to recognize that law enforcement resources are inadequate, inexperienced, and overwhelmed. The same cannot be said of the United States or, for example, developed countries in western Europe.

Maxim 5: It is important to determine the ratio between the informal economy and the formal economy. That is of little relevance. Every country is affected by money laundering. Everything related to money laundering is relative to the opportunities available. Opportunities are infinite, and the chances of spending time in jail are, as the saying goes, one in a million.

Maxim 6: The adverse effects of money laundering also undermine the trust of customers. Therefore, the trust of customers and related institutions is essential to building a stable financial sector and economy. The impression of fraud in relevant institutions, such as depositors, investors, and society in general, as well as customers, is a major obstacle to trusting them. In other words, money laundering damages the image of financial institutions; as a result, the customer loses his trust in the relevant institutions. How many customers lose trust in their financial institution? Do they leave in droves if there is a regulatory breach or even if the bank has been fined for participating in money laundering? No. The reputation of the institutions is more likely to be judged on service, charges, and good interest rates.

Maxim 7: Indices track and rate the laundering of money on the potential risks and regulations available. In other words, the indices can determine how vulnerable a country is to money laundering. The annual Basel AML Index evaluates structural factors by quantifying regulatory, legal, political, and financial indicators that influence jurisdictions' vulnerability to ML/TF. Of what use is this when the actual enforcement of the regulations is not considered?

All well and good, but what is the value of the money laundered? Surely that is the key? Haiti, as an example, is more vulnerable to the risks of money laundering—evident in its weak economy, number of poor people, fewer industries, and less sophistication overall. The United States is seen, of course, to be far less risky. But vulnerability does not measure the value of the money being laundered or how it is being laundered. A bigger economy opens many more opportunities to launder money (and much more of it), given that it is well recorded how ineffective we are globally at both prevention and prosecution.

For example, the value of money estimated to be laundered globally is anything between 2 and 5 percent of GDP. Well then,

5 percent of GDP America	2020 is	US$20.94 tn =	1.047 tn
5 percent of GDP United Kingdom	2020 is	US$2,708 tn =	0.1354 tn
5 percent of GDP Peru	2020 is	US$202 bn =	10.1 bn
5 percent of GDP Haiti	2020 is	US$13.42 bn =	0.671 bn

In the 2021 Basel Index, the index noted that "broadly, countries are getting worse at effectively countering and preventing the trillions of dollars in illicit finance flowing around the world each year."

A summary of why the index says this is due, chiefly, to four overarching challenges: "weak or non-existent compliance rules around cryptocurrency, not preaching on prevention and floundering on effectiveness, failing to boost beneficial ownership and tackle corporate opacity, and continuing to leave certain nonbank groups unbound by AML rules, like gatekeepers" (https://www.acfcs.org/basel-aml-index-2021-an-ounce-of-prevention-and-being-less-effective-on-effectiveness/ September 17, 2021).

I do not agree with these being the main challenges. The current legislation to control money laundering is simply not working. In terms of the challenges mentioned above, to pin cryptocurrency to compliance rules is just another product to pin to rules that are not working anyway.

In a recent scam (Washington/New York, February 8, 2022, Reuters), the US Justice Department "unraveled its biggest-ever cryptocurrency theft, seizing a record-shattering $3.6 billion in Bitcoin tied to the 2016 hack of digital currency exchange Bitfinex and arresting a husband-and-wife team on money laundering charges." The Lichtensteins, who hold dual US-Russian citizenship and are in their early thirties, have been accused of collaborating to launder 119,754 Bitcoin stolen after a hacker broke into Bitfinex and initiated more than 2,000 unauthorized transactions in 2016. Bitfinex allocated losses of more than 30 percent to all customer accounts and applied a convoluted mixture of BFX tokens or later exchanged them for iFinex capital stock and created another coin for that conversion (reported by Aljazeera, February 10, 2022). Not all customers have been satisfied.

It is interesting how they got caught. A bust of an underground digital market used to launder a portion of the funds in 2017 gave the clue that some of the money was transferred to AlphaBay, which is hosted on the dark web. In taking the site down, the US authorities found that AlphaBay's transaction logs (with the help of a digital currency tracking company, Elliptic) were connected to a cryptocurrency account in the name of Liechtenstein.

While it is said that blockchain technology facilitated the tracking of these transactions (following the trail of money "just as we have always followed it within the traditional financial system"), the complexity is now about "who walks away with the $3.6 billion in Bitcoin that the US recovered from the Bitfinex currency exchange hack has become the crypto sphere's favorite guessing game." Cryptocurrency is just as complex as ever about who owns the cryptocurrency that has been laundered.

Money laundering opportunities are enhanced because of the exponential growth of cryptocurrencies, flexible payment and innovative remittance options, e-wallets, and NFTs.* As an example of the speed with which these transactions take place, a fintech enables users to send money from one continent to another in seconds, with near-zero fees.

*NFTs are non-fungible tokens. Bitcoin is fungible, which means that you can trade one Bitcoin for another. A non-fungible token means you trade one thing for something completely different. In reality, it is usually dollars paid for something digital considered artistic or a collectable, e.g. $6.6 million for a video by Beeple, or $3 million for a tweet by the founder of Twitter.

Back to the Basel Index, which refers to challenges: it is also indicated that the other three issues of corporate opacity, ultimate beneficial ownership transparency, and preaching prevention are needed to address the fundamentals.

Corporate opacity and ultimate beneficial ownership do not need more legislation and more investigation; company structures need to be clear and simpler, shell banks made redundant, and offshore transparent.

Preaching prevention? How is that going to help? Compliance is an all-out attempt at prevention now, and where exactly has this got us? If opportunities keep presenting themselves, how will more legislation prevent that? Legislative impact is huge on institutions affected by AML/CFT laws, but it is equally ineffective and costly, using intelligent and expensive resources only to lose the fight against laundering of cryptos and money.

The sources of laundering are so entrenched in our world that we will struggle to get out of it. Great minds need to put their efforts into simplifying company structures, making shell banks redundant, providing for offshore transparency, simplifying financial and corporate accounting, and simplifying taxes. The more complex, the easier to confuse, confound, and obfuscate society and the less privileged. It makes it harder *for most people* to meaningfully contribute to the economy and to understand how best they can partake in it. In most countries, governments are seriously compromised by their inability to collect taxes because of the complexity of it all (and therefore the loopholes that present themselves) and the ability of the launderers to easily escape detection.

Just as one example: Every audited financial statement varies from how the figures in the books of entry are transposed into financial accounting and finally "correctly" displayed in the financial statements. Auditors please their clients, and if the financial statements are approved, we accept them at face value. The swapping of financial statements between financial institutions and regulators for anti-money-laundering purposes is an absolute joke. In most cases, they should be (and usually are) available on websites anyway, but how many investors, compliance officers, and even regulators will understand the financial statements of Credit Suisse, for example? It is a complicated company structure just like millions of other company structures. The sad fact is that only very few people have the experience and knowledge to understand those financial statements. The only figures that raise concern to regulators and, indeed, bankers are when there is less income than expenditure and liabilities exceed assets. Otherwise, audited financial statements are good to go.

Then there are trust structures, especially discretionary trusts, which defy the ultimate beneficiaries and their taxation requirements, estate duty with its fideicommissary and other complex calculations, shell banks with their legal status but used to hide taxable income and assets, and offshore tax havens, which offer secrecy and sophistication in money protection from predators and regulators, and so the list goes on—all of which are not simple for the average person to understand. And mostly, the average person in his or her lifetime will *never* get to use these complexities. It is just designed for the privileged and wealthy to make them more privileged and wealthier.

In an interview with National Public Radio, *All Things Considered*, Deborah Schenk, the Ronald and Marilynn Grossman Professor of Taxation and editor-in-chief of the *Tax Law Review*, when asked why the American tax system is so much more complicated than tax systems in other countries, replied, "We're a very sophisticated, complex economy, and that requires a very sophisticated tax system. And the other reason is attributable to incentives. Congress loves to provide incentives to the Tax Code."

Shenck went on to say that for any problem that needed solving, the decision always starts with using the Tax Code. Changes are then made to the Tax Code, making it more complex as every year goes by. She quoted the example of the current year's stimulus bill which had more than 300 changes made to the Internal Revenue Code. She acknowledged that perhaps the code was correctly designed to stimulate the American economy, but those changes certainly "mucked up the code." Tax simply gets more confusing, and cryptos have complicated taxation even more.

Government and tax offices around the world are still at odds on how to deal with crypto and its taxation. What this means is that there's a lot of discrepancy between how crypto is viewed and therefore how they are taxed around the world. In some countries, you'll pay multiple taxes on your crypto—while other countries do not tax cryptos at all. Of course, we already have some ten crypto tax havens, such as Germany, Malta, Belarus, Singapore, Switzerland, and then some.

The vast majority of countries (*excluding El Salvador, which uses it as its day-to-day currency*) do not recognize cryptocurrency as a fiat currency—like dollars or pounds. Instead, it's most often viewed as a kind of asset or commodity—like a property or a stock.

Why this has relevance is because of the way in which tax is applied to cryptocurrency. In many countries, cryptocurrencies will be subject to income tax and/or capital gains tax. (Is it that easy to get proof of earnings on capital gains and income from cryptos?)

If taxation needs to be sophisticated as Schenk indicates above, then we must produce something equal to that description. But that reference to "sophistication" in this context is discriminatory, given the growing inequality in our world.

America is not the only country with complex tax laws, of course. Tax is a serious key component of a strong economy and provides for a good physical working infrastructure for a country and the ability to bring about fairness and equity among its people.

The minds that draft these tax laws should apply their minds to simpler systems that are fairer and result in equitable outcomes for an economy. It will be easier for governments to budget for taxes and every business and individual could be tax incentivized if the government achieves its budget. And since the world is so global, how about aligning tax regimes, rather than here, there, and somewhere, there just happens to be double taxation agreements between countries.

The time-consuming but ineffective part of money laundering legislation should be dropped. The essentials of identifying the bigwigs of money laundering should be replaced by encouraging delving into transaction trails and account behavior. An identification document is more for the regulator than the business. If you are doing business with a client, especially big business, you take the risk of not knowing enough about your client. That surely is more of a business imperative than the regulator checking to see if any passports have expired and, if so, issuing a fine. Also, stupid things like making an assumption that if a person's passport is not renewed, then it cannot be proved that they are who they say they are. Really?

In general, as much as anti-money-laundering legislation gets stronger, the gaps between the legislation and the outcomes of money laundering have widened.

Problems experienced by the economy also have social consequences. The increasing enrichment of specific individuals and groups causes social degeneration. One of the most critical damages of dirty money to be determined is its negative effect on income distribution. Although the negative impact of the decline in income sources and the differentiation in income distribution is difficult to measure, it is also challenging to compensate for social damage. The gap between individuals in terms of income distribution increases the tendency to commit crimes and makes money attractive.

The availability of money adversely affects competition because people and businesses operating in the registered sector are punished somewhat. Since tax evasion is common in informal and formal economies, the tax burden of those operating in the official sector increases, and income distribution is adversely affected.

Many completely ineffective controls enforced by regulation are time-consuming and take the resources away from following the real money launderers. (An example of an AML audit by the regulator includes nonsensical issues such as an insufficient client address or a transposed name and surname of the sender of a transaction to a family member in another country for a small value.)

> Despite the consistent efforts adopted by banks to fight money laundering and financial crime, fines for AML breaches have hit an all-time high. In 2020, financial institutions were fined a grand total of $15.13 billion (€12.79 billion) worldwide, a 51.3 percent increase compared to 2019, with US banks accounting for 73.4 percent of the issued fines. As compliance departments continue to face regulatory and internal challenges, it is projected that fines will continue to grow in the coming years. ("Why do most AML programs fail?" Pideeco.be March 15, 2021)

The public does not care about fines paid by financial institutions because they are (ho-hum) business as usual, and from a reputational point of view, people continue to bank with their bankers because every financial institution at some time or other will be fined for regulatory breaches and even for money laundering. So what?

The world is on the wrong treadmill from a regulatory point of view to clamping down on money laundering. It was Oscar Wilde who said, "It is always with the best intentions that the worst work is done." More of the same in an increasingly complex world will not change the outcome.

Yes, there has been excellent investigative work, both by investigative and law enforcement authorities, agencies, and journalists, and also individuals; there have been some good legal wins and a few high-profile people locked up. But it is nowhere near enough. The offense or the crime committed is one thing; the money laundered is what we are trying to find, and it is unlikely to be found in the money launderer's bank account. KYC seriously impacts law-abiding individuals; bank account transactions and the movement of money reveal more than an identification document.

It is indeed a struggle to implement a global legislative regime that does not work in every country, regulators who do not always understand or have the experience of newly applied options and movement of money, or prosecutors and law enforcement with often less-than-required resources to investigate and prosecute these cases. Trails of money are complex, interconnected, and interdependent; money-moving operators and fintech are growing exponentially.

What needs to change?

Our focus needs to shift to the sources of the cause of economic inequality—fight or fix those sources. Without them, the opportunities to launder big money will never be curtailed.

With no change and the continued "add another Band-Aid' approach to money laundering, we will join the climate change deniers and ignore scientific predictions already proving to be true. Money laundering will continue to weaken governments financially while their holders of power get stronger in their personal right. The power of democracy and well-being lies in a strong middle class, which is being eroded by greedy individuals.

A world where 1 percent of humanity controls as much wealth as the bottom 99 percent will never be stable. (President Barack Obama in his departing speech in September 2016 to the United Nations General Assembly)

Any stability that we have now—in May 2022—is being threatened by the power of likely the richest and most powerful person in the world. The money is not enough to satisfy his insatiable need for power. (We have no idea where his money is either.) He wants his country to be bigger. His name is Putin. And there is many more power-hungry waiting in the wings.

He will never get convicted for money laundering.

It is time to acknowledge
that money laundering
is as inherent in society as money is.

It swirls around the world
faster and faster
free for some, punishment for more.

The rich are richer and poor are poorer
powerful and irreverent launderers
leaving governments' coffers weaker.

It is time to acknowledge
the frustrations, the cost, the efficacy
of looking for money long gone.

Face the defeat of looking for one
when it's interconnected to more
devised to complicate, muddy, and confuse.

It's time to acknowledge
that we have it wrong
looking for money when legislation provides
for the places where it is hidden.

Dawn Pretorius

INDEX

G

Gadhafi, Moammar, 118, 196
Garcia, Alan, 67
Gekko, Gordon, 318
Gertler, Dan, 90–91
Glencore, 90–91
globalization, 162–64, 167, 174
Global Laundromat, 106
Gnodde, Richard, 100
gold, 11, 17, 21–23, 65, 74–79, 90, 97–98, 104, 191, 278, 280
  South African, 22
Goldman Sachs, 100–101, 216, 218
Gold Scheme, 76, 78
gold trade, 22
government corruption, 47, 98
government funds, 33, 43, 102
government officials, 33–34
  money laundering by, 33
gray list, 199
Greece, 65, 304, 308
Green, Jeremy, 175
Groupe d'action financière (GAFI), 181
Group of Seven (G7), 180
Grupo Odebrecht, 41, 67–68
Guaido, Juan, 91
Guardian, 8–10, 35, 37–38, 63, 87, 90, 116, 125, 150, 241, 272
Guatemala, 8, 65–66, 173
Guatemala mafia, 8
Gupta brothers, 34–35, 55–56, 58, 211, 271, 290, 327
Gurría, Angel, 177
Guzmán, David Eduardo Helmut Murcia, 48
Guzmán, ovidio, 7

H

hackers, 52, 118, 138–39, 283, 324–25
Halkbank, 74–80, 97–99
Hamilton, Lewis, 85

Hanekom, Darren, 142
Hardach, Sophie, 172
Hasheminejad, Syed Ali Sadr, 114
hawala, 80–81
hawaladars, 81
Hermitage Fund, 107
Hinds, Stephanie, 140
Ho Kok Yong, 208
Holmes, Elizabeth, 323–24
Home Affairs Select Committee, 37
Horn of Africa, 73, 81
HSBC, 108, 110, 124, 126, 216, 218, 234, 239–41, 301–2
Humala, Ollanta, 67
human rights groups, 294
Human Rights Watch, 21, 279
human trafficking, 12–15, 38, 47, 82, 154, 165, 277, 286
"Human Trafficking in the Community Banks" (Lake), 14
hydrocarbon crime, 24

I

Iceland, 66, 199
illegal miners, 22
illegal trafficking, 25
illicit economies, 1, 32
illicit trade, 1, 47, 92
impeachment, grounds for, 282
India, 56, 58–59, 77, 103–4, 119, 133, 138, 168, 175, 254, 271–72, 313–14
Indian Enforcement Directorate, 59
inequality, ix, 162, 166–67, 170, 172, 176–77, 303, 317, 330
  economic, 32, 34, 177, 340
ING, 119
International Consortium of Investigative Journalists (ICIJ), 123, 239, 302

U

ultimate beneficial owner (UBO), 251–52
Unione Siciliane, 4
United flight 93, *30*
United flight 175, *30*
United Nations Office on Drugs and Crime (UNODC), 12
United Overseas Bank (UOB), 208
"US Report Names Bahamas as Money Laundering Jurisdiction," 71

V

Varoufakis, Yanis, 304
Vbs south africa, 108–10, 270, 273
Venezuela, 22, 85–86, 90–93, 124–25, 308
Vienna Convention, 182–83
Volkswagen, 245

W

Wall Street (movie), 318
Wall Street Journal, 296, 302, 323
water companies, 29
Weisberger, Dave, 136
Wells, Joseph T., 124
Westpac Banking Corporation, 111
whistleblower, 78, 103, 115, 284, 292–93, 296–98, 303, 328
whistleblowing, 248, 292, 298
white paper, 203, 208, 286
wildlife, 15, 18–19, 57, 70, 73, 157

wildlife trafficking, 18, 157. *See also* animal trafficking
Winslet, Kate, 59
Winters, Jeffrey, 304
wire fraud, 324
Wisconsin Project, 74
Wolfsberg Group, 216, 234
Wolfsberg Questionnaire, 216, 221
World Bank, 166, 189, 191, 199, 251, 320–21
World Trade Organization, 162, 165

X

Xhafaj, Fatmir, 44

Y

Yamaguchi-gumi, 82
Yengeni, Tony, 54
Yes Bank, 119
Yuancheng, 9

Z

Zambada, Ismael "El Mayo," 7
Zambia, 32, 63–64, 109
Zarrab, reza, 74–79, 97–99
Zimbabwe, 16–17, 32, 70, 173, 199, 211, 305
Zondo Commission, 56, 295, 328
Zuckerberg, Mark, 26
Zuma, Jacob, 34–35, 54–57, 271, 289–91, 295, 326–27